Letters to Kelsea

Life *After* Death

TRACY LYN LAWLER

Mitey Mo Unlimited
EL CAJON, CA

Published by:

Mitey Mo Unlimited

EL CAJON, CA

ISBN: 978-0-69283-935-5

Cover and interior design: Gary A. Rosenberg

Printed in the United States of America

it's hard to cope
when you know you're sick
all the ups and seldom downs
a day in life is such a trick
when society is ignorant
and you can't explain
makes me mad but not insane
i'm not an outcast
no matter what you all might say
because i know i'm sick
and all i do is go day by day
i'm smart and funny
creative and pretty
intelligent, even witty
despite what you say
i can independently cope
with my loving family
prayer and hope

Kelsea Lyn Phelps
August 12, 2006

DEDICATION

I am now approaching the "3rd Marker" of Kelsea's going Home. Over this last year, I will say that this journey I entered into on August 22, 2006, continues to soften. The progress and place I am in today is different from even 8 months ago. I am better able to function on a daily basis and I have actually begun to live again. I am able to think clearly, work for longer periods at a time and go out places without wanting to run home and hide in the safety of my home.

The first year was the year of surviving. The second year was the year of fighting: the fight for justice for Kelsea, and I deemed the third year to be my year of healing and prospering. I can say I am healing. However, I say that with guilt. I think to myself, how can I be healing when I don't have my daughter with me? I think, *how dare I heal?* I have come to realize how irrational these thoughts are and now I understand it is okay to feel life once again. I want to continue living.

I have said in the past, God has a sense of humor and His timing is perfect.

After I finished *Letters to Kelsea,* I knew I needed to have someone read it and give me feedback. I asked a man who goes to my gym and who knows what has happened in my life to read it for me. He agreed.

Over the next several weeks I would see him periodically in the gym. He told me one day that he could only read a couple of pages at a time and had to put it down because it was just too difficult to read. I told him it was "OK" and that whenever he finished would be fine. I did have some concerns though that maybe it would be too difficult for people to read.

Then, one day he asked me to go outside to talk to me about my book. I was excited and thought he had finished and wanted to share with me what he thought. We sat on a wall outside and he began to open up, wholeheartedly, about his past. It was at that very moment I completely understood WHY it was so difficult for him to read.

This man had not dealt with something from his teen years and this book brought things to the surface of his life again. But now he was dealing with it all. It was my book, my pain, my anger, my thoughts and absolutely everything within that was helping him now.

Upon speaking with him, he suggested that I try to weave some kind of hope throughout the book. He said that people want to know there is hope. I understand but if I was to do that then what I wrote through that first year would have been a lie. I want to speak the truth. As hard as it is to read, my hope is that *Letters to Kelsea* will educate both the griever and the supporter of those who grieve.

I say, God has a sense of humor because out of all the people in my life that I could have asked to read this book, I chose a man whose life the book had impacted and helped. I know this is a difficult book to read but I can say that you will benefit from it. You will come to understand the heart and soul of a grieving mother. Hopefully, you will be able to identify with, or possibly learn from, my journey through a senseless, choiceless, ruthless, and seemingly hopeless event.

I dedicate this book to the Lord. It is He who has given me the strength each day I wake up to walk, talk, function, focus and breathe.

I dedicate this book to my son, Digger; my psychologist, Susan, who has become a trusted friend; and to Dr. Ken Druck. Dr. Druck not only helped me through this hell I entered on August 22, 2006, but continues to help people each week with his compassion, kindness and understanding of the pain and to Roger, my therapist, who I turned to when I began to enter darkness again three years into my grief. He has helped me for over 4 years now, to process not only this loss, but also to help me accept and embrace the healing that occurs with each minute, hour, week and year that passes.

I also dedicate this book to the parents of children who have gone home. It is the greatest loss a person can experience. It is choice less. I hope that through these letters, understanding will emerge in each soul, knowing one is not alone.

My thoughts are not those of one. My pain is shared by others. My confusion and my anger are not out of the ordinary. I am simply part of a group of people who never asked for these new lives, never asked for our children to be taken. I am a survivor.

GLOSSARY OF TERMS

KCD: Kelsea charisma dust

KZ: Kelsea zone

Pad: Where Kelsea was laid to rest, cemetery

Hawaii: Kuuipoaloha Lawler, my husband

ECAL: East County Academy of Learning

IEP: Individual Education Program

ADD: Attention Deficit Disorder

EMOTIONAL SCALE
THROUGH THIS JOURNEY OF GRIEF

As I began writing my letters there came a day when I wondered how I was doing. Where my emotional state of mind was from day to day and how high a roller coaster I was sitting on from moment to moment. Almost 6 weeks into this journey of grief, I started rating my days. It helped me to put a number to my day. It helped me to see my "good" (although I refused to use that word at that time) days as well as my bad days. It enabled me to see as days, weeks and months passed that the numbers were slowly climbing. On the following page is my scale of emotions.

Scale of Emotions from Day to Day

8. The closest I have been to having my life back again

7. Surviving for two years and able to function daily

6. Kelsea's 18th Birthday, a complete day of honoring

5. My first day of not crying and every day with no tears

4. Moments of peace, some laughter, strong love for Kelsea

3. Existing, walking, talking, functioning to my best ability for the day

2. Just want to be alone, with Kelsea, lonely, crying, deep sadness

1. Feeling hate, crying, cannot breathe, think, function, live; in utter darkness

PROLOGUE

August 22, 2006

I woke up and looked over at the clock. It was 6:14 a.m. and I knew I should get up to check on Kelsea to make sure she was up for school. It was the first day Kelsea was going to attend her new school for her senior year. As I walked down the hallway to her room, I heard the alarm going off and I just smiled because she always slept through her alarm.

I opened Kelsea's door and walked straight over to the alarm at the end of her bed and turned it off. I told her, "Kels, it's time to get up." I turned the alarm off and grabbed her foot, shaking it, and again said, "Kels, get up." I looked at Kelsea and realized she wasn't moving. I rushed to the side of her bed, now yelling for her to get up, shaking her shoulders and body to get her to respond to me.

I noticed that Kelsea looked pale and had what looked to be something dry on her face, coming out of the side of her mouth. I reached down and began trying to feel for a pulse and I couldn't find one. I yelled out to my husband, "Call 911. . . . Kelsea doesn't have a pulse!" I screamed again to call 911 and I heard my husband, Steve, on the phone. Steve came in the room and immediately tipped her head back and gave her a breath. Some fluid, rust in color, came out of her mouth after his breath and he panicked. He stepped back and I grabbed a shirt on the floor, wiped Kelsea's mouth, tilted her head back again and gave her a breath. I heard a deep gurgling sound in Kelsea's chest as I watched more fluid come out of her mouth. Again, I wiped it away and tried another breath.

Again, gurgling.

I remember a deputy taking me out of the room as other deputies and paramedics were everywhere. I dropped to the floor *right there* outside of Kelsea's room and began to pray. I looked up and into Kelsea's room and saw the paramedic's machine that Kelsea was hooked up to. I saw a 40 for her blood pressure. I saw a flat line on the monitor and I dropped my head again praying, begging, and crying.

I continued praying until a deputy said, "Tracy, come on with me." He got me up off the floor and onto my feet and took me by my hand to the living room and sat me on the couch. I'm not sure how long I had been sitting there completely numb and confused. What was going on right now? None of this could possibly really be happening, right?

I walked over to the front door and looked outside. There were sheriff units, a sheriff SUV, an ambulance, a fire truck and yet I could not remember hearing one single vehicle pull up; no sirens, nothing. Again, I was confused and my mind was completely empty. I walked over to the kitchen table and sat in a chair. There were deputies, firemen, paramedics all buzzing around my house and I was trying to figure out what was happening in my home.

The paramedics were on the phone in Kelsea's room. I could hear them. They were all working so hard to save Kelsea. They worked on Kelsea for approximately 45 minutes. When I looked up, all the firemen were walking down the hall toward me, their faces so sad. I looked at them and one of the firemen said to me, "I'm so sorry," and that was it. They all walked out my front door so quietly with their heads all down as if they felt my pain.

One of the deputies told me that a medical examiner was on their way. Kelsea needed to be checked out by a medical examiner before anything else could take place. I asked the deputy, "Can I *see* her?" The deputy said, "Yes" and walked me to Kelsea's room. I took a step into Kelsea's room and the paramedics had pulled a blanket up over Kelsea's head. I instantly got angry and stepped out. I demanded that the deputy pull the blanket off Kelsea's face. He went into Kelsea's room and removed the blanket down to her shoulders.

I walked into the room and looked at her lying on the floor, motionless. I got down on the floor next to her and I told her how sorry I was for what happened. I lay down next to her and I wrapped my leg around her. I touched her face and I stroked her hair and I professed my undying love to her. I cried as I looked at her lying so still next to me. Her hands were becoming cool to the touch. Her eyes were closed and I was numb. A deputy came into the room and asked me where my son, Digger, was. I told him at work. This deputy sent another deputy to Digger's work to get him. Apparently, my son's friend Skip was going to work when he saw all the vehicles in the street. Skip had already told Digger something was happening at his house. Digger had left work and was on his way home already.

As I was lying next to Kelsea, I heard a soft voice say, "Tracy." I looked up and there was a woman kneeling down next to me. She was unfamiliar to me and looked sad, too. She took my hand and quietly said, "Come on, let's go." I slowly got up, looking at her, still not understanding what was going on right then. As we left Kelsea's room, she said to me, "My name is Sandra and I am the medical examiner. I will be taking care of Kelsea." It was then that Digger showed up and asked to be alone with his sister. Sandra allowed this for Digger. Digger entered Kelsea's room; he shut the door and what happened in the room was between him and his sister. Sandra took me into the living room and told me what she would be doing. She sat me back on the couch and told me to stay there. As Sandra walked toward Kelsea's room, Digger finished his quiet time with his sister. He came into the living room and sat beside me.

Several minutes passed before Sandra came out to me with a back pack and asked if it belonged to Kelsea. I told her yes. She then showed me a prescription bottle with no label and a yellow sticky note attached to it. Sandra asked me if the prescription bottle belonged to Kelsea. All I remember was looking at the note with red hand writing and knowing it was not Kelsea's hand writing. I looked at Sandra and said, "That's not Kelsea's." Sandra showed me two different pills that were in the prescription bottle and asked if they were Kelsea's and I told her no, they were not. Sandra told me she was going to take the pills and note back to her office and try to identify what the pills actually were. She then went back to the room.

I sat in the living room completely in shock. What is going on? What just happened? Why was Kelsea laying in her room on the floor, not breathing. . . . I hate to even use the word *dead*. Sandra came out of Kelsea's room again and told me she wanted me to go into my bedroom now. Sandra took my face in her hands gently. Sandra looked at me and very softly promised me she was going to take care of Kelsea. Sandra was going to take Kelsea to her office where an autopsy would take place. Sandra promised me she would stay with Kelsea and take good care of her.

Sandra looked at me before she walked out of the room and said, "Do you want to donate any of her organs?" I remember getting so angry at that question and thinking to myself, *how can you be asking me that question?* Before she even finished the question I was saying, "No." I was still in such shock; my brain was not processing anything that was happening or being said to me. All I knew was I was supposed to stay in my room till Sandra came back again. It was while I was in my bedroom that Sandra rolled Kelsea out of my home and placed Kelsea into the medical examiner's van to take Kelsea away. She did not want me to see Kelsea rolled out in a body bag. Minutes passed as I stood in my room unable to move, then Sandra came back into the room. She softly said to me, "I'm going to take Kelsea now and I will call you. I'll take good care of her for you."

I walked out of my room and all of a sudden the house was quiet, *completely* quiet. I walked down the hall to Kelsea's room and looked in. Kelsea was gone. The blanket she was covered with was just laying there in the middle of her floor. There were tubes from the paramedics on the floor and the rug was stained. Still, my brain was trying to process. I walked around the house aimlessly. I kept thinking, *now what?* I walked into my bedroom and entered the bathroom, looking in the mirror. I did not recognize the person I was looking at. I stared at myself, looking into my eyes, and I was dead. I had just died with my daughter. My eyes were empty. My eyes had lost any life in them and it was as if I was looking into absolutely nothing. I was dead.

I walked back down the hall into Kelsea's room and I made my first phone call. I called Cara. If anyone would have understood my pain it was Cara. She lost her beautiful 17-year-old daughter 2 years ago. I knew her daughter, Melissa. I loved her daughter. Kelsea and Melissa were raised together in the same apartment complex and played together forever. Kelsea had a tribute to Melissa on her walls in her bedroom and now, well now Kelsea was gone, too. How can that be?

I told Cara, "Kelsea's dead." Cara was at work and I heard in her voice the pain she was just reminded of when she lost Melissa. Cara said she was going to come over as soon as she could leave work. Next, I called Jamie, the girl Kelsea had been with the day before. I also told Jamie, "Kelsea passed away through the night." Jamie let out a loud scream. As she was crying she asked me how? I told Jamie I didn't know and she hung up the phone. Those were the only two phone calls I made that day.

Within the hour, Jamie came to the house. Jamie was upset and sat with me on the couch. As I cried, I tried telling her no one knows why Kelsea died. I explained the medical examiner said Kelsea had a bad throat infection but did not know what exactly happened to Kelsea. Jamie left and went home.

I had people at the house who were trying to figure out what happened. I had several friends who were deputies stopping by my home to give me their condolences. At one point, we were all trying to piece together what happened the day before. I know I talked to Kelsea several times throughout the day and made plans to pick her up at her boyfriend's house in the evening at 8:30 pm and that's what I did. Kelsea grabbed her backpack from out of her boyfriend's house after she gave his mother a hug and kiss and said, "I'll see you tomorrow."

We drove home and she grabbed her backpack out of the car. As we walked into the house, she said, "I'm tired Mama, I'm going to sleep." I said okay and goodnight to her. A half hour later I went to her room to check on her. She was lying in bed with the lights off and already sleeping. Little did I know that would be the last time I saw my daughter alive, and those would be the last words I ever spoke to Kelsea Lyn.

At one point, one of my friends, Teri, was calling the kids Kelsea had been with, trying to get information about the night before. She called Kelsea's boyfriend's house and left a message. Later in the morning, Kelsea's boyfriend, Josue, and his mother came to the house. They walked in the front door and the pain on Josue's and his mother's face was evident. After all, they were the last two people who hugged my Kelsea before she died. They both loved Kelsea, too. Josue stood there motionless, tears in his eyes, as I stood up and hugged his mother. She sobbed in my arms. Josue asked, "What happened?" I explained to him and his mother, I did not know. I told them about the medication bottle with pills in Kelsea's backpack.

Josue looked at me and said he had to show me something. Josue said that he had received a text message from Jamie that morning, saying, "I'm so sorry what happened to Kelsea. Please don't tell anyone where she got the pills." Apparently, Jamie had text messaged Josue after she left my home and knew something more than what she had told me.

At that point, I realized that this might now be criminal. If Kelsea had gotten these pills when she was with Jamie, then we needed to find out more of what was going on. We called back the deputy that was first on scene and told him the new information we had. He appeared uninterested and at one point said to me, "Why can't you just accept this as a tragic accident?" What the hell did he just say to me? How *dare* he talk to me like it was no big deal and just an accident?

The other deputies were questioning if the deputy first on scene had called homicide and he had not. Again, his attitude was that of pure laziness. At one point he actually became rude and told us not to call homicide or anyone else. He finally did make a call and got some direction. Then, he explained to us homicide would not be getting involved at this point and he left.

As the day progressed I walked down the hall to Kelsea's room constantly.

When Cara arrived, we went to Kelsea's room and sat on Kelsea's bed together. Cara told me what to expect. She was in shock also. How could this have happened to the both of us? How was it that both our baby girls were now in heaven? I didn't cry with Cara because I was simply in shock. I was numb. I think Cara must have been, too.

At one point during the day, later in the afternoon I went through Kelsea's room. I'm not sure what I was trying to do or look for but I was just going through her closet, her dresser drawers, everything. I found a pile of poems Kelsea had written. They were lying on top of her television in her closet. I began to read them and cry. They were an array of poems from professing her love to her friends to very dark poems of despair, hurt, loneliness and suicide. My heart broke. I wasn't sure when she had written the poems but they were a mirror image of her bipolar illness, the moods she swung to and from daily. I carefully put them all together and shared them with Tom, one of my closest friends.

My husband had called and left Tom a message in the morning, and he came to my house in the late afternoon. At first he asked me if I thought Kelsea killed herself. I instantly said no. I told him of the events that took place and it was as if a light went off in his head. Tom looked at me and said, "She didn't commit suicide. She set her alarm to get up in the morning and she wouldn't do that if she was going to kill herself," and I felt better because he was right.

The rest of the day consisted of more people stopping by. I think that saved me because with all the commotion going on, I didn't have a lot of time to think about things. But, as the night rolled in and people left, I came to the realization once again that Kelsea was gone. I walked down to Kelsea's room and sat on her bed. I lay down and began to cry uncontrollably. I felt empty.

There are no words to express the pain, confusion, shock or any of the emotions that ran rampant through me this first day.

Digger came to the room and sat me up. He asked me if he could sleep with me that night and I said, "Of course." I grabbed my pillow and blanket and went into the living room and lay on the couch. Digger lay below me on the floor. We finally fell asleep and the first day of this choice less life had ended. I slept that night out of pure exhaustion.

August 23

As I woke up the next morning, my first thought was *now what?* The house was so quiet and still. My head was quiet, my thoughts seemed numb. I walked down the hall to Kelsea's room and again sat on the bed. All I could do was look around her room at her things, her clothes and the emptiness of it all. I got up and I walked back into the living room to the front door. I opened the front door to find the sun shining brightly, the air warm. There were cars driving by on the street we lived on, *swoosh, swoosh,* and *swoosh* as they drove by, as if *nothing* was wrong.

I got angry. I thought to myself, *don't you people know what just happened? Don't you people know I just lost my daughter? Don't you people know how broken I am right now? How can you all be just driving around like nothing is wrong?* It was one of the strangest things I had experienced: seeing life going on right before my eyes when my life had just been taken away from me. I died yesterday with Kelsea. I knew at that moment that I would never be the same woman that I was a short 24 hours ago.

My task for this first day of my life without my daughter was to go pick out a casket for Kelsea. I was blessed that day to have my husband and Teri with me. We went to a place specializing in caskets. I walked in and it was like a dream. We sat down and told Scott, the salesman helping us, that I needed a casket for my daughter who had just died yesterday. I began to cry and my life felt unreal. He took me into a back showroom and began showing me the different caskets. There were so many to choose from. I looked over at one Scott pointed out and immediately knew it was the right one. It had 4 beautiful gold angels: one on each corner of the casket.

We went back to his desk and I didn't realize I also had to decide where I was going to lay Kelsea to rest. He had a list of plots available with prices.

Steve, Teri and I left the casket store and drove to the first cemetery. It was nice but expensive. I didn't have any money saved for this. I didn't plan on having to bury my 17-year-old daughter. We drove to the next cemetery where a double plot was available. It was cheaper than the other cemetery and, since it was a double plot, I could be there with Kelsea one day.

As we walked over to the exact place with the grounds keeper, I looked at Digger and said, "What do you think?" He looked at me as he pulled his cigarettes out of his pocket. He took one cigarette out and dropped it on the ground. He took another cigarette out and lit it for himself, then he said, "This is good." My heart ached. That was Digger's way of having another cigarette with his sister.

I told the grounds keeper we would take this spot. I filled in the paper-work, and the groundskeeper gave me the names of a few mortuaries to check into. I was done for the day emotionally and knew the next day would be full again. We drove back to my house. I hadn't eaten yet and Steve sat me at the table and made me eat. I had no appetite. I didn't want to eat, yet he knew I had to. I took a few bites of food and went to the bathroom. I looked into the mirror and my eyes again were dead. I had no life in my face; it was as empty as my heart and soul.

I spent the rest of the day wandering between the living room and Kelsea's room. I opened up Kelsea's bedroom door at one point to find Digger sitting on her bed smoking a cigarette. I went in and sat on the bed with him. He said to me, "Mom, I think we are the ones that are living in hell now" and I agreed with him. We walked out of her room and found our places, me on the couch and Digger on the floor below me. This was now our second day of life without Kelsea.

August 24

As I woke up on day three, I was still numb. This day ahead of me consisted of driving from mortuary to mortuary looking for the perfect people to give Kelsea a perfect burial. Again, I was glad I had people around me to make everything happen because I was on autopilot; I got in the car when I was told to, I walked in the businesses I was led into, I listened as best as possible to what was being said . . . yet, my mind did not quite comprehend what was taking place.

Steve and I stopped at McDonalds between mortuaries, and he sat me down like a child and made me eat a simple cheeseburger. He watched my every bite and I had to force every bite down. I couldn't finish it, but I did my best. My appetite was null, as was my ability to understand.

We left McDonalds and after visiting several different mortuaries, we finally found the right one. The mortuary was responsible for picking Kelsea up from the medical examiner's office and bringing her to the church for the service. They were going to make Kelsea look absolutely beautiful for the open casket service. I wanted a police escort for Kelsea from the church to the cemetery and the mortuary helped to set that up also.

Dave from the mortuary was working with me on the paperwork for Kelsea. I took out a picture of Kelsea and softly placed it on his desk for him to look at the little girl I had just lost. He pushed the picture to the side, barely acknowledging it and I got angry. I was so angry I wanted to leave and go somewhere else. How could he be so insensitive and just push Kelsea's picture aside when I was in so much pain?

He realized he had upset me and apologized to me. He explained to me that this was his job and he deals with death every day; it is simply "business." I understood, somewhat, but was still very angry. He told me he needed a picture of Kelsea so the make up artist could make Kelsea look like herself. He reminded me then that I also had the task ahead of me to pick out what I was going to bury Kelsea in. We finished, and Steve and I went home as Teri returned to her home.

Over the last 2 days as I was picking out a casket, a plot and a mortuary, Kelsea's Godmother, Tawnia, was putting together the perfect funeral. I wanted to have a slide show at Kelsea's funeral. I had to pick out the pictures I wanted in it and the songs to go with it. I wanted two DVDs made:; one of all Kelsea and one of Kelsea and her brother because that is what her life consisted of. So, I got out all the pictures I had in a couple of bins and began going through them. I could only pick out between 35–40 pictures for each DVD and I just kept thinking to myself, *how am I going to honor Kelsea's life in 35 pictures? How do I put 17 life-filled years into 35 pictures?* I knew I couldn't possibly show her life in such few pictures but I had no choice. So, I carefully went through the pictures and chose the ones I wanted.

Once again, Tawnia was my savior. If there was anyone who felt my pain in this loss, it was Tawnia. She was in Kelsea's life from the age of 3, after I divorced Kelsea's father. Tawnia was just as much Kelsea's mom as I was; Kelsea and Digger were her first two children.

As the day came to an end, I wandered again from Kelsea's room to the living room. I spent time in Kelsea's room in the dark laying on her bed. I stared out the window at the stars above and I cried and cried and cried some more. I talked to Kelsea out loud and I prayed to God. I just did not understand why this happened; how my beautiful, vibrant, full of life little girl was not here anymore.

My son came into the room and he took my hand. He led me out of Kelsea's room back to the living room where we laid down to go to sleep, me on the couch and he on the floor below me, where he felt safe.

August 25–27

I woke up today knowing I had things to do to prepare for Kelsea's funeral.

I want it to be perfect because she deserved that. The days are all running together now. I spent the weekend in the house. I didn't have anything I had to really do. Everything was getting all in order and it wasn't being done by me, it was Tawnia. I can't think. I can't wrap myself around what is happening. I keep waiting for Kelsea to walk in the front door again all bubbly and smiling . . . or I think she is just spending the night at her best friend's house. Yes, that's it . . . she is just spending the night at Jeanie's house.

But, then I walk to her room and sit on her bed constantly throughout the weekend. I didn't think one person could cry so much. The house is so damn quiet. I don't know what to do. I know my parents will be here in a couple of days and on Tuesday we are going to the church to actually plan the service. I know in my head what I want and how I want the service to go.

I know Digger wants Kelsea to wear a beautiful prom dress and I told him he could pick it out. I think that will be on Monday. I have been spending a lot of time on the phone with Cara. She knows my pain. She has answers for me. I don't know what to expect. Hell, I don't know how I am surviving right now. I don't know how I am able to function. Maybe I'm not?

I know my son and I are still finding refuge in the living room; I on the couch and he right below me on the floor when we sleep at night. I don't think he likes hearing me cry while I am in Kelsea's room. He always comes down to the room, takes my hand and walks me back to the couch and sits with me till I calm down. . . .

My first weekend without Kelsea is over. When I look in the mirror, I still see nothing. I have no emotions on my face. I look at myself and I look dead. My soul is lost. My life that I knew is gone forever. . . .

August 28

It's Monday now and my parents arrived from Arizona late this morning. My task today is to meet with Pastor Tony Jr. at my church to plan the funeral. My friend Tom came to the house to see how I was doing and for the first time since Kelsea passed away I smiled. Tom had the ability to always make me laugh or smile when I needed it most and he did it as soon as I opened the door.

He walked in and hugged me. I introduced him to my mom and dad, then we walked down the hall to Kelsea's room. Tom sat on the bed with me and I picked up some of the poems Kelsea had written. I read him a few of them. One was very loving about her friends, yet the other was very dark and talked about death. I cried when I finished reading them. He put his arms around me and just held me till I finished.

It was time to go to the church, so my parents, Steve, Tom and I all got into two cars and drove there. I rode with Tom by myself. As we drove down the street, I saw Jamie walking down the road toward her house. She lived so close to us. She was talking on her cell phone, sporting a short skirt, dark sunglasses and just walking along like life was peachy. I became so angry. I could not believe Jamie was fine and walking around while I was on my way to plan my daughter's funeral.

We got to the church and went upstairs into the pastor's office. We all sat down and Pastor Tony Jr. gave his condolences and asked me to tell him about Kelsea. Where do I start when my daughter was 17 and so vibrant and full of life? Tom and I both spoke at different times about Kelsea. As we spoke, Pastor Tony Jr. was taking notes and asking many questions.

After I spoke for a bit, Pastor Tony Jr. asked me what I wanted to do for Kelsea's "celebration of life" service. So I told him exactly what I wanted; an open casket. I explained I wanted a DVD of Kelsea and a DVD of Kelsea and her brother playing to music on a screen up front. I told him I wanted to speak and that Tom would be giving her eulogy. I wanted the longest procession there has ever been for Kelsea because she would want that. I wanted a graveside service after the church service that was open to everyone that attended her service. I wanted each person to be given a hot pink balloon to release together at graveside. Yes, that is everything I wanted and I told him in detail. We finally finished; I gave my thanks and Tom and I drove back home and my parents and Steve followed us.

I spent the rest of the day going through Kelsea's room again. I'm not sure where the strength came from but I began going through her closet, drawers, clothes, everything for the second time. I found 3 cameras in her closet that were not developed and knew I had to get them developed immediately. I folded her clothes and put them away in her drawers. I straightened up her closet, papers, books, and I was looking for anything to bring me comfort.

Before I knew it, the day turned to night. Steve was still forcing me to eat and he sat me at the table and almost spoon-fed me. My parents were telling me I had to eat. I didn't want to. How could I eat? Kelsea was not here and I kept waiting for her to walk in the front door still. I kept telling myself she was just at her friend's house and would be home soon.

Digger and I were still sleeping together in the living room. We lay there watching TV in silence. I thought about still having to get her dress and outfit together for the funeral home. That was my task tomorrow. I just want to get through this night. I just want Kelsea back. I just want to know how this could have happened. I took a Xanax and went to sleep.

August 29

When I wake up in the mornings now, I am afraid to look at the clock. I am afraid to see 6:14, the time that I woke up and my life changed. Today I have to go pick out Kelsea's dress. Digger, Tawnia and I went to the mall today to a store with beautiful dresses. As I was walking toward the store, my cell phone rang. I answered it and it was Chris, Kelsea's psychologist for the last year. He had been out of town when all this happened and just returned to his office to receive the news.

Chris loved Kelsea and she loved him. I walked over to this wall outside the store and I leaned against it, talking, and slowly made my way down to the ground to sit. It was surreal telling Chris what had happened. He was very upset because right before he left for his vacation, Kelsea had a session with him.

They talked about what was going to happen the next couple weeks until she saw him again. I think he felt like he failed Kelsea, but he didn't. He was a positive influence in her life and she loved him. I finished my conversation with Chris and walked in the store where Tawnia and Digger already were.

Tawnia had called ahead to the store and spoke to the manager, Barb, and explained to her we would be coming in and what we were there for. I sat down in a chair that Barb had brought over for me. I began to cry. How was I going to do this?

Barb began bringing different dresses over to where the three of us were sitting. Digger would just say, no, no, no and then finally a yes. She brought over a beautiful white dress with hot pink accents. It was to the floor, fitted to the waist and perfect. It looked just like a prom dress but then Tawnia thought about something I never would have . . . the autopsy and the scars that would be on Kelsea's chest. The dress was low cut so we had to now pick out a scarf to wrap around her neck and chest to cover any scars.

Barb brought out gloves next, ear rings and a tiara. Yes, Kelsea was my princess and we wanted her to have that tiara. My goal was to have Kelsea look absolutely beautiful one last time, for all her friends to remember her. I knew that with what Digger just picked out we could accomplish this.

When we were done, I walked out of Prevue completely drained. Tawnia drove Digger and I back home. I decided I wanted to make a poster to put up in the hall at the church to educate people on Kelsea's bipolar disorder. I don't think too many people knew Kelsea was bipolar and I wanted them to know. I went on the internet and printed up several different facts on this disorder.

I went through Kelsea's pictures again and picked some different ones to put on the poster. I had everything laid out on the dining room table and was talking to my mom when all hell broke loose. We were talking about one of my brothers being diagnosed bipolar several years ago. I told her I understood his choices in life with having to live with this disease.

My parents were not well educated on this disorder and didn't understand that my brother's life and choices he made were part of his bipolar disorder. I understood his pain because I saw it in Kelsea at times. I got frustrated with my mom and told her she didn't understand. I told her that my brother was sick and I understood his pain. My parents took that as an attack on them and all hell broke loose.

All I know is I looked at them and said, "I just lost my daughter," and I ran out of the room into my bedroom bathroom. Steve followed me and was yelling at me. I fell to the ground in a fetal position, screaming and crying. Digger came into the bathroom and asked what was wrong. He had just fallen asleep on the couch when this happened and my screaming woke him up. Steve looked at me and told me he was going to walk down to the 7-11. I stayed there in a fetal position unable to move.

I don't know how much time lapsed before Steve came into the bathroom again. Digger was still with me. Steve got me up off the floor and told me my parents were leaving. He said they decided to drive back to Arizona that night because they were so upset. I said okay. I couldn't really understand, but I was too exhausted to even care. I just needed some rest so I took another Xanax, and Digger and I found our way back to our spots of comfort—the couch and floor—and we went to sleep.

August 30

I woke up today and knew all I had to do was make it through one more day till the funeral. Everything was in order. The flowers were taken care of, the collage of pictures, the DVD's, the balloons, the police escort, the music, absolutely everything but my parents. I called my sister to see if she had heard from my mom or dad and she said yes and they were already home. I really didn't care today though because my daughter just died and if they didn't want to go to the funeral that was their choice. Hell, I don't have the strength to care.

I spent a lot of time on the phone with Cara today. I've also been arguing a lot with Steve. He told me his biggest fear was that he just lost his wife. Yes, that upset me because I just lost my daughter and he did lose the woman I was nine days ago. He kept telling me, "This isn't all about you," and he was completely wrong. This is about me. This is about me losing my daughter; the girl I spent the last 17 years raising. My children are my life.

The woman I was on August 21st is gone forever. I will *never* be the same. My heart is broken, shattered and will have a hole in it forever. No one or nothing will ever take Kelsea's place or fill that hole. I am dead right now, too. I do not know how I am surviving. I do not know how I am waking up every morning able to take care of all this "business" because that is what planning this funeral has been, business. It's like over the last eight days I have been on an autopilot mode, and although the tears flow freely and frequently, I still have the numbness that has allowed me the sound mind to plan this funeral and make it perfect.

Today is almost over and tomorrow I will be waking up and attending the funeral of my only daughter: my beautiful, loving, vibrant, free-spirited 17-year-old daughter who did not deserve to die. So as night comes upon me once again, I set my bed up with my son still below me on the floor, hoping that tomorrow I will be able to function. Again, I took a Xanax and somehow fell asleep.

August 31

I woke up today still breathing and knowing I had to begin getting ready for Kelsea's funeral. I cried in the shower, of course. As I stood before the mirror putting on the little bit of make up that I could, my eyes were cold and empty. I put my black dress on and Steve, my son and I got into the truck and began the drive to the church.

As we pulled up to the church, there were several people out front talking and standing around waiting. I knew that once I got out of the car, they would all be looking at me and I didn't want that. Luckily, an old boyfriend was right there when I got out of the truck. He took my arm and led me into the church. I kept my eyes down so I didn't have to look at the great sadness on all the faces.

He walked me into a room off to the right side of the church. The doors to the church were still closed so I did not see anything at that point. In this room were a couple of my close girlfriends. They were all hugging me and giving me their condolences. I was doing "okay" until the reality of where I was and what was about to happen slapped me boldly across my face. I completely lost control of myself. I cried so hard I couldn't breathe. I was shaking and heard voices all around me but didn't hear what they were saying. All I knew was I couldn't breathe or think or feel . . . then Pastor Tony Jr. came into the room.

He saw the pain and suffering I was experiencing and he asked us all to join hands and he prayed for me. By the time the prayer ended my sobbing was short and subsiding. I wiped my eyes and put myself back together. Pastor Tony Jr. said he would start whenever I was ready.

I took some time, then I slowly got up off the couch. I walked into the lobby where Tawnia had done everything perfectly. There were tables set up with pictures of Kelsea everywhere, and the poster I made was placed right before we walked into the church. There were people walking around in the lobby looking at everything and talking quietly to each other.

I walked into the church and before me lay my daughter. I slowly began the walk toward the front of the church and my legs were weak. As I approached I had to stop. I couldn't walk forward anymore. Someone took my hand and walked up with me, closer till I was beside the casket looking at how beautiful Kelsea looked. I couldn't move. I just stared at her. She was so still. I walked closer and I touched her face. It was so very cold.

I looked at her from head to toe and my son stood beside me silently. He just looked at his sister as tears filled his eyes. People were coming up and looking at Kelsea, placing flowers near her. On the big screen above her was the DVD playing with pictures of Kelsea from the time she was born to now. I could hear people crying and sniffing and the sadness permeated the church.

Pastor Tony Jr. was sitting in a chair by the altar and patiently waited for me to finish admiring my daughter and her beauty. I looked at him and I simply nodded my head that I was ready. My son and I took a seat. Pastor Tony Jr. began the service by explaining that this was going to be Kelsea's "Celebration of Life" service. He knew that I was going to speak twice and he asked me to come up to the altar. I brought with me what I planned to say. I stood there and looked at all the people there honoring my daughter. I looked down at my paper and this is what I said:

"Kelsea was diagnosed bipolar manic depressive at the age of 12. Never in my life would I have ever thought being bipolar would have been so devastatingly difficult. As the years passed, this illness progressed, leading to the last 2 years of my baby's life.

I know that on the outside, Kelsea always had a smile for everyone, and a witty comment to make you laugh and not a care in the world. But then, she would come home to me and sit on the couch with tears in her eyes saying, "Mom, I need help. Not just Chris and Usha." They were her doctors.

I would kneel down and ask her to tell me what she needed, I would do anything. She would simply respond, "I don't know."

Every minute of every day was a struggle for Kelsea. She was a very sick little girl and no one knew it or understood it like I did. She was not the party girl that everyone thought she was . . . she was self-medicating all the pain that lived within herself. She never shared with anyone this illness because she thought no one would understand.

At times her thoughts raced so fast, she couldn't speak. She could be up for days with no sleep . . . she would sit there and have to cover her mouth because she couldn't stop giggling no matter what the mood of others. She would come home and lay down and sleep for 2 days or at the drop of a hat become so angry and irritable, yelling, screaming, crying.

My daughter suffered every day of her life. For a very long time, I have prayed that God protect my children from harm, evil and wrong doing, that He would deliver them from evil, and that He would take away all my daughter's pain and give it to me. That Monday night when Kelsea said goodnight, she lay down and the Lord answered my prayer. He took her with Him in the most peaceful, loving way, and she has no more pain.

He may not have answered my prayer the way I wanted Him too, but I trust Him. Hebrews 11:1 says:

Faith is being sure of what you hope for, and certain of what You cannot see.

I fought every second of every minute of every hour of every day for my daughter. My life has been forever changed but I find solace in knowing that one day, I will resume my job of mama for my baby girl, only then it will be for eternity."

I was able to speak without a single tear. I sat back down and the service went on. At one point the song, "Jesus Take the Wheel" played and I raised my hands in worship, crying and singing so loudly. I couldn't take my eyes off Kelsea. This was completely surreal, as if I was dreaming.

I also wanted to do the eulogy with Tom. Tom knew Kelsea and loved her since she was a very little girl. We walked up to the altar together holding hands and again, I looked out at all the people. Tom spoke first, then again I pulled out my notes that I had written to read to everyone. I wanted everyone to know what Kelsea loved and what she was about. I also wanted everyone to hear Kelsea's love for me in something she wrote for me one Mother's Day . . . as she professed her love to me. This is what she wrote:

Happy 2nd Mama's Day.

Mommy, I know that yesterday was the worst day of your life. And I would give the world to make it better and or to go back in time and change what happened. But the most important thing that I want you to know and remember is the love I have in my heart for you is indescribable. Like the church guy said, we have to pray and open up space in our hearts to allow and accept Jesus in us. My heart is wide open and ready for Him but there's more than enough room for you as well. And no this Mother's Day was not something to be remembered, but I do want you to know that I am always here for you and that will never change.

When I am off at college and something goes wrong . . . your fingers can still hit the digits and call me and you can expect me there! I guess that point I am trying to make is . . . just because Digger's head is in his @$$, doesn't' mean you have failed at raising him . . . it means he is just dumb. One of these days he is going to look back on what he has done and put you and I through and he will realize what an ass he was. But I am always here by your side mama, and that will never change. And the reason I hate being around you when you cry . . . is because it makes me cry when I see you in pain, and when I see those tears of pain roll down your cheeks, I JUST CAN'T STAND SEEING THE MOST IMPORTANT PERSON IN MY LIFE HURT! I JUST CAN'T! and money can not buy love and mama I am going to do WHATEVER you ask me to for you today . . . let's just call this your . . . "second mama's day!" From me to you. and I would love to go to church with you again sometime. But see words can't describe the love I hold for you in my heart! I just can't. But this I can say . . . and I say with joy, and LOVE and pride . . . I love you more than the law allows!!!!! And indeed I do! Mama . . . if you want a foot massage when you get home. . . . YOU GOT IT! If you want the house spotless when you come home. . . . YOU GOT IT! When you come home and say I love you to me. . . . I know I GOT IT! I love you mama . . . have a GREAT day at work. And I hope you stay safe there and I will talk to you later, okay mama. I love you more than the law allows. And remember . . . *God is always with you mommy* I love you.

Love always and forever,
TAT

As I read that aloud, I heard loud cries from people because they were able to see Kelsea's heart and soul at that very moment. I went and sat back down and Pastor Tony Jr. continued the service. At one point in the service Pastor Tony offered the prayer to be "saved." This was a prayer that Kelsea participated in every opportunity she got and that is why Pastor Tony thought it was important to offer. Kelsea "saved" 45 of her friends today.

At the end of the service, people formed a line to give their condolences to me. I realized during this time that I seemed stronger than the people coming up to me. I didn't cry, not once. Since Pastor Tony Jr. said that prayer for me in the room prior to the service, I had an incredible amount of strength. Maybe it was shock still too; I'm not sure.

As I shook people's hands and received hugs, I was unaware that Kelsea was being removed and placed into the hearse. When the line ended I looked and she was gone. I was told they were ready to go to the cemetery. As everyone left they were handed a hot pink balloon to take with them. I walked outside the church and our truck was right behind the hearse. I looked around and saw cars lined up in the parking lot ready to go and the police escorts were ready.

We pulled out of the parking lot and I looked behind me. I wanted Kelsea to have the biggest procession from the church to the cemetery that anyone had every seen. I realized I was actually smiling as we began the drive because the line of cars was so long, I could not see the end of them. I smiled all the way to the cemetery.

It took several minutes for everyone to arrive and park. Kelsea had already been placed above the spot where she was to be laid to rest. As everyone gathered around, Pastor Tony Jr. gave a very short service and blessing. I asked everyone to step out into the center of the cemetery with their balloons. As we stood there I spoke once again and thanked everyone for their love, support and honoring of Kelsea Lyn. I asked everyone to hold their balloons up high and we all let them go together. We watched in amazement as they all floated up together staying in a tight-knit pack as if Kelsea's arms were around them all saying, "Come to me, now."

I stayed as they lowered Kelsea into the ground and people threw flowers on top of her casket. It was so damn surreal. People again approached me with their condolences. Slowly, everyone left until I was the last one there . . . and it was now time for me to go back to my home without my daughter.

When I got home people were already showing up. They brought food, more flowers, and cards and just wanted to show me more support. I walked around my house not able to think yet what had just transpired because there was too much going on around me. As the day progressed people left my home and before I knew it, my house was completely silent, COMPLETELY silent.

I walked down to Kelsea's room and sat on her bed. I sat motionless. I sat emotionless. All I could think was "Now what?" Now what am I supposed to do? Kelsea was gone now, really gone. I had no funeral to plan now. I had nothing to keep me busy anymore. Now, I have time to think about the fact that my daughter died.

I went to Kelsea's room and I lay down on her bed in a fetal position and began to cry. Eventually, my son came in the room and sat down. He looked at me and he said, "Mom, I think WE live in hell." I had to agree with him; this new place where I reside is hell. He took my hand and led me out of the room, as he had done all week long, and sat me down on the couch.

I eventually lay down with him below me and realized the day was coming to an end for me and I had no idea what to expect when I woke up again.

CHAPTER ONE

August 31, 2006, Thursday

I miss you honey, you looked so beautiful. Your service was absolutely perfect and you gave me strength to not cry when I spoke. You made me strong. So many people were there that loved you, including Chris. You touched his heart and he cried at your loss. I can't believe you popped Adam's balloon at the cemetery! As soon as I mentioned your name, you had to make it known you were with us, thank you. Lot's of people stopped by the house this afternoon and I wish you were here with us but I know you are with your Heavenly Father now. You have the dad you always wanted. I promise you, I am going to do my best job ever to keep your legacy going. I want to help as many kids as I can and help guide them. I will see and be with you soon. I love you. I will say this, too, Kels, there are times I truly "feel" your presence. It's almost as if every day something is jumping out at me screaming "you" and I know you are with me. I know there will be days when I will not feel anything and those days I will miss you. I am going to try to honor you in different ways as often as possible simply because I love you, miss you, want you and need you, still.

"Each day brings Kelsea, each day brings new things, each day we will see, feel and know; She Is Here." It will be those special times that I am aware of that I will share with all. One of the most obvious times was today after the funeral at the graveside.

As each person left the church after Kelsea's service they were handed a pink balloon. After the graveside service everyone gathered in the center of the cemetery in completely open air and I began to speak. The sun was warm and the air was still. As we lifted our balloons into the air, I began to speak. The very second I began to say Kelsea's name a balloon popped! It was Kelsea's Godfather, Adam! I said, "See, there she is now. . . ." She Is Here!

September 1, 2006, Friday

I went to church first thing for grief counseling, Kels. I wish I didn't have to. I came home then and looked at all your pictures and I miss you. I lay on the floor and cried and cried. The house is so quiet now and I don't like it. I prayed last night for God to help me feel your presence and here came your spunky black kitty, Sassy, and she crawled on my chest and lay there and I felt you. I'm afraid for my marriage. I wish Steve would have loved you more and showed it more. I'm angry with him for that. All you ever wanted was to be treated nice and played with and respected. I'm sorry it didn't happen. I know you're respected in heaven. This is the longest I've ever gone without you honey and I miss you. But, before you know it, I'll be with you again forever. I love you, Kels.

She Is Here

I prayed tonight for God to show me, somehow, that Kelsea is with me, so I can feel her. Through the night as Kelsea's kitty, Sassy, lay above me on the window sill, she crawled down four times on top of me and snuggled so closely to me like never before and I felt comfort. Kelsea's love came to me through Sassy and I felt her.

September 2, 2006, Saturday

Thank you Kels, for the beautiful sky tonight filled with hot pink cotton balls. Sasha's mother called me and said it was you. I hope you know how many people's lives you touched. People you didn't even realize loved you. Digger is going to church with me tomorrow again. He misses you and cries every day for you. I cried a lot today again. I don't think another day will pass in my lifetime that I will not shed tears for you. I hope you will guide me in my writing because Sasha's mom called you a genius tonight with your writing. You truly are a brilliant writer and I promise to publish everything you have ever written. I miss your voice, your smell, your mouth, tickling you, yelling at you, YOU. I love you more than the law allows. Kisses, Mama.

She Is Here

Sasha's mother called me in the evening. She said Sasha called her on her way home from work and told her to look at the sky. It reminded her of cannonballs and Kelsea. Her mother said they were hot pink because of the sunset.

September 3, 2006, Sunday

How is my baby doll doing up there in heaven? Are you busy? I know you are happy. I'm sure you're with Melissa most of the time. Do you miss me as much as I miss you? Digger said today, this is too "awkward," thinking you're gone forever. I don't like saying that because it makes me sick to my stomach.

Sometimes I don't think everything has really sunk in yet. I get a sick stomach, chest pains and my finger writing is back. It would be driving you crazy right now. Digger went fishing with Adam and Payton today. He misses you terribly, Kelsea, and always loved you. I put all your pictures back today and it was hard. I also made a poetry book for Chris and your dad. They love you, too.

Please come into my dreams, Kelsea, so I can remember your laugh again. Love, Mama.

She Is Here

We stopped at 7-11 on the way to church. As we got out of the truck, Digger asked, "Where's Kelsea?" I looked down at the ground and there was a single cricket. Kelsea hates crickets! After church I went to the cemetery. As I lay with Kelsea and talked to God and cried, I sat up and looked at the flowers on her site. A small butterfly flew over and landed on a flower right in front of me, so still, as if it were looking at me.

September 4, 2006, Monday

I am so sorry I sat and watched Hillary Duff in her movie today. I walked into the wrong theatre and as I sat there for 5 minutes watching her, all I could think of was how much you hated her! You're so much more beautiful than she. I found out today Melanie is pregnant. I would give anything for it to be you that were pregnant. I'm so sorry that you didn't get to experience getting married and having children like I know you wanted. Maybe that's your job in heaven?

Watching all the babies up there? Did you meet the Australian Alligator TV guy Steve today? His death was crazy. I know how much you loved watching him and now you're with him! I cried a lot today and I don't foresee that changing. Please don't be mad at me though. You're my life, forever. Kisses.

She Is Missed

I missed you today—where were you?

September 5, 2006, Tuesday

Hi pumpkin! I tried going back to work today. Actually, Steve made me feel like I had to and I didn't want to go. I stayed a couple hours and there are so many people at the gym that don't know. I cried a lot today: in the bank, in the post office, at work, at home, in the car. I can't help it. In my head, I know you're in heaven and happy but my heart is empty and broken. I did send my book to Walmart and hopefully they will want it. I'm going to start on our book again soon. I have to get all your journals together though. It's going to be a #1 best seller; I know it. I thought today that if God ever took Digger too, I would kill myself because there would be no point to life. I can't wait to see you again. I long to tickle you, touch you, smell you, hear your voice. I'm so sorry, honey. I love you.

She Is Here

As I was putting gas in my car, the biggest, fattest, flying moth hit my arm and landed on the gas nozzle. I screamed, jumped back and chills ran through my body. Then, when I went into work for the first time today, I sat at my desk. I opened up the drawer and there were cotton balls and Q-tips in my desk. I smiled because I know how much Kelsea hated even the cotton on the Q-tips and there was absolutely no explanation or reason for those two things to be in my sales desk!

September 6, 2006, Wednesday

Hello Kelsea Lyn. Have I told you today how much I love you? More than the law allows. I got a letter today from a mom whose 12 year old daughter was diagnosed bipolar last year. They want to help me with our book. See honey, we are already starting to help people. I wish you were here with me though. I cried today. I got angry today and Cara and I talked a lot about not understanding why this happened to you and Melissa. I only hope you two are hanging out together. I still don't think it has sunk in yet. When I'm out places, it's as if I'm just going through the motions. At times, I get sick to my stomach. I get chest pains, my back hurts and I feel lost and empty without you.

Sometimes, I don't want to wait 40 more years before I see you but I have to take care of Digger. Kisses.

She Is Here

Today, Sassy walked over to the chair I was in and jumped up into my lap. She lay there all snuggled up tight and gave me love. Colleen said when she got home from work yesterday the song "I Believe" was playing from her CD player in her kitchen as she walked into the house and she knew you were there.

September 7, 2006, Thursday

Hello baby doll. Well, at work tonight I had to deal with a lot of members asking where I've been. It sucked. People are still in shock, honey. No one believes that you'll never be here with us on earth again. It's called denial. Everyone does know though that you are in heaven. Your dad called me tonight and told me he still loves me. I knew he did. Digger said he called him, too, and told Dig he is worried about me. Can you believe it? I spent most of the day crying. I cried all the way home from work. I hate to tell you this, Kels, but it's going to be awhile before that stops. I believe there is no greater job than that of a mother or father. It makes me wonder what God has planned for me that is more important than being your mama. I'm sure you already know. Can you let me in on your secret? I love you, miss you, and need you . . . soon.

She Is Here

Digger wanted an omelet for breakfast. I opened the refrigerator door and knelt down to get the eggs. For a moment, I got an overwhelming smell of Kelsea, so strong I began looking for flowers in the refrigerator, in the trash and found none; just the sweet smell of Kelsea.

September 8, 2006, Friday

How is my baby? You know you are the baby of the family just like I was . . . spoiled, too. You know you were! It never mattered what you had done or how mad I was at you; all you had to do was sweet-talk me and give me that smile and I would cave in! I got a call from Jo today. She has become close to God again and believes He has just put her back into my life to help me because I'm not doing well. At the gym, Jane asked me if I was sleeping because my face looked so bad. I just told her that's called pain. What you see on my face is all pain. I don't think the pain will ever leave me for good. I miss watching Sassy chase you around the house and hearing your loud screech followed by your laugh. Please, come into my dreams, Kelsea, so I can see you again and hold you and smell you. I'll love you forever.

She Is Here

If all else fails, I feel Kelsea through her kitty and I know she is with me.

September 9, 2006, Saturday

Hello Angel, another rough day. I called Cara and asked her why every day gets harder, not easier? It's because I'm still numb and in denial. She said I will be for a long time. I lost it in the bank today. Some idiot was rude to me and I let him have it. The bank was packed and I started yelling at him. I made it to my car and sat on the concrete and cried. A nice girl put her hands around me till I stopped crying. Then, she told me how beautiful you were. Dig and I went to the beach with Colleen today. He took me into the water. We wish you could have been there with us. It's starting to get cold. I wish you were here to cuddle with. I'm going to come see you tomorrow. Colleen said you talked to her today about what you want for me, to be happy. Guide me honey, work with God and help me. I love you more than life itself.

She Is Here

I feel your love through Sassy every day. Her affection and love for me grows every day. Colleen said you spoke to her today while we were at the beach. She said you told her what will make me happy.

September 10, 2006, Sunday

Hello Kelsea Lyn, how was your day? Mine was long. Dig went to church again this morning. I had a hard morning. I was looking at our picture crying, touching your face. Did you feel it? Do you see me every day and all I do? I wanted to go see you today but I couldn't. I watched your funeral today with Jo. It was hard, very hard. I cried more today than the actual day. I guess it's more a reality now or at least as real as it can feel. 19 days without my baby girl and I miss you every minute. I still can't eat really and haven't been back to the gym. I don't know when I will; I have no desire. I'm seeing a therapist on Tuesday. I know I'm going to be wiped out after. Are you truly happy now, honey? Is it as beautiful as the Bible says? Do you miss me? Please don't make me wait till 2063. I love you.

She Is Missed

I missed you today. Where were you?

September 11, 2006, Monday

Wow, honey, what a shitty day. You know how I have no patience for rude people? Well, now that you are not here with me, it's even worse! At work, on old lady was rude to me. I told her, God bless you today and she got mad. I ended up having to leave work after an hour. Do you like your hot pink rose and black teddy bear? I got it at 7-11. At least I got to spend an hour with you today. I yelled at God for awhile . . . told Him I just don't understand. I keep asking Him to tell me what I'm supposed to do now. Do you know? Will you tell me? I also told God I didn't think anyone, including Him, could love you more than me. I started a photo album tonight with all your pictures. You look so happy in all of them. I feel bad that I never provided you with a real "family." I'm sorry you never felt loved. Please tell me you're loved now or, maybe please let me know that you know how much I love you. Kisses.

She Is Here

Not once, but 3 times while typing on the computer, wanting to type *Digger,* you came through my little digits and typed *Kelsea.* Then, at the cemetery today, during my crying, praying, yelling and talking—I heard you tell me the title of our book: *When Society Is Ignorant;* a book to educate people about your bipolar disorder. The book we were writing together. I heard you so clearly.

September 12, 2006, Tuesday

Dear Kelsea, I forgot to thank you yesterday for telling me the title of our book: *When Society Is Ignorant.* I saw a therapist today, but she was an intern like Candace was and won't work for me. I am seeing a guy on Tuesday though. I showed a lot of people your memorial card today and can you believe 2 of them were bipolar, too? I'm telling you honey, this book is going to be BIG. I only wish you were by my side here, not in heaven. I was asked today about how I was able to get through each day and I had no answer. I think I'm just going through the motions of each day right now, not actually living. Once again I cried a lot today. Cara said I looked bad today. It's the pain coming out in my face; my eyes are empty, like they have no life anymore. I hate waking up each morning without you. One day though . . . I promise.

She Is Here

At Walmart, I found your perfume. I bought 2 bottles. I drenched myself in your scent . . .

September 13, 2006, Wednesday

Hello Sweetness, it was another long day. I went to Dr. Johnson for the pain I have in my back. He gave me a cortisone shot then I went to another therapist. No luck. All I keep getting are rookies and we both know we are way above a rookie. The therapist said I looked extremely depressed. Really??? I thought you would, too, if God just took your life away from you. The rest of the day was at home. Miss Ramie stopped by and we talked a couple hours. She's going to have an entire page dedicated to you in the yearbook and see if I can't walk for you at your graduation from Westhills. Yes, I cried a lot today again. You better get used to it because I don't see it stopping for awhile. I can't believe it's only been 22 days. My Lord better not make me wait another 57 years to see you.

Please come into my dreams tonight, even if only for a second. I miss you so much; it hurts so badly. I love you, Tat.

She Is Missed

I missed you today—where are you?

September 14, 2006, Thursday

Well, Honey, I found a group of parents who feel the same as I do. I was the new one to the group and I cried so hard when I first walked in the room and all during the group. It was nice to have people who all understand. I actually felt a little better driving home. They all agreed that I need to go live with Tawnia for awhile, so I can be in a stress-free environment because, as you can see, home here sucks right now. Steve just doesn't get it and probably never will. I'm sorry he treated you the way he did. I'm sorry for a lot of things. I'm sorry your dad abandoned you, his family ignored you, your brother yelled at you. But, I know you knew deep down how much I love you. I would have died for you. I'm not afraid to die now at all. I can't wait to hold you again and see you scrunch your nose and freckles! Hugs and Kisses, Mama.

She Is Here

As Jeanie told me she raised her hand to be saved, I got chills and so did she.

September 15, 2006, Friday

Hi baby. Did you enjoy our visit with Jeanie and Jackie? Do you see how much you are missed? Today was the hardest day yet. I cried all the way to work. I came home and just wanted to lie on the couch all day. I'm still waiting for an "easier" day. Can you tell me if I will ever have one? Here's another weekend and I know you're safe . . . but I wish you were sitting here with me, flinging your body across mine as I tickle every part of your body except your stitches! I look at your pictures and I long for you. I just don't understand why God needs you more than me? Your dad called me today again. Why couldn't he have been here for you? I'm so sorry. Is it nice in heaven? Do you wear make up and do your hair? What is your job? I can't wait to hold you again and kiss your pretty little cheeks. My heart is so broken and my pain is so deep. I love you, Mama.

She Is Here

Sassy slept with me all night and she had to lie on my chest with her head nuzzled in my neck. So much love.

September 16, 2006, Saturday

Well, Sweetness, I met Nick today. He was nice, he was cute and you made such an impact on him in one short day. He really liked you. He wants to come see you with me next week. It was tough being at Tawnia's today without you. It just wasn't right. No one knows, honey, what I am going through. Everyone is just living life normally and I can't. I was told today by a pastor to take as long as I need to mourn your death. I try being strong in the mornings but if I don't cry right away I feel guilty. I'm afraid to accept this because I still don't want to believe it. My chest hurts, I can't eat and I don't want to eat. This is the skinniest I've been. I just have no desire to eat. I wish you were here so we could share some Carne Asada Fries but you're not. Please tell me you see me, watch over me, protect me, love me, and miss me. . . . I ache. I love you forever.

She Is Here

Morning came, my mind woke up, my brain is already singing, "Suds in the bucket and the clothes hanging out on the line."

September 17, 2006, Sunday

My Dearest Kelsea, I love you more than the law allows. I heard your knock on the door at 3:09 am! You were here. Church was hard today, but I got the DVD from when I dedicated you to the Lord. I'm afraid to watch it though. I know because it makes me sick to my stomach. It's the only thing

I have of you living. I talked to Josue's dad tonight. He told me you were Josue's first true love. His dad cried with me on the phone. You were so loved and are still so loved. I cried a lot today and tried praying more. Can you ask God to help me through this, because I am struggling so badly? Digger is doing okay. He looks at your pictures a lot and is quiet. I hope Chris can help him, too. You know I will always have a hole in my heart. Like Cara said, the day you died, a part of me died, too. I will never be the same Tracy. Steve can't handle that. I need a man to love me through this all. I miss you.

She Is Here

3:09 am, I awoke to a very loud double knock on the front door to my home. So loud it woke me up, my heart pounded. As I opened the door there was no one there.

September 18, 2006, Monday

Hi Baby doll, it was good going to see you today. I hate how sad I am at first, but I feel a little better when I leave. Did you like the pretty rose? That was Bessy with me; she's a client. Wasn't that sweet of her to come out with me? I wrote in our book today. I'm going to try writing a little bit every day. I know you will work your wonders through me when I write. Please give me the words. Do you know how much pain I feel now? Do you know how sad I get when I look at your picture? And yet, I have to have it in my hand all the time. I know, I cried a lot today. I'm going to see a therapist tomorrow and I hope he can help me.

Sometimes I think I'm not going to be able to make it, but I know I have to for your brother's sake. I know; he's even more spoiled now. I wish it was you I was spoiling. I ache for you. Love, Mama.

She Is Here

As I spoke to Tom about Kelsea's time with Josue and his family and I explained the love Josue felt for Kelsea, chills ran rapidly through my body.

September 19, 2006, Tuesday

Hi Honey, do you know how much I hate Tuesday now? It's been 27 days and still no one truly knows the depth of my pain for the hell I am in. I found my own therapist today. He asked about you and I showed him your picture. He said that you are beautiful. Everyone says you are beautiful. I knew how beautiful your inside was, your heart, your soul . . . under all that pain you had was such a loving, caring, considerate and polite girl. A day can't pass, an hour, a minute that I do not ask God, why you? Why take a girl from a mom with the deep love I have for you? Did He take you because you truly are an Angel? Do you have wings? I lit a candle for you tonight; did you like it? I'll bet you're at heaven's gate greeting all the new people, just waiting for me and Digger. My stomach is sick, my chest hurts and my face shows the pain in my heart. I feel as if I will never smile again or feel joy. I asked God to bring you back to me. Will He listen? I want you. XOXO

She Is Missed

I missed you today . . . where were you?

September 20, 2006

My Dearest Kelsea, I'm so lost without you. The very second I think about you being gone brings tears to my eyes and since I think of you constantly, I cry. I wrote to Josue today on his Myspace and thanked him for loving you and told him you loved him, too. I know he was good for you. I haven't been working out and I have lost about 14 lbs now. I need to get into the gym but I have no desire. I don't want to accept your death. I told God I want you back. I'm pretty mad at Him right now. Has He mentioned it to you how often I talk to Him? I missed tickling you all during *Deal or No Deal*. Remember how much fun we had watching that? I talked a lot to a pastor at work tonight. We talked a lot about heaven and how when I get there my first question to God will be, Why? Do you think the hole in my heart will ever mend? I don't. I love you.

She Is Missed

It's been two days . . . why can't I feel you. . . .

September 21, 2006, Thursday

Hello Angel, what a day. It started out "okay," but, like always, as soon as I got in my car to drive, I started crying. I had to go to court to change your child support.

Can you believe what your dad wants to do for me? It's going to help Digger and me a lot. I wrote to you on your Myspace. Did you like it? Someone wrote you a poem, too. I went to group tonight and left so drained. Everyone kept talking about "images" of their child. No one found their child like I did. I will tell you this though, honey, I'm glad the Lord took you when you were home here. Someone told me, "She came home, to go home." I'm trying to learn as much about heaven as possible. Is it really like a paradise? Will you greet me at the gate?

Is your hair still black? Can you believe how skinny I'm getting? Thanks Kels! I love you, need you, miss you. XOXO

She Is Missed

I need you, please come to me. . . .

September 22, 2006, Friday

Sweet Angel, it's tough down here without you. I can't believe you have been in heaven for one month. The pain hasn't gotten any better. Your brother said he thinks we are living in hell here on earth. Digger and Steve got into it bad today. I believe God is guiding me toward Tawnia. I can't live like this, Kels. I wish you were here to help me through all this. Tawnia told me you really didn't care for Steve. I'm so sorry I couldn't see it. Please forgive me. You know there's' a lot of people here for me, who love me, but it still doesn't really help. I cancelled your gym membership today. I always dreamed of the day you would want to start working out with me every day. I was always so proud to have you there with me. You're so beautiful and built just like me and you have my appetite! Do you eat in heaven? Are there good desserts? Please, come into my dream, knock on the door, tickle my arm, SOMETHING. I need you. XOXOXO

She Is Missed

Why won't you come to me? I miss you too much. . . .

JOURNAL: ONE MONTH MARKER

So, it's been one month since Kelsea went home. I can't even fathom this. I'm still in shock. I can't even enter into denial because I haven't accepted this yet. It's like a bad dream. It's like she's just at her friend's house and she'll be walking in the door anytime now. It's crying more than I ever thought one person could cry; it's never ending.

It's talking to God one minute and being so angry and confused the next minute with Him. It's visiting Kelsea every week and, instead of being able to lie on the couch with her or in bed, I have to lie above her, alone on the cold ground. I can't even think about it being like this for the rest of my life. I can't think past this minute. What will the next month bring me?

PSALM 34:18
The LORD is close to the brokenhearted.

CHAPTER TWO

September 23, 2006, Saturday

Hello Sweetness, I miss you. Today sucked. I hate the weekends because the days seem so long. I mean I am supposed to be trying to track you down or pick you up at 3 am at the 7-11 in Lakeside. You know I would come get you anytime, anywhere, for any reason because I am "in love" with you, still. I watched *Pay It Forward* tonight. Colleen said I should. The boy died in the end and I cried. To watch the actress on TV, acting about losing her son . . . it just sucked because I actually lived it. I still don't understand, Kels. Tawnia is really struggling. I called her tonight and we agreed how hard today was. It makes me so sad to know you did not feel the joy of marriage or having a baby. It kills me.

I lay in your bed today, crying. I look at your room and just want you back. But you're not coming, are you? Why are you in Jeanie's dreams? Come into mine.

She Is Here

As I sat at breakfast with Digger, I pinched the end of the straw paper and blew . . . right past Digger to the next table, hitting the man reading his paper, and I laughed, remembering when I took you and Sherry out to eat for dinner. I blew the wrapper there and it flew to the next table hitting the dad in the head! We laughed so hard we almost cried!

September 24, 2006, Sunday

Dear Kelsea Lyn, that is such a beautiful name. I spent some time with Tawnia today. She showed me the room that you were going to live in. Guess what? It's going to be my room now. I can't stay in this house. I can't heal here and I know how much Tawnia loved you, Digger and me; she is our family now and we miss you so much. I came home from church today and ran to the toilet. I felt like throwing up. My chest pains have been bad today. I saw pictures from your funeral. You really did look beautiful but I cried, hard. Do you think I will ever truly accept you're gone? I know you're in my memories, thoughts, heart and soul but I want your physical body. I want to feel your hair, tickle your legs, and see your smile. Jeanie dreams about you all the time. Why can't I? How can you be gone 32 days already? I'll visit you tomorrow though, always. I'm sick without you. Why me?

She Is Here

I sat in the chair talking away to Colleen. Jeanie sat quietly watching TV. Jeanie looked over into the kitchen and saw some boxes moving; then WHAM! They all flew all over the floor scattering papers, clothes and nails everywhere. I got up to scoot the cat away from the boxes she just knocked over only to realize the cat was outside.

September 25, 2006, Monday

Hello little girl. I worked more today than I have been able to. I actually trained 3 people and did okay. Of course, once I got home tonight I broke down and cried in the shower, on the floor and in the chair. I cry driving in the car, always. I know it's because I pray then. Did you like the flower and the teddy bear? It's hard to go see you because I lay on top of your grave and can't believe you're buried below me. It turns my stomach when I think of it sometimes. But, I will never stop coming to see you. I will never move away from you, ever. Josue wrote to you today. Do you miss him? Do you miss me? Do you even think about the life you had here? Did God take you because you would have had a tough time here? I don't want to wait so long to see you. I'm not afraid to die. I will be buried with you. I want to hear your voice, see your smile, watch you eat, sleep and live. Why? Why? Why? Why me Lord?

She Is Here

In the words of Nina: "She may be gone from here—but she lives forever and you love her in here," as she touches my heart.

September 26, 2006, Tuesday

Dear Kelsea, I love you with all my heart and soul. I miss you every second. I actually didn't cry today as much as I have been, but I will tell you I feel guilty about that. I did lose it though when I saw the pastor at church. I read in the Bible today about everlasting life. I understand all of that, but it doesn't help lessen at all the pain I feel of purely missing you. If I think about finding you that morning, I cry and get sick, so I try not to do that. It's hardest when I drive somewhere because that's when I pray the most. It's hard for me to think I have to wait to get my answer. Was that really you knocking over all the boxes? I think it was. I bet you're mad Digger and I are moving in with Tawnia. I need to be around her right now because I can't heal here. Digger said tonight he misses you. I'm sorry you never got a driver's license or went to prom or to college. I get angry about all that. Not at you but at our heavenly Father. XOXOXO

She Is Here

It's as simple as Sassy jumping up in my lap, licking and loving me.

September 27, 2006, Wednesday

How is my Angel doing in heaven? Are you busy up there? I wish I knew what it was like, but someone said to me that if we knew how wonderful heaven really was we would be stepping in front of trains! I miss you, Kelsea. Today was a very hard day emotionally. I didn't just cry, I sobbed loudly. I try not to think about when I found you and what you looked like but it's hard sometimes. I get sick to my stomach when that happens. I finally went to workout today. It was tough. I thought about you walking on the tread-mill next to me and how you complained because you were sweating! I just knew one day you and I were going to workout together and now we can't. Do you workout in heaven? Have you seen your Myspace? It's beautiful. I miss you, Kelsea. I don't want to spend the rest of my life here on earth without you. I just have to believe in our everlasting life together one day . . . tell God hello. Love you.

She Is Here

I open the sliding door; in runs Sassy and I know . . .

September 28, 2006, Thursday

Kelsea Lyn Phelps, I can't believe you cut up my favorite stretch jeans into a skirt!!! When did you do that? I began going through your room and clothes today and found so many cut-up clothes. It made me smile. Thank you. Another hard day, lots of crying, questioning and wondering. The sunset was so beautiful tonight. Tawnia called me to see if I saw it. Did you do that for us? I read a lot in a book on heaven today. I wish you could tell me what it's like. I wish you could tell me you're OK. Maybe once you do that I will move a little bit forward.

In group tonight we all talked about how we just miss our children. I shared your "Happy 2nd Mama's Day" letter because it shows the real Kelsea, the healthy girl, the girl I love no matter what. Unconditional love is all I ever had for you. No matter what, I was always proud of you and bragged about you. Till tomorrow, I love you.

She Is Always Here

I realized today, even if nothing jumps out at me, she is still in my heart.

September 29, 2006, Friday

Hi honey, how was your day? Mine was different. I went to the gym to workout and I had no head phones so I had to deal with people. I found myself getting angry. Someone tried to compare their divorce with my loss of you. What a joke? No one, Kels, has a clue what I go through. Sometimes I get mad at all the life going on around me. Don't they know how miserable and sad I am? Are you happy now honey? Do you feel better? Do you really have no pain or sadness? I guess I just get mad that I couldn't do that for you. I couldn't make you well. I want you back. I'm trying not to think about you being gone because it makes me sick. But, I think you are the one who is giving me the strength to get out of this bad relationship. I know it's what you want—my happiness here on earth. I'll never be really happy till I am with you in heaven.

She Is Here

Sassy was MANIC tonight!

September 30, 2006, Saturday

Hi sweetness, how's my baby? I'm okay this minute. Of course, I just got done crying, too. Your Myspace is still pretty active! There's a picture of you and Jeanie that just kills me. I was pretty nauseous this morning and I wish this dang lump in my throat would go away. Jeanie is going to church with me tomorrow.

You know you helped in her salvation and will see her again. I have a lot of questions for the pastor. I read Hebrews tonight and I pray this didn't happen to you because of my past, my punishment. I did not sleep at all last night. I didn't take a Trazodone. I thought I could sleep. Steve and I have drifted so far apart but it's okay because it confirms what I know and need to do. I look at your pictures on the wall and get so sad. I hope one day I can look at them and feel joy. I'm putting, "I love you more than the law allows" on our gravestone. One day, honey, we'll be together again. Can't wait!

She Is Here

A manic Sassy kitty and cotton ball clouds.

October 1, 2006, Sunday

Hello Angel, did you see who went to church with me? Jeanie wants to go every Sunday with me now. Another save you helped make. How I wished, though, it was you with me. Digger and I are going to see Chris tomorrow. I made a book for him in your honor. I also met Megan and Tracy today at Dog Beach. I think Megan may be schizophrenic, not bipolar. She's a sweet girl and I hope I can help her and her family. How about that fight with Steve? I can't do it anymore, honey. I don't have to put up with things now that you're gone. I know you want me happy. You know I wasn't happy. Can you ask God if he took you as a punishment to the lifestyle I lived before? I thought I was forgiven for that?

Why, Kels, did He take you when I have been so obedient and faithful? Can you help me to understand? Lots of crying again and sick when I saw this mom and daughter in the grocery store. I miss you. . . .

She Is Here

The choir sings of Angels and I drink Propel water.

October 2, 2006, Monday

My Dearest Kelsea, each day on earth here without you is horrible. At times when I'm busy, like training someone, then my mind returns to you not being here with me and I get so sad. I ask myself how I am going to live the rest of my life without you. I yelled at God tonight. Can you have Him explain to me how He can cause so much pain to His obedient child? How all this pain given to me is out of LOVE for me? I cried all the way from work to Josue's house. I can't even remember the drive home. I don't cry first thing anymore; I am sick to my stomach. Digger saw Chris today and it went well. I also gave Chris all your poems in a binder. I'm sorry I didn't visit you today but I will this week—I promise. It's only been 41 days and yet it still feels like yesterday. I hate the images of when I found you. I hope they go away. Will I ever feel joy again, honey? Or look at your picture and remember all the good times? I'm still waiting for you to walk in the front door. I love you.

She Is Missed

I'm sorry—I missed you today. . . .

October 3, 2006, Tuesday

Dear Kelsea Lyn, do you know I haven't cried today? Well, I cried with no tears in the car once today. I've been so busy though with everything going on in the house that I really do not have an opportunity to grieve. We're moving out in a week and I wish you were with us . . . in with Tawnia. I got to the gym again today for a half hour. It's just not the same at all now. It's like I don't really care, I'm just going through the motions. Jeanie and I cleaned your room out today. Were you with us? She's going to go see Chris, too. He is really a blessing and I know you loved and trusted him. So do I. I feel weird today, honey. I almost feel as if I don't feel anything. It's strange how different your life becomes and how much your wants and desires change. Nothing is really that important anymore, just Digger. I hate waking up every day without you and can't imagine the rest of my life now. Please enter my dreams tonight and let me know you're happy. XXOO

She Is Here

The scent of you, Mystical, so strong everywhere.

October 4, 2006, Wednesday • Scale (1/worst, 10/best): 2

Hello Angel, I'm sorry I cried all day. I know it makes you upset to see me cry. I woke up, though, crying and I prayed for an hour. So you ever talk to God about what I'm saying? Has He told you yet when I'm coming home? I can't even imagine another 40 years here, not seeing, holding, touching you. It makes me sad and sick. It's getting harder to go in your room because all I can think about is finding you. Part of me is thankful it was me who found you but part of me wonders—why me? How can I live with those images? Digger is sleeping and staying home a lot but I'll keep an eye on him, promise. I sent off all the information to the medical examiner now. I just want justice, honey. If someone is responsible, I want them to be held accountable. I hope you're okay with that.

I'm sorry you went to sleep and didn't wake up. Peaceful or not it shouldn't have happened. Yah, I'm PISSED. I also thought today, Kels, about how much of a roller coaster my days are. I thought it would be good for me to be able to say on a scale of 1 to 10, What kind of day am I having? What do you think? Yes?

Kisses 2 you.

She Is Here

Sassy crawled up onto my chest, nuzzling my face. As I picked up Kelsea's bag of sympathy cards and memory cards, laying quietly under the bags hidden was a half smoked cigarette.

October 5, 2006, Thursday • Scale: 2

Hello Sassy girl . . . that's you. You were a sassy, spunky, out-spoken young lady. You saw how hard today was didn't you? Why don't you talk to God when you see me struggling? I saw your dad today. We went to court and actually agreed on something. I also gave him the book I made of all your poems. Do you have any idea how talented you are? Your writing is going to blow people away in our book. Tracy emailed me today and said you and I are her angels and she thinks we will be able to save Megan from this illness. At group tonight, I shared that if someone broke into my home and brutally stabbed me to death, I would welcome it. Because, honey, now that I have felt the pain of losing you, I could look at them and laugh because nothing they did to me could compare to the pain of losing you. It's kind of like I want the physical pain. It would feel better than my pain right now. I miss and love you. I will see you again.

She Is Here

All the pictures I share with strangers . . .

October 6, 2006, Friday • Scale: 3

Hi Pumpkin, how is heaven these days? Is it really a paradise? It's hard to believe you are living in a place of no sin. Can you believe you have 45 days sober? So does Jeanie. I'm proud of you. I know you could have done that here, too. I would have helped you. I know you were struggling but I really believe you were on the right path. Did God want you because you would have had a hard life with your bipolar? Today, I wanted to go see you but couldn't. I'm sorry, I will see you tomorrow. Thank you for helping me shop at Walmart. I heard you singing when I walked out, "In the Arms of an Angel." Kels, can you help me get rid of the images? I think getting out of this house may help. I try to keep my mind busy. The hardest thing is when I drive anywhere. I constantly cry when I drive. I miss you more than anyone could imagine. No one, except my group, knows the pain I feel. Thank God for them. I just want us back in the apartment again, the 3 of us. Do you miss me? Think of me? Love me? At least I know you're safe.

She Is Here

I asked Kelsea to be with me, help me shop, guide me where I needed to go in Walmart. As I was walking out the front door, there was the music and song I heard, "In the Arms of an Angel . . ."one of the songs on Kelsea's CD.

October 7, 2006, Saturday • Scale: 2

Hello Love, I did some research on heaven today. Was your white stone beautiful? And your new name? I also bought another book on grief. I want to know everything I'm going through is normal: the crying, impatience, crying, anger, denial, crying. It's like this roller coaster ride. One minute I'm okay, the next I'm sick to my stomach, crying. It all passes to just return again later, over and over again. I cried loudly today but I know you already knew that. I trained Colleen today; I'm going to work out with her awhile. She has become my most supportive person. Can you ask God to bless her for me? I wrote an email asking for help for your headstone. I'm tired of you not having the proper stone to honor you. Soon though, I promise. It's hardest when I'm here alone, I hate it.

I'm looking forward to being with Tawnia. What is it like living with peace and joy? Do you ever sleep? What color is your hair? So many questions; I hate waiting. How long do I have? I want you back. I love you too much. XOXOXO

She Is Here

Each time I hear those words . . . in the arms of an angel.

October 8, 2006, Sunday • Scale: 4

Hi Baby. So, today's message at church was "press on." Jeanie went with me again and I know you saw us at the gravesite together. We miss you. Jeanie talked to a psychic today. The psychic mentioned our book and said you told her that is my mission and that if you were still here I would not be able to help everyone else because I would be too focused on you. I understand that but I would rather have you here than to help everyone else. I know that is selfish. We had fun at Colleen's watching the Charger game. We all talked about you awhile. I know you loved that. I actually had a fairly good day with minimal crying. I heard you're with Melissa and a few others. Do you love your everlasting new life? I couldn't imagine life with no tears or pain or sorrow. Is the food good? I want to honor you every day honey; help me do that. Speak through me in writing our book. Help me to help others. I love you, miss you, and want you. XXXXXXO

She Is Here

As Jeanie waited in line at the haunted house, up on the screen a truck and a cross on it said: "Phelps."

October 9, 2006, Monday • Scale: 2

My Dearest little girl . . . so I woke up feeling okay and by the time I got in my car for work, it's like this wave came over me and I cried so badly and hard. By the time I walked in work, I should have turned around and gone home. Then at the gym, Steve M. made me so mad complaining about his girlfriend. My patience, honey, is so thin. I've never had road rage before and now I do. I need to pray for patience. I'm not sure either how to answer this question: "How are you?" Shitty is what I want to say to everyone. I really have no answer. It's harder and harder to walk into your room, too. I did tonight and I flashed on you lying on the floor, when I laid next to you and you passed. I hope those images go away and that one day all my thoughts are good memories. But it's only been 48 days now. Does it seem like a long time to you, too? Do you miss me from up there? Are you with me here and I don't know it? I need a hug from you, please. . . . XOXOXO

She Is Here

Re-fries all over the ground, Sassy lying by my feet and me singing, "I wonder, who you'd be today . . ."

October 10, 2006, Tuesday • Scale: 3

Hi Honey, thank you for being with me so much today: the door shutting quietly, your smell, the windshield wiper! I was pretty busy today with the move and all. I know you wish you were moving into Tawnia's with us. I wish you were, too. I did well today until I didn't have something occupying my mind, then WHAM . . . here comes the wave. I'm sorry I cried in the bank. I know how much you do not like me crying, but I know you understand my pain, don't you? I cleaned your room completely tonight. I hate being in there now. I hate the stain on the carpet where the firemen worked you. I hate the images. I want to remember good memories but it's too fresh, too real, and too painful. I hope God can help me understand one day, Why? Cara's sister's friend lost his daughter (18) last weekend at the desert. Have you met her yet? She loved the desert, too. Be good to her, honey; show her your big heart. I miss you. XXXXXOOOOO

She Is Here

A door softly shut and I wake up to no one. I begin to pray and I smell you . . . as I am driving a friend's truck, the windshield wipers turn on high in a truck I've never driven, *swoosh, swoosh, swoosh* . . . and I didn't even know how to turn them on!!!

October 11, 2006, Wednesday • Scale: 3

Hello Love, long, long day here. How about you? Wait . . . there is no time in heaven! You're lucky with that because I have to wait what seems like forever to see you and yet it will probably seem like no time at all to you. Today was too busy to grieve. Except, why do I not cry when I am writing to you each night, yet when I read this to someone, I ache? I was a wreck reading this to Colleen and Jeanie. They helped me move out today. It should all be done tomorrow. I wish you were here with us to live with Tawnia. I woke up with Digger at 4 am and couldn't sleep so I prayed for a long time. What is the weather like there? Does it rain because I know you love the rain! I'm sorry you never got your license or got to work, or go to prom or graduate or really be loved by a boyfriend. I'm sorry I never took you on a good vacation. I'm thankful though I got to share my bedroom with you for 2 years. I loved sleeping with you. I miss you. X

She Is Here

All your friends at Tawnia's house, reminiscing . . .

October 12, 2006, Thursday • Scale: 2

Hi Baby, busy day today. I finished the move; we are now in with Tawnia and the boys. I only wish you were here, too. You're supposed to be here with us. I feel relieved being here, no stress, no turmoil and no more arguing. Did you see who I met tonight? Ken Druck, Jenna's dad. Have you met her yet? Can you tell her how thankful I am for her father and how honored

I was to meet him tonight? I left group wiped out but feeling good about my decision to leave Steve. Do you know Ken is the first person I have ever met that understands my life in raising you with your bipolar? He was so compassionate. It was amazing. He said it's okay to cry and to feel the pain I am feeling. He said I need to be in a safe place and now I am. I cry when I look at your pictures, but yet I have to have one with me wherever I go. I'm still in denial I think. I don't think I realize this is a forever thing. Forever is such a permanent word. I love you tons. Kisses and hugs.

She Is Here

A song plays on the radio . . . "I wonder, who you'd be today . . ."

October 13, 2006, Friday • Scale: 2

Hello Angel, I heard your voice today for the first time in 52 days. Desiree brought me the tape she made of your voice messages that you left me. I cried. Were you with me today at the cemetery? Did you like the rose? I can't wait to get your headstone. Today was our first full day at Tawnia's. You should be here, it's just not fair. I hate still having to tell people what happened. Except now, sometimes I don't cry. I just have this blank stare on my face. I'm emotionless. I don't know why. Can you believe I haven't heard from Steve yet? Are you ever with him? I wish I could feel you with me all the time. I need to talk to Pastor Tony. I have so many questions for him. I just don't know, Kels, how I'm supposed to just go on living day to day without you. I don't want a different life. I want my old life back with you. I would do it all over again, every second of your 17 years, good and bad. Please come to me, come in my dreams tonight. Bring me comfort.

Help me heal, please . . .

She Is Here

As I tickled my arms and chills ran through my body . . . I knew.

October 14, 2006, Saturday • Scale: 4

Hi Baby doll, wow . . . could you have been with me anymore obvious than at the gym, doing cardio? Thank you, I needed that. This was actually one of the best days I have had. I cried of course, but maybe I just kept busier than usual.

Maybe it's being in a healthier atmosphere, too? Greg's partner looked at your picture tonight and said you were gorgeous. I should have gotten you into modeling. Maybe this wouldn't have happened then. I'm so sorry. I hope you realize I always did what I thought was best for you. It makes me sad you couldn't graduate, or get a driver's license or work or go to prom or get married and have a baby. Are you happy enough in heaven that those things don't even matter? Jeanie's going to church with me again. I still haven't heard from Steve yet either. Sassy is starting to get used to this house. Please watch over me and ask God to guide me in my purpose here without you. Help me to understand. I love you. XOXO

SHE IS HERE!

As I ride the bike at the gym, I hold your picture in my left hand and hold the heart rate sensors with both hands. My heart rate pops up . . . 141 . . . as sweat drips down my face, I wipe it away with my right hand and my heart rate stays up on the screen . . . 140 . . . my heart rate stays constant even when I take BOTH my hands off the sensors. I look around and no one is near me anywhere. I wait for the last 30 seconds of my workout and count my heart rate and it's right on track with the computer . . . 141 . . . for 30 seconds without me touching the only thing that should have made the heart rate show up. And more than ever before, I knew without a doubt.

October 15, 2006, Sunday • Scale: 4

My Dearest Kelsea Lyn, I love you. I miss you. Now that I am with Tawnia I'm much busier with the boys and all and that's good. But, when everything settles and I'm alone, the pain is so fresh. I got all your Halloween pictures out for Tawnia and I cried the whole time. We're putting them on your Myspace. It still hasn't hit me when I think about you; that here on earth I will never see, feel, touch, and smell you. Can I do all that and feel all that when I'm with you in heaven? It's just not fair that you are gone. I try not to think about it all because I get sick. I mean it though when I say no one can even hurt me because to lose a child, honey, is the worst thing a person can ever experience. I know people look at me and know I lost you and wonder how I am even able to function and I don't know how I do it either, other than by the grace of God. He gives me strength but I'm tired of being strong. I miss your laugh and taking you to see Chris. He misses you. I love you.

She Is Here

The blow dryer wouldn't work in the bathroom yesterday even after flipping all the breakers in the house. I thought, Kels, be with me today. I plugged in the hair straightener and it worked. I plugged in the blow dryer and it worked; thank you.

October 16, 2006, Monday • Scale: 1.5

Hello Sweetness, I'm sorry. Today was one of the hardest, emotional days yet. I really felt like I was in another world when I walked in the gym. Rod called me and I was staring at him and didn't even recognize him. It was very strange. I cried half the day. I hated having to set up a payment plan with Cingular because my bill should not be that high and you should not be in heaven. You should be here with me and Digger and Tawnia. Everyone keeps telling me that you want me to be happy but I can't feel it. They just don't understand. They don't know my pain, my loss, my loneliness, the hole in my heart; if I even have one left. I won't quit praying because that is what keeps me going. Digger is doing okay. I know you're watching over him; he needs you to do that. Do you have any idea how much I miss you? I wonder how I am supposed to go on with life, without you. I watched the trolley go by today and I flashed on stepping in front of it. When will my life feel right again? I just can't foresee happiness. When will it come? I need you. XXX

She Is Missed

I ached for you today. . . . I miss you . . . where were you?

October 17, 2006, Tuesday • Scale: 3

Angel, better day today . . . is it because I asked you to be with me all day? Did you see Brian today; how he hugged me and told me that it does get better? He didn't even know me but saw my pain and sorrow and cried with me. I was told today, too, that I am very insightful. I know what needs to be done to heal. I'm trying to do all of it, but it's still such a long road, a never-ending road. I believe I will be able to help other people down the road. The girl at hospice today said our book is going to help so many people. She also said she likes the fact that I refer to it as "our" book. Well, that's what it is, OURS. How come you never knew how stunningly beautiful you were? Didn't I tell you enough how pretty you were and how proud I was of you? Do you have any idea how much I used to brag about you to everyone? I love showing your pictures to everyone now. I want all the good memories to be vivid in my mind. I want to dream about you. Why can't I? At least let me dream . . . I love you.

You Are Missed

I missed you today; I need you every day.

PSALM 34:17
*The righteous cry and the Lord hears,
and delivers them out of all their troubles.*

October 18, 2006, Wednesday • Scale: 3

Hi Honey, how is my Angel? Today was a much better day. Did you see how good I did with not crying? I can't help but cry though when I visit you. The last rose I left you was still there, too. Did you hear me when I talked to you? I had really bad chest pains all day for some reason. I mean, I know it's anxiety. I was also a little sick to my stomach. The easiest way for me to describe things is one day I'm okay or one hour I'm okay then this huge tidal wave comes over me and sweeps my legs out and wipes me out. I can't imagine the rest of my life like this, but I know it will be. I love being with Tawnia and the boys. Tawnia and I talk about you a lot and that's good. I try not to think about what has happened because I'm not ready to accept this all. I love you forever and ever. XXX

She Is Here

At your gravesite, I hold a single rose and spread its petals open so beauti-fully. . . .

October 19, 2006, Thursday • Scale: 3

Hi Tat, haven't used that in awhile; I miss my Tat . . . so does Digger. Digger asked me if I believed everything happens for a reason. I said yes but right now, honey, I am having a hard time understanding this. In my group tonight I said that whenever I start to think about what happened, my brain can't process it. I push it away and stop. I don't want to and can't accept this. I cried the whole time I was in group. I read to them all our dedication to our book and they loved it. Digger said that maybe God needed you for His glory. Pretty amazing out of Digger. You know, honey, I drive around and do things every day and for brief moments a day, life seems "normal." Yet, it's not. It will never be normal again.

I feel like a broken woman and feel like I wear a mask around people and when I'm alone it comes off and I grieve. It's almost Halloween. What would you have been this year? I wish I was taking you trick or treating. Do you miss me? I do you. I love you.

She Is Here

As your picture is passed from person to person, I read our dedication, so beautiful, and I know as they know. . . .

October 20, 2006, Friday • Scale: 4

Hi honey, not a bad day today . . . at least as long as I don't think about you. I want to be able to think about you and not have bad thoughts, but all I think about is finding you or you at the cemetery and it kills me. That's when the chest pains come on. It's been hard with Tawnia gone. I hate being alone and Digger's been out all night; so I have spent the night crying. What do you do in heaven on the weekend? There probably are no week-ends up there, hah? I haven't talked to Jeanie all week, but I think she's get-ting to the angry part. I want her to see Chris. Digger and I go on Monday. I need to start writing more in our book. Can you give me the strength to do that more? Talk to me when I write and help me, please? I can't process this. I don't want to. It's almost been 2 months and I can't believe I haven't held or touched you in so long. Remember how I would give you a kiss every day I dropped you off at summer school? I should still be doing that. IT'S NOT FAIR OR RIGHT. YES, I'M PISSED. I need you.

She Is Here

As I sweat on the treadmill, I smell you radiating around me. . . .

October 21, 2006, Saturday • Scale: 3

Dear Kelsea Lyn, today was confirmed what I thought. Sandra called me today. Now, I can move forward in making sure the person responsible for taking you from me is held accountable. Your death is officially an accident. I knew you were dirty for marijuana but no other drugs or alcohol. I knew you were doing better. Methadone was in your blood only; it was your cause of death. Yes, I'm pissed. If Laura didn't give you that medication, you would be here with me now. Anger today, a headache, chest pains, a sick stomach, and diarrhea. I had a hard day, waking up crying. 60 days today and it's unbelievable to me. I just try not to think about any of it. I know I will have to one day, though. I'm just not ready yet. I hate my new life. I'm pissed, too, that no one in my family has supported me or called me since your funeral. Tawnia once again is my savior. I'm sorry I didn't know and didn't help you that night. Please forgive me and let me know you are "ok" and happy in heaven. When will I see you again? Soon? I love and miss you.

She Is Here

Jimmy Stewart, *Anatomy of a Murder*, watching it because of you and your love for him.

October 22, 2006, Sunday, 2 Months • Scale: 4

Hello Sweetness, I can't believe it's been 2 months today since you went to live with your heavenly Father. I know He loves you and is making sure you are cared for and loved. But, even knowing all that does not make it any easier. I guess I'm trying not to think about it right now. I think I'm in denial. At first, I thought about it all the time and now I can't. Church was hard today.

Sometimes the songs are hard to sing. Pastor Tony talked about our trials and tribulations and how God is here with us for them and those blessings will come out of even the hardest storm. I have a hard time thinking ANY blessing can come from your passing. It was an accident. If she wouldn't have given you those pills, you would be here with me. I pray all day asking for strength. I think that is the only way I make it through each day right now. I wake up every morning crying now. I'm seeing Chris with Digger tomorrow. I will give him a hug for you. I can't even put into words how I feel. I miss you. I miss every fiber of you . . . your stitches, your smart-ass comments . . . YOU.

She Is Here

As I stroke Sassy's back, petting her fur, I get 2 electrical shocks.

JOURNAL: COMPLETELY BROKEN

It has now been two months since my daughter's death. I hate that word, *death*. I find that when I speak of what happened I refer to her as "passing away." I think that sounds more peaceful and less final. Of course, at this point in my life I do not believe in finality yet. I have come to a place in which, when I even remotely begin to think about finding Kelsea that morning, my mind immediately pushes it away, not wanting to think, not wanting to relive it all over again in my mind. But, do you know how hard that is?

The first month after Kelsea passed, I spent in that place we call numb. That place that no one can even fathom. I barely remember the first month actually. I know Digger asked me the day we lost Kelsea, if I would sleep with him and I said, of course.

I remember more now that I am in the second month of this hell I reside in. Every morning I wake up, I hate it because it means another day without my Kelsea. I find myself afraid, too, to look at the clock. I was afraid it would read 6:14 am, the time I woke up, walked down the hall and found my Kelsea, unresponsive. Even that word, turns my stomach.

I got up and walked to the front door to open it for the first time in several days. As I opened the door, everything hit me. Life was going on right before me. It was a beautiful, warm sunny day and cars were zipping by the house making that sound cars make as they drive by . . . *swoosh, swoosh, swoosh* . . . I hated that sound.

I looked outside at life going on and all I could think to myself was, *Don't you people know what just happened to me? Don't you know my daughter is gone? How can you just be going on like everything is okay?*

Then there were the sounds of the police cars and fire trucks. I was never really aware of them before all this happened, but I found myself hearing every single siren going any time of the day, and, once again, I hated that sound. I don't even remember hearing them coming to my home that morning, but I knew they were there and what it must have sounded like as they drove up to my house.

I remember the day it happened: laying with my daughter on her bedroom floor as we waited for the medical examiner to arrive. When I was told I could go in the room to see her, they had her blanket pulled up completely over her body, including her head. I was so angry. I stepped back and told them to take that off of her and they did. They gently pulled the blanket down to her shoulders. I went into the room and lay beside her. I touched her face, felt her hair, held her hand and wrapped my legs around her body. I cried and I told her how much I loved her; how sorry I was this happened.

Then, the medical examiner arrived. When it was all said and done, I remember the medical examiner holding my face in her hands and looking at me. I wasn't there. I don't know exactly where I was, but I was not with her.

She told me slowly and gently, holding my face, "I'm going to take Kelsea with me now. I'm going to take very good care of her for you." I said okay and they took me back into my bedroom. Once she had left, I was allowed back out and I went to her room. The rest of the day was unbearable.

It's strange how, when this happens and you know you have a funeral to plan, you can go from grieving to business in a second. I knew what I wanted for my beautiful Kelsea. I told the people around me what I wanted and they all made it happen.

For the 10 days between her passing and her funeral, things were hectic and I was busy preparing everything for her burial—another word I hate.

But after the funeral it is so true what happens . . . all the phone calls, visitors, cards, support basically diminishes, practically overnight. Then, you are left with the reality of what has just happened: you have lost the most important thing in your life, your child.

I know I sound so selfish when I say what I am about to say, but it is the God's honest truth . . . there is NO greater loss than the loss of a child. You see, I know that most people have lost a loved one or a friend sometime in their life. I, however, have not lost anyone until now. I struggle with that, too.

I remember being in the bank one afternoon. It was a Friday and the bank was very busy. I was talking to one of the tellers about what had happened.

Kelsea had been in the bank with me and people knew her. We were talking when a man walked by me and made the comment, "Real important bank business."

It took me a moment to realize what he had just said and then it hit me. He was standing at the window next to me. I looked at him and told him, "You have no idea what we are talking about." He made another comment back to me and I lost it. In a moment, I was saying to him as my voice got louder and louder, "I just lost my daughter. Are you happy now? Does that make you feel better?!" I grabbed my keys off the counter and began to walk out. It took everything in me not to throw my keys across the bank.

The bank was silent and I assume all eyes were on me as I walked out the front door. I barely made it to my car when I collapsed on the sidewalk, with my head against my car, hysterically crying. A young girl came up to me and sat next to me, asking me if I was okay. I put my arms around her and I cried and cried. Once I calmed down, I showed her Kelsea's picture. She told me how beautiful she was and how sorry she was for my loss. I finally calmed down enough to get into my car and drive home.

I'm reading my second book written about losing a child. I have seen my pastor several times, a therapist a couple times, attended church every Sunday, and I participate in a parent support group every Thursday night, which is strictly for parents who have lost a child.

That is bitter-sweet. You see, I know I need the group and the support, but at times I can barely walk to my car afterwards because it is so emotionally draining. I find myself all week long doing as expected, but when that Thursday night comes along, it is the only place that we can feel each other's pain, someone to understand. We discussed the first time I attended the fact that this was a "group" that none of us asked to be in and none of us wanted to be there but we had no choice. This was a choiceless group.

I have gone back to work and am trying to do "normal" daily living things. Nothing social though or with a lot of people. I couldn't handle that yet. I have gone back to the gym to work out because I know that I have to take care of myself. At least, that's what everybody keeps preaching to me. The first day walking back into the gym was tough.

I wear an iPod, basically so I do not have to talk to anyone. I was sitting in the corner of the gym when a guy walked up to me. He bent down and asked me if that was my daughter he read about in the obituary. I told him yes and the tears began. His eyes filled with tears and he told me, "I lost a son at the age of 23. I can tell you that for the first couple years I walked around on autopilot. I didn't enjoy life, or things. I didn't smile or laugh and I don't know how I made it. But, it does get easier and I just wanted to let you know that." He held my hand, squeezed it and walked away.

I have spent the last month with a perpetual lump in my throat.

Sometimes, it feels as if I am choking. I have chest pains; I know it is anxiety. I have headaches and no appetite to speak of. Of course the crying is daily. The easiest way to explain the crying is you never know when it's coming. It's like one minute you're okay and the next this big tidal wave comes over you, sweeps you off your feet and takes you down. Different things will trigger the waves or they just come on their own.

One night I was at the grocery store standing in line. I looked over at the line next to me and saw a mom with her 11-year-old daughter. My eyes filled with tears and they began streaming down my face. Another day, I was in Starbucks with my son. I saw a mother sitting there with her 12-year-old daughter. I walked over to her and placed my hand on her shoulder. I showed her Kelsea's picture and said, "I just lost my daughter, love your daughter every single day." Tears were pouring down my face. Sometimes I feel compelled to say that to every mother I see with her daughter just because they have no idea how long they have with her.

The second month has been no different from the first. All the pain is still here, all the physical ailments, all the racing thoughts, all the "what ifs." I still wake up, breathing every day and realize I must get up and do something. At first I gave myself 1 task a day to complete, but if I didn't complete it I was okay with that, too.

I have found that now, I consciously know I am repressing what has happened. I don't know if that is a good thing or not, I just know that is what I have been doing. Whenever I find myself beginning to think about all of this I feel my face, my eyes, squinting as if trying to think hard about something, then pushing it away. I don't want to deal with this right now.

I have Kelsea's pictures all over the place. I have laminated several pictures and I carry one of her everywhere I go. Sometimes, I am able to just hand her picture to someone and say, "I'd like you to meet my daughter." I did this at Walmart last week and the woman who was checking me out, said she lost her daughter also. I had no idea and I told her about my support group. She gave me her business card and I hope I am able to help her in some way.

Sometimes when I look at Kelsea's pictures, it kills me and other times I just relish in how beautiful she truly was. Everyone tells me that she should have been a model. She always wanted to be a model. I find myself wishing I would have pursued that more with her because maybe, just maybe this wouldn't have happened if she was a model. But, there go the "what if's."

It is still very hard for me to believe it has already been 2 months since she has been with her heavenly Father. I can't even fathom the rest of my life without her. I was never really frightened of death but now I desire it. The best way to describe the way I feel about myself as a woman is simply that I am broken.

The relationship that I was in at the time of this tragedy has been destroyed. I don't know if it is because he did not know how to grieve or did not know how to help me grieve. We grew apart every single day. I know it is difficult to be in my shoes and to understand my life now. I think being a step parent is completely different also. All I know is that within a short two months, it was over.

I can't say I blame him though because as I said, I am now a broken woman. I do not feel whole and I know I am hard to live with and handle right now. I don't know how many husbands could truly be in it for the long haul or "till death us do part." So, for now I grieve alone, with my son, and realize that one day I may be able to feel whole again, unbroken.

I don't know what the next month holds for me but I will see. I will also tell and write because these are the memoirs of a grieving mother.

PSALM 6:2

Have compassion on me, Lord, for I am weak.
Heal me, Lord, for my body is in agony.

CHAPTER THREE

October 23, 2006, Monday • Scale: 4

Hi Pumpkin, I got to see Chris today. It was nice but you're supposed to be in there with me. I got lost on the way there. Crazy how scattered your brain gets. Digger said, "Mom, you've been there 100 times." I told Chris the results of your toxicology report. We both feel so frustrated that we should have prevented it all. What is the hardest on me is thinking you were just going to sleep, ready to start your new school. The school you believed to be a blessing, East County Academy of Learning, ECAL. You had no idea that your heart would slow down and stop beating. You had no idea. That KILLS me. It makes me sick and crazy. My chest pains have kind of gone away. I don't think I have cried a lot at all today. Chris said it's okay and normal for me to repress the thoughts and to not want to deal with it right now. I know we have a lot of work ahead of me and I don't care really how many people you and I have helped and will help. I want you back. I don't just want you in my heart and thoughts. I want your physical being with me. Please, come in my dreams. I love you. XOXO

She Is Here

Scattered clouds in the sky, imagination at work, your voice in the tape recorder professing your love to me.

October 24, 2006, Tuesday • Scale: 2

My Dearest Little Girl, I love you. As the days go by, nothing seems to change. I keep getting asked, "How are you?" It's such a hard question. Fine, okay, good, would all be a lie. Shitty. That's what I want to blurt out and do sometimes, "Not well, broken." I'm not a whole woman anymore. I wonder if anyone will be able to accept me broken. I'm still not doing much in public. Sometimes, most of the time I just don't want to talk to people. My brain can't really have a conversation about things. Unless I'm talking about you, I really don't want to talk. I got all your reports in the mail today. I cried reading the autopsy. I just can't believe it's all about you. It's still surreal. I cried a lot looking at your Myspace. Do you have any idea how beautiful you were? Not only on the outside, but in your heart, too. I know that's why God took you. I still am upset though and don't understand why He needed you more. What is His plan, Kels? What am I supposed to be doing? Will I ever be happy? Will I see you soon? I love you tons . . . hugs and kisses.

She Is Here

As I drive down the road, I am forever praying. Praying that you are happy in heaven. I look in your eyes in your picture in my car and your picture moved and jumped as if the car made a startling sound.

October 25, 2006, Wednesday • Scale: 2

Hi Babydoll, hard day at the cemetery, I know . . . I think partly because the other funeral was going on. I haven't ever cried that hard. I have so much information about what happened to you and I promise I will not let your death go. I will make who ever is responsible be held accountable. Justice is all I want; the truth. . . . people to know the *whole* truth. You were doing so well and I was so proud of you, even through your struggles. It's nice to see people still writing to you on your Myspace, too, but it also seems like people are forgetting and I don't want that. That's why I have to finish our book. It is so that people know your legacy. I want people to know your struggles with being bipolar and your strengths. You were so outspoken and stood your ground like no one else ever has and I loved that about you. The funny thing about it, too, is you were usually right! I will make you proud, I promise. Headaches and chest pains today. I want you at the gym with me, next to me sweating. I love you, tons. XOXOXO

She Is Missed

I missed you today so badly, where are you?

October 26, 2006, Thursday • Scale: 4

Hello Little Girl, how's my baby? What kind of fun stuff did you do today in heaven? Do you have a boyfriend or are all the boys in love with you? Because I know you're like the most beautiful girl up there. Group was tough. I told everyone your story. They are all as pissed as I am at what was done to you. Do you have any idea how sorry I am I didn't save you? Can you tell me if God would have taken you that day even if you had not taken the medication? I just don't know what to believe. I get confused because I think that if God is such a loving, caring God, then why would He put me through all this pain? Tell me what His "big plan" is for me now and why I couldn't have done it with you by my side? Life is so unfair and confusing. I wish I knew just how happy you really are in heaven. Maybe then I would feel a little better. I just don't know. I miss you and love you.

She Is Here

Sassy girl sleeping all night, cuddling, biting me . . . loving me.

October 27, 2006, Friday • Scale: 3

Hi Honey, what a night! You should be here with us all; having so many kids to take care of is a good thing. It keeps my mind busy. What's so different is that any spare moment is dedicated to you. I met with an attorney today. I will not let your death go in vain. I can't say enough how angry I am at what happened to you, how wrong it is. I wonder though if God would have taken you a different way that night. Did He really know He wanted you on the 22nd of August? I hate that number now. It's almost Halloween and I wonder what you would have been this year? I know you would have gone somewhere dressed up. I can't even imagine yet Thanksgiving and Christmas or your birthday. It's been 66 days now and it still feels like yesterday. Don't people know that you need them more AFTER the funeral then before? It's sad I have had no family support. I have forgiven them all, but it still hurts. I hope you're having a great Friday night. I bet you met Scott today, hah? Tell him his mom is okay and loves him as I love you.

She Is Here

The love from Sassy is so strong when I hold her, love her and kiss her.

October 28, 2006, Saturday • Scale: 4

Hello Angel Girl, how was your day? They just all run together, don't they? I saw you at the gym with me today. Thank you. I also got some skull socks today in your honor. I hope you like them. Things here at Tawnia's house are good.

Did you see the 3 kids we have now, too? Pretty crazy, hah? It was really nice today being with Colleen because she lets me talk about you a lot. We laughed at the things you did. Do you have any idea how witty you were? I'll never forget your "shellfish" story! Or how you stood up for me at the 7-11 or remember when you stood right behind me because you did not want that guy looking at my butt!? You really loved me, didn't you? Not as much as I loved you. Today was probably one of my most "okay" days and I think because I asked you to be with me and I talked to you a lot today. You did hear me didn't you? It would be nice if you answered. You can when I get there with you—k? It will never be soon enough though. I love you.

She Is Here

At the gym, riding the bike with Colleen. . . . I asked you in the morning to go to the gym with me. Again, my heart rate shows up on the screen without holding the sensors. Colleen looks in disbelief. The chills run through me as the tears fill my eyes.

October 29, 2006, Sunday • Scale: 2

Hello Sweetness, I missed you terribly today. Church was harder than it has been and I'm not sure why. I am able to sing some songs now, but others I can't because of the words. Desiree saw my pain and came to sit with me. Another woman told me she knows God's plan for me is to help other people. I struggle though at why I couldn't help them all with you by my side? Will you tell me the answer as soon as I see you again? Being home alone today was tough. Jeanie put a new picture of you on her Myspace and it is stunning. It killed me. Tawnia and I talked about how surreal it all is. We both wonder if that surreal feeling will ever go away. I don't think so. I believe you just learn to live with it as well as all the pain. It's been 68 days now and the wound is still so very open and fresh.

I'm just so very thankful for Tawnia. Now I know why you loved her so much. I need you this next week to give me strength and determination to do what needs to be done for you, your justice. I miss you baby. Love mama.

She Is Here

Again at the gym with me: cardio, heart rate and not touching a sensor.

October 30, 2006, Monday • Scale: 4

Hi Honey, how was your day? Mine wasn't too bad. I found myself, though, thinking about all the things I hate now and I never hated before. I've been getting more headaches than I ever have. The chest pains are still here. It's like all I have to do is talk about you and what happened and the chest pains are here. I think I've figured out heaven. I think right now you're in heaven but you're outside the gates. I think people go to heaven and they are there and can communicate with loved ones. I think once the person is able to accept the loss, then you enter the Kingdom and meet your heavenly Father . . . then all peace surrounds you. I think you and I will go through the gates into the Kingdom together. My new motto in life is "bring it on" and all it really means is I am so NOT afraid to die and I welcome it, once I fulfill God's plan. I missed you today and every day till eternity. Everlasting life is you and me.

She Is Here

As I pay my phone bill and I need to enter my pin number, the 8 pops up without my help. I hit cancel and smile at the employee because I felt her. . . .

October 31, 2006, Tuesday • Scale: 4

Hi Honey, I love and missed you tonight for Halloween. I saw a girl in one of your old costumes; it was hard. We had all the kids there and I just kept picturing you playing at the carnival on all the slides. It's like as long as I'm busy with lot's of people around I'm okay but as soon as I'm alone, I'm done. I almost made it through the day without crying, almost. It was a tough cry though. I find myself coming up with a large list of things I hate. I have really learned to hate the "how-are-you" question. I've also learned that the days aren't getting easier. I am simply learning to live with all the pain. Still chest pains, headaches, crying, praying and more praying. I just pray the Lord has mercy on me and does not take Digger from me; I could not go on living if you were both taken. I've never been as frustrated as the day I tried to cut my wrist. You made me so angry and I just snapped. But you know what Kelsea Lyn? I would do it again to have you here. I still have the scars on my wrist from that day and I'm sorry if I upset you. Please, forgive me. I look forward to entering the Kingdom with you. I love you.

She Is Missed

Halloween . . . you should have PHYSICALLY been here tonight.

November 1, 2006, Wednesday • Scale: 2

Dear Kelsea Lyn, I woke up crying. I cried all the way to work. It was a trigger going to work today. The last meeting I went to at that hotel was the last day I had with you, 70 days ago. They sent me home right away. I cried at my attorney's office and the receptionist held me as I sobbed. I'm having bad chest pains whenever I talk about all this. My list of things I hate is growing and I hate the fact I have to have an attorney. All the receptionist asked was your date of birth and I lost it. It's crazy how one day you're "okay" and the next you're a wreck. You never know when the wave is going to hit. I hate people looking at me knowing you're gone. I hate how strong God has made me to get through this. I flashed today on hitting a cement guard-rail. The flashes seem to be coming more frequently. I don't think I could actually follow through but I think about ending it all. "Bring it on." I was an emotional wreck today—why? And to think I have the rest of my life? I love you more than the law allows.

I Samuel 16:7
God sees not as man sees, for man looks at the outward appearance, but the Lord looks at the heart. Amen.

November 2, 2006, Thursday • Scale: 3

Hi Precious Girl, some incredible things happened at group tonight. You know Jenna's dad—Ken? He said he sees me helping a lot of people one day and maybe even with him. Tawnia says hello and misses you terribly. The only thing that makes me so angry, though, is why couldn't I help everyone with you by my side? I learned tonight that exhaustion is grief's biggest enemy. It's so incredible when Ken runs the group. Colleen says she thinks this is just all part of God's plan for me. Is it? I had another "bring it on" moment. I'm finding myself day-dreaming more and more about hitting a guard rail or crashing my car. I was told there is a difference between wanting to die and wanting to kill myself. I'm ready to die but I'm seeing maybe how needed I am right now. I think Digger had a bad day. Watch over him, honey. He needs your guidance. Still have the chest pains and headaches and am crying terribly. I have to learn self-compassion. Can you help me? I love you more than the law allows. XOXO Mama.

She Is Here

Your beautiful pictures I carry without ceasing . . .

November 3, 2006, Friday • Scale: 4

Hi Honey, do you realize 2 months from today you will be 18? I hope a lot of your friends come to the house that day. I am going to open it up to everyone. I can't imagine though how hard it is going to be. I went to the house for the last time. That will always be the house I lost my baby girl in. I hate driving by that house. I'm sorry I didn't come see you today. I was so tired and couldn't handle the emotional stress there. I'll come see you tomorrow. I was super busy at work today. It's probably the most I've worked since you left. I hate Friday and Saturday nights because I'm supposed to be worrying about you and, knowing you're in heaven, I don't have to. But I'd rather be worrying. I've come to the conclusion that nothing about this gets easier and time does not heal all wounds. You simply learn to live with all the pain. I hate it. I hate the pain, sadness, crying, chest pains, loneliness, and brokenness . . . all of it. Please come back.

She Is Here

Each day at the gym, each cardio session, each heart rate that comes up.

You're so funny. . . . 187 heart rate and going up. No sensors touched, and Colleen and I know and smile.

November 4, 2006, Saturday • Scale: 2

My Dearest Little Girl, I love you more than the law allows. I woke up not feeling well today, nauseous actually. I couldn't place my finger on why but assume it is my undying sadness and loneliness I have for you. Colleen tells me all the time she just doesn't know how I do it. The bible says God won't give us anything we cannot handle. It must be my praying without ceasing and the prayers of all my friends that enable me to live. I'm struggling right now to sleep, even with the Trazodone. My head is spinning on so many things. I pray one day I will be able to not think about the day I found you. Why that way? Why me? Lying with you on the bedroom floor, holding you, kissing you, touching your hair, your face, holding your hand. Did you feel my pain? The whole day is a blur, sketchy. I will never forget 6:14 am though or the number 22. I hate them both. 22 was my favorite number my whole life. Why did you die on that day? Why did you leave me? I need answers. Hugs.

She Is Honored

Sometimes it's not as obvious you are with me so I have decided to honor you in some way, each and every day. I shared your picture with a girl in the nail salon. Your beauty is what she saw and you were honored.

November 5, 2006, Sunday • Scale: 4

Hello Tat, how was your day? Did you like your hot pink roses and balloon? I spread them out so pretty on your site. I'm going to call it that because I don't like *grave*. It was very peaceful out there today. That doesn't make it any easier though. I can't wait to get your headstone there so I can make you have the prettiest one there. All your friends around you will be jealous! I promise I will keep it beautiful in your honor. I've decided on your birthday, I am going to get my "In Memory Of" tattoo. So is Tawnia; we'll go together. I've actually had an almost okay day. It will never truly be okay because you're not here. I was so busy and I know that's why. Any downtime becomes hard. I prayed a lot in church today. Do you ever talk to God about my prayers? Did He take away all of your pain like I asked Him to do? I think he gave it all to me. I'm sorry you had to live with so much pain. I would have taken your place for you. It makes me sick to think of all the things you didn't get a chance to experience . . . come into my dreams.

You Are Honored

A visit to your graveside, a dozen hot pink roses, a "Thinking of You" balloon, prayers and tears.

November 6, 2006, Monday • Scale: 2

Hi Honey, what a shitty day. I was just so depressed at work and sad, then I came home and took a nap. On the way home from work I cried all the way home. I cried in Food 4 Less and this sweet girl asked if I was okay and I said no. She asked if I needed a hug and I said yes. She hugged me and I told her your story and showed her your picture. I had been standing there looking at this family, asking why you and not one of them? Then she came over. She was 17 and pregnant. She looked at me and said, "He only takes the best." It makes sense but doesn't make it any easier. Life does not get better because how can it when you never come back? I'm learning life is different and the pain doesn't go away, you just live with it. I wish people would learn to not ask me, How are you? They should just look at me and say, "It's good to see you." That way there's no pressure, no thoughts of how I am: shitty, broken, lonely, sad, sick, empty, angry, confused, frustrated and tired. I love you.

You Are Honored

No matter where I go you're with me in a picture. I jam Kottonmouth Kings and I love Sassy.

1 Corinthians 12:10
For when I am weak, then I am strong.

෴

November 7, 2006, Tuesday • Scale: 2

Hello Angel, yet another tough, emotional, crying day. What's going on with me? Can you tell me? I think a big part is that I didn't get the hugs and emotional support the first 50+ days and now I'm getting it wherever I can. I saw Lonny at the gym and cried. I saw Steve M. and sobbed in his arms. I have figured out one thing though. . . . I don't want people to ask me anymore, How are you?

Instead I want them to simply say, "It's good to see you." It takes off all the pressure of having to share how I'm really feeling: sad, broken, lost, empty, angry. See, that's another thing, too. I'm very forgetful these days. I think because my mind spins on everything. Have you ever known me to forget my cell phone anywhere? I have lately. You know I'm actually starting to like that Kottonmouth Kings song, too. You know, the one you would JAM every morning while getting ready for school? The one I hated! I miss you; it kills me. XXXOOO

She Is Here

Once again, at the gym on the tread climber . . . your picture resting on a 5-inch ledge. I look away and, as I turn back, your picture is floating ever so softly down onto the ground. There is no wind, no air, and no breath to move it and right away I know.

PHILIPPIANS 4:13
Whatever I have, wherever I am, I can make it through anything in the One who makes me who I am.

November 8, 2006, Wednesday • Scale: 3

Dear Kels, how was your day? Mine was still emotional but better. I find myself at certain times so compelled to show people your picture and tell them you're my beautiful daughter. Sometimes I can tell your story and sometimes I just can't. I've found myself accepting hugs from complete strangers. I don't care; I need to be held and I need to be able to cry as hard as I want to. It's now 78 days and I've cried every single day. Do you think

I'll ever go a day without crying? I'm afraid if I do, I'll feel guilty as hell. I guess I shouldn't, or at least I've been told I shouldn't feel guilty if I don't cry. But how can I not? To me, not crying would represent moving on and I don't want to move on. I want you back. I want you to walk in the front door. I want to go on a sugar-eating binge with you or share Carne Asada Fries with you. Do they have them in heaven? Have you eaten them yet in heaven? Will you share them with me there? Do you still love me? I miss you bad.

She Is Here and She Is Honored

I love you being in the gym with me every day; showing your presence in the heart rates. Then, I go right into honoring you. I introduced myself and you to the guy next to me on the lifecycle bike. I showed your picture to so many people in the gym because I'm so proud of you.

November 9, 2006, Thursday • Scale: 3

Hey Angel, a little better of a day if *better* can be used. I got pretty pissed though tonight when I was getting ready for group. I got so pissed I even had to leave. I was getting a picture to take and the biography part to our book and I was just pissed. I drove to group crying and praying. Then I got pissed that I am going through all this alone. Pissed that Steve failed me through this. My hands were clamped hard on the steering wheel and I just wanted to drive right into the guard-rail. I started praying right away for God to take away that anger. I know if I ever hurt myself, Digger couldn't survive and that would not be fair. I had a dream last night that the sheriff's department wasn't going to help me. I was so pissed in the dream. I will not let this woman get away with what she did to you. I promise you that. I love you more than the law allows and more.

She Is Honored

Sharing our book at group tonight. . . .

November 10, 2006, Friday • Scale: 4

Hi Baby girl, another Friday night with nothing to do. What I mean by that, too, is my head is empty. I hate that you know and understand what

I mean. That's been one of the biggest things to get used to. Before, you consumed my thoughts in my head. I don't ever have to worry about you now and so my head is so quiet. I hate it. I would trade it for all the worries in a heartbeat. It's Jarrod's birthday, you know, and his party was hard. I had to come into the room, drop to my knees and pray. I'm afraid for the holidays. Jarrod's birthday was tough . . . I just feel so alone, honey, like I have no family. Digger is always gone now. I love Tawnia to death, but it's still her family here. She said to say hello to you today. Did you see me close to you tonight? The stars were amazing and I saw a falling star. It was you, wasn't it? Thank you. My life is getting so different now. What does God have planned for me? Can you tell me somehow? I love you tons . . . sweet dreams.

She Is Honored

Little Miss Riley brings me flowers today to the gym for you.

November 11, 2006, Saturday • Scale: 4

Hi Honey, so tonight was my first venture out into the real world and life. There were 10 of us women, a huge party bus and we went to The Shout House downtown. I was afraid to go out and feared someone coming up to me and asking me, "Do you have any kids?" Luckily, it wasn't that kind of a bar. We celebrated Tawnia's birthday and I didn't want to ruin it for her, so I prayed for God to allow me to enjoy myself with everyone and He did. So many times, Tawnia and I would look at each other, raise our glasses and drink that drink for you! We knew you were up there looking down at us, laughing so hard. I must say, too, I didn't or don't feel guilty for having fun and I think because you were there with us so much. I had Big and Rich, "Save a Horse, Ride a Cowboy" dedicated to you, did you like it? I hope you did. I'm sorry I will not be able to share a drink with you on your 21st birthday. I'm sorry there is so much I can't do with you now. I love you tons.

She Is Honored

The Shout House Bar and Grill: Big and Rich: "Save a Horse, Ride a Cowboy" up on stage for you.

November 12, 2006, Sunday • Scale: 4

Dear Kelsea, I love you more than the law allows. Today was a peaceful day. After church, Jeanie was at her Gramma's. I came to see you. Did you like your pink flowers? One from me, Digger, Tawnia, Jeanie and your dad. Did you like the Tweedy Bird balloon, too? It was nice that Brenna showed up with pretty flowers. I know she visits you a lot, too. I think today was the easiest time I have had yet at your grave with you. Brenna and I walked around and looked at some headstones to get an idea. I want yours to be perfect just like you are now.

What is it like now to suffer no pain, no tears and just feel joy? Do you like your new life up there? Do you have a lot of friends? I'll bet you get along with all the girls now; no jealousy or drama there, hah? I'm not looking forward to the holidays. I can't fathom them without you PHYSI-CALLY here. I'm repressing my thoughts again because I just don't want to believe again. Come into my dreams tonight. Kisses and hugs.

She Is Honored

A Tweedy balloon, 5 beautiful pink flowers and $1^1/_2$ hours at your grave-side.

November 13, 2006, Monday • Scale: 2.5

Hi Sweetheart, talk about rage today. . . . I found myself watching TV, raging and yelling at the TV, cussing. You see honey; I don't understand why God doesn't punish parents who don't take care of their children like the drug addicts on TV with the 9-year-old girl? Why me, who lived every second of the day for you, believing that between God and me, we would raise you through life? I will admit today I felt true anger for the first time. I had chest pains today and a bad lump in my throat. Did you see me and Digger playing catch tonight with the football? I think I've been neglecting him. He needs me badly to be strong and I haven't been. I t was good for us. I love playing your CD, too, in the car. That one song about being on the wrong path is so you! You were so misunderstood. But, I knew you, your moods, your heart, and your ups and downs. I still have a hard time think-ing. I couldn't concentrate for anything today. I need to pay my bills, too. Oooops. I love you so much—it hurts.

She Is Honored

New laminated pictures to carry in my pocket wherever I go, to share your beauty.

November 14, 2006, Tuesday • Scale: 3

Dear Tat, it's crazy how one minute I can look at your pictures on my dash and yet another minute I have a major breakdown. When I cry and no one is there with me I get so sad and think, *Why do I have to go through this alone?* I look so forward to my group on Thursday nights. It's like I'll be driving along and for a few seconds at a time things seem "normal," but then it all hits me that you're not here and I just don't get it. I had a long talk with Lonnie at the gym. He said, "Why would God take someone who's not 'saved'?" He wouldn't and we know you were saved. Is that why He took you? Would you have had a hard life here on earth? Did God actually bless you by taking you? You are better off in heaven than here on earth, a living hell? I just don't see how you can be. I'm your mom. I'm supposed to be taking care of you. I miss you so much. It's not fair. I hate this.

She Is Honored

Listening to your song "Always on the Wrong Track"; always doing what you want to do . . . Miss Independent Girl.

November 15, 2006, Wednesday • Scale: 3

Hi Honey, did you meet Craig today? Barb's cousin went home to heaven today and I know he's there with you; take care of him, okay? I picked out your headstone today: black with gold flakes and angel prayer hands, "Tat, Jesus Freak"; it is going to be totally you and me. I had to go alone and was doing great until the end. I had massive chest pains and a headache. But I promise you will have the coolest headstone on the block! The days aren't necessarily getting "easier." It's like for a little while you feel somewhat normal, then WHAM you realize what has happened and you feel your face looking confused. I also wondered today if I'm going to use Trazodone to sleep for the rest of my life. I woke up crying with a dream that I couldn't find you anywhere. I know that's why I woke up crying. I know you'll come in my dreams one day. I love you.

She Is Honored

The most beautiful, perfect headstone created for my most beautiful, perfect little girl.

November 16, 2006, Thursday • Scale: 4

Hello Sweetness, busy day . . . sometimes it's good, though, because it doesn't give me a lot of time to think about reality. I met someone at the gym today whose best friend lost his son two years ago. Have you met him yet? Do you know what the hardest thing is right now? Sleeping. I can't do it without my pills. My head spins in every direction there is and I hate it. We talked about Thanksgiving at group tonight. I don't want one this year. It's just going to be another day to workout. I also talked to Dr. Druck about asking people to say, "It's nice to see you." He said that was brilliant. I think one day I am really going to be able to help him in some way. I talked about my rage this week, too, at the TV, getting the headstone alone, filing for divorce . . . yep, hon, I'm gonna do it. I hope you are having some good talks with your Father about hooking me up with a good man to love me the way you want me to be loved and treated. Sprinkle that dust. . . . I miss you Tat. Kisses.

She Is Here

As I wake up from my nap, your smell is so strong.

November 17, 2006, Friday • Scale: 4

Hi Honey, how's my little girl? I'm not sure how I am. It's been an emotional day. I filed for divorce today. Although, I know it's the right thing to do, it still feels like a loss. They were very good to me at court though. Remember the girl who was really rude to me with your dad? She remembered me and asked if I was doing okay. At first I said yes, and then she smiled and said, "Really?" Then I shook my head no. I can't believe I am going to be spending the rest of my life wearing all these different masks. It pisses me off. It's like, how come I can't believe it's almost 3 months? Yet it feels like forever already, but also like it happened yesterday??? I guess it's the pain that feels like yesterday. I try picturing you in heaven, running around with a big smile on your face. I'm sorry I don't talk to you a lot. I find that hard to do. Do you want me to talk to you more? Please, let me know somehow and I will. I just need to know and feel you with me. Please! I love you tons. XXOOXX

She Is Here

Everywhere I go, so goes Sassy Girl.

November 18, 2006, Saturday • Scale: 4

Dear Kelsea, it was nice seeing you today at the cemetery and talking to you. I know I don't talk to you as much as I should. It's just really hard still, you know? I notice your ground isn't even close to settling. I think you're just being really stubborn. How come all your neighbors who have moved in after you had their ground all settled? You're just waiting for your headstone aren't you? You're staying visible for me, thank you. I feel, Kels, like I am stumbling through life. So many changes have come about since you went home. I hate this. This week is Thanksgiving. Do you celebrate it? Maybe I'll go to the beach for a bit. I'll bet every day is Thanksgiving in heaven. I love jamming your song, "Misunderstood." One day the whole world will understand you. My heart still aches for you. The chest pains aren't as often and I haven't had a lump in my throat for awhile. I believe that's a good thing. The tears still flow though. I love you more than the law allows. XOXOXO

She Is Honored

A single rose at the cemetery. Your picture shown to the 7-11 guy who said you are beautiful.

November 19, 2006, Sunday • Scale: 4

Hi Sweetie Pie, how was your day? Did you see Jeanie at church with me? Did you hear the message; about being "thankful?" The whole time I kept asking myself, am I supposed to be thankful? So, after the service I asked Pastor Tony Jr. that question and he couldn't answer me. He said his heart breaks every time he sees me. Yep, the service was tough . . . it was Tawnia's birthday today and I gave her your perfume so you will be with her always. When I gave her the present and card, we held each other and cried because we both miss you so much, words cannot describe it. I think I have been, not intentionally, but ignoring Digger. I have been putting forth an effort to be affectionate with him.

Today he wanted Tawnia to take pictures of us together. He put his arms around me and was home all day with us. Please be his guardian angel above all else. He needs you. I need you but I guess for whatever reason, God needed you the most. I really want to hear why and understand. It sucks I have to wait to get there for my answer. I love you.

She Is Honored

Tawnia's birthday, Mystical Perfume and your scent.

November 20, 2006, Monday • Scale: 4

Hi Honey, good news today . . . justice may prevail. It was my blessing of hope I have been praying for; your case has been picked up. I know it's just the beginning of a long road but it's a start. Today has actually been a fairly "okay" day. I have been busy. I met Spencer today. He lost his little boy, Tyler, a couple years ago. I know you're with him and probably hold him for God . . . he's a baby. It's nice to meet someone who understands my thoughts, pain and feelings. I have an idea. I am going to have business cards made up that say, "Love your child like there's no tomorrow" and give them to people when the Holy Spirit guides me. I want to make a difference in some parent/child's life. Will that make you proud? I want you to look down on me every day and smile and be proud to say I am your mama because I am very proud to tell everyone you're my girl. I need you and can't have you here. Why? I love you, kisses.

She Is Honored

Business cards: "Love your child like there's no tomorrow."

November 21, 2006, Tuesday • Scale: 3

Dear Kelsea Lyn, some answers are coming to me slowly. I believe them although I am afraid to accept them because I am afraid that would mean I have accepted you being gone and I have not. Did God take you to save you from a horrible life? I guess I just get mad because I think I could have done everything with you here with me. I showed your picture to a girl in the gym. Her daughter is at Westhills, too. She asked me how I get through each day and function. I told her I really didn't know. I guess it is my constant prayer. I don't know how someone can lose a child and NOT turn toward God. If it weren't for Him, I would have killed myself by now or just never gotten out of bed. The holidays are coming up and I'm afraid of the tidal wave coming; you just never know when. I hope you're going to spend Thanksgiving day with Melissa, Brittany, Tyler, Martin, Red . . . too many of you there in heaven. I love you.

She Is Here

Again at the gym with me on the life cycle, heart rate's going strong.

PSALMS 4:1
Answer me when I call to you, O my righteous God. Give me relief from my distress; be merciful to me and hear my prayer.

November 22, 2006, Wednesday • Scale: 2

Dear Kelsea Lyn, it's now 3 months and still unbelievable. Still pain as deep as that day. There are so many people that still think of you and know today is 3 months. So many messages on your Myspace. I think the 22nd of each month is going to suck. I don't see how it can't. It's just a reminder of another month gone without you. Maybe I should start looking at it as another month CLOSER to being back with you. It still doesn't make it easier not having your physical body, voice, smell here with me. You saw me spend the day crying, too. But, all the changes in my life now wouldn't have happened if God hadn't decided He needed you more. I always knew He had great plans for you and Digger; I just thought and trusted it was here on earth with me not there with Him. Please talk to Him Kels, and ask Him to have mercy on me and do not take Digger from me too. I would have nothing else to live for. Half of me is dead and the other half is trying to survive for your brother. Be with me on Thanksgiving. It's my first without you. I hate this all. Kisses.

She Is Missed

I missed you today—it's been 3 months . . . please come to me.

JOURNAL: THE MASK

I ask myself, How can 3 months have passed already without my little girl? How can 3 months feel like an eternity, yet still feel like yesterday? How can the pain be as deep as the minute I lost her? The sorrow? The brokenness and emptiness? How am I supposed to wake up on the 22nd of each month, knowing another month has gone by and Kelsea is not with me?

I find myself still waiting for Kelsea to walk in the door, or call me on my cell phone. There are moments that go by now that she is not on my mind, simply because I am "living" and doing things that I have no choice but to do. I have to work. I have to work out. I have to pay bills. I have to continue loving my son. I have to eat. I have to go to my support group. I have to go the bank, the grocery store, the post office. These are all things that I have no choice in doing; it is the same as I had no choice in the loss of my daughter.

I'm sure that if I chose to stay in bed, keep the house dark, not go anywhere, do anything, I would be in a worse place than I am right now. I know if I did not constantly drop to my knees in prayer, constantly, during the day, I would be in a horrible place.

I still hate the question, How are you? Anxiety still sets in when I anticipate that question. I still can't answer; okay, good, fine, and I wonder if I will ever be able to and *really* mean it. I have begun telling people, for my own sanity, to not ask me that question. I tell them to simply look at me and say, "It's good to see you."

That makes me feel good. That leads to no thoughts of how I am feeling, no reminders. The response has been overwhelmingly positive when I tell people how to address me.

Over the last month I have been told how much "better" I am doing. That's a funny statement because I ask myself, how can I be "better" when Kelsea has not come back? I think people want to think I am doing better and my outward appearance may demonstrate that at times, but I assure you, I will never be "better."

You see, the best way to describe this grief "thing" is in the way of putting on a mask. You have several different masks that you carry around with you everywhere you go. It all depends on where you are, who you're with, what you are doing. However, rest assured that once I am alone in my car, in my room, wherever that mask gets ripped off, then you can see the true me. I am the mother who still does not understand, Why me?

I left work one evening and was on my way to the grocery store. As I left the parking lot at work, the tidal wave came and took me out. I began crying so hard, I could barely see the highway; the lanes and all the car lights were a total blur. I'm sobbing, praying, yelling at God and talking to Kelsea. I'm a wreck but I have to go into the store. As I'm doing my shopping, tears are rolling down my cheeks. I don't care though, I have to cry. I have learned that I really don't care where I am, who I'm with or what people think when they see me crying, I just do it.

I finished my shopping and I was standing in line to pay. There was a family of about 6 or 7 a couple aisles down from me. The mother had a Walmart smock on and was sitting in an electronic chair; she was a heavy-set woman.

The children were loud, dancing around and basically annoying me. I know, though, it was only because of the place I am in right now, "hell."

I watched them all for a few moments, deep in thought. I thought to myself as I have several times now, *Why me and not one of them?* The guilt hit me immediately for the thought. I dropped my head and asked God to forgive me. Again, tears were streaming down my cheeks. My head was bowed so no one could see my pain. Or so I thought.

As I said my prayer for forgiveness, I heard a soft voice say, "Are you okay?" As I looked up, one of the girls in the family I had just questioned was looking at me. I did not say a word but simply shook my head no. She asked me, "Do you need a hug?" I shook my head yes, as tears poured out of my eyes. She walked over to me and wrapped her arms around me, tightly, and held me.

I reached into my pocket and showed her a picture of Kelsea. I told her that I just lost her. She told me how beautiful Kelsea was, then she looked at me and said, "You know, He only takes the best. God bless you," and she walked away. For a split second, I believed her. For a few moments, I felt peace.

She came back over to me and asked me how old Kelsea was and I told her, 17. She was 17 and pregnant. As her family finished bagging the groceries to leave, they all turned and looked at me and every single one of them smiled, waved and said good-bye. She was my angel that very night.

It's Thanksgiving eve and I don't even care. Although I have many, many things to be thankful for, I still do not have my daughter and cannot be thankful for that. I wasn't quite sure how the holidays were going to go or how I could handle them. This is the first year in 17 years that Kelsea will not be here. As I write that I still find myself not able to grasp that concept. My eyes squint and my forehead wrinkles and it's as if I can feel myself in my mind, not comprehending this. That's when I push the thoughts out of my head and decide to not believe it, not deal with it, not right now. I just can't.

I was told that I had permission to skip the holidays for the next 2 years. Because this is all so fresh, the wound, it's not a holiday for me; it's a hell day.

I don't want to go far from my home. I don't want to be around a lot of people. I want to be able to retreat to my bedroom. My bedroom has become my place of comfort. I can cry, isolate myself, drop to my knees and pray, and sleep. We had a birthday party for Kelsea's Godmother's son, Jarod. He turned one. It was at this little party that I realized what the holidays ahead of me were going to hold . . . pain.

Although I love this family with all my heart, I could not handle it all. I retreated to my room. I cried and prayed and Tawnia came into my room because she understands. It was at that moment I realized I didn't want a Thanksgiving or Christmas; I want my room, my son, and I want my daughter back.

Psalm 61:1–2

O God, listen to my cry! Hear my prayer! From the ends of the earth, I will cry to you for help, for my heart is overwhelmed. Lead me to the towering rock of safety.

☙

CHAPTER FOUR

November 23, 2006, Thursday • Scale: 2

Hello Dear, here I sit on Thanksgiving at your grave site. Someone else brought some beautiful flowers, too. It warms my heart to know others come see you, too. I decided not to do anything or go anywhere today. I can't be around a lot of people. I feel bad for Digger but he's off with Oso doing okay. Watch him for me, please. It's very peaceful out here. Do you do anything special on Thanksgiving? I would imagine every day is a Thanksgiving in heaven. I may go see Jeanie today but that might be too hard. Jeanie and her mom are still devastated, too. Are you happy for me that I filed for a divorce? I know Steve is a good man but our hearts are different. He deserves a woman to love him and I just can't now. I know how you felt about him. I am happier and more at ease now. Life is so different. I'm going to talk to you for awhile and I'll write more as the day unfolds. So far, it's been a rough one because I miss you so deeply. I have not had an appetite at all today. Digger and I went out to eat and we both brought everything home. At least I won't gain any weight these holidays. I'd rather have you here and be getting fat with you. Adam came home today. This day has been hard. I can't imagine Christmas. The craziest thing was having no appetite. I just spent the day like it was another day. Society builds up these holidays when it's really nothing special. I'll be honest, hon, I've been drinking beer more then I should. But I promise I will be careful. I took my Trazodone with a beer because I want to sleep well. My cough's bad so I decided to drink some cough medicine, too. Probably not a good idea but I really don't care; know what I mean, baby doll? I love you. I hope you spent the day with me. I love you and today SUCKED. See you soon in a better life, an eternal life.

She Is Here

Thanksgiving . . . Sassy so loveable tonight, kissing, cuddling and biting me. So much love, I knew.

November 24, 2006, Friday • Scale: 3

Hi Babydoll, better day than yesterday. All the hype and lead up to another "holiday," gone. I'm not looking forward to Christmas. I know I have to think of Digger, but what about you? What about putting your stocking on your bed in the middle of the night? What about giving you your Almond Rocha's? Please help me that day and the next month. I am already dreading the next month. Help me. It's been 94 days now, unbelievable. It's nice being able to talk to Tawnia about you. I know the more I talk about you, the better I am. Sometimes, I can tell stories about you and laugh but other times I can't even think. Know what's hard? Not having anyone to go through this with. I just wish I had someone to hold me at night so I can just lie in bed and cry. Someone to hold me tight. I think things could be more bearable but no. Tomorrow is a birthday party at the park. Will you be with us? It's not right that you're not here. I love you.

She Is Honored

Showing your picture, your story, my love for you with a complete stranger.

November 25, 2006, Saturday • Scale: 4

Hi Sweetheart, I've been lagging and not being disciplined lately with things. I've gotten really bad at paying my bills. I don't know; I just don't care. We had Brayden and Jarod's birthday party at the park. You were supposed to be here for it. I kept waiting for you to get there and you didn't. They were all playing football and I could see you right in the mix, kicking everyone's butt, playing tackle with all of them. You truly had such an innocent side to you at times, a pure child at heart. It pained me to see you in pain. I know you struggled in life and I was trying my hardest to help you. I thought I was helping you. Is there anything else I could have done for you? I wish you never would have tasted that rebellious, wild side of life. I wish I could have provided you a complete family. I wish I would have checked on you earlier. I wish I could go back 95 days and change the course of your life. I wish I could be in heaven in your place or, better yet, with you. I love you so much. XOXOXO

She Is Missed

I spent the morning in prayer . . . help me understand.

November 26, 2006, Sunday • Scale: 3

Dear Kelsea Lyn, can you talk to your heavenly Father and ask him how I am supposed to be thankful through this trial in my life? Hard message at church today to swallow. I've been spending a lot of time at the gym every-day. I mean, it's not like I really have much else to do. I've been training Colleen and she's been my savior with Greg. I tell people that my life was consumed by you: where you were, who you were with, doctor appoint-ments and now, I have nothing to fill my head. Nothing to worry about. I hate it. My head is so quiet now. I want it loud. I want worry, stress and you. Then the tidal wave came. It always does when I'm driving and start praying. It was bad tonight. I lay in the room alone, crying and praying. I haven't had any chest pains lately but the lump in the throat is here. Please, guide the investigator in the direction to honor you. I will fight to the end to make sure people know the whole truth about your death. You are my world. Love you, kiss.

She Is Honored

The search for your tattoo . . . on your birthday. I can't wait . . . such a beau-tiful tribute.

November 27, 2006, Monday • Scale: 3

Dear Angel, did you love the rain today? I stopped by the church after the gym. I was drawn to pull in, so I did. The church was so quiet. I knelt down at the altar and as I prayed for you, it rained harder and louder on the roof. You were there with me, weren't you? I had chest pains twice today again. It's crazy the physical pains that come with grief. Lots of tidal waves the last few days. I have to get pictures ready for your yearbook. It's pretty cool they are making a memorial page for you. If anyone deserves it, it's you. You know I'm going to walk at your graduation for you in your honor. I ran across pictures of your funeral. You looked perfect. It was so hard but you did look peaceful. I wish people would quit telling me things are going to get better. No, you'll never be here with me so it's not better. It's different. So many masks. I'm so tired of being told how "strong" I am, too. I'm not; I'm tired. I want to dream about you. I want to hug you and tell you how much I love you. I want and I can't have.

She Is Here

Sassy lying in your basket—so loveable, purring so passionately.

November 28, 2006, Tuesday • Scale: 5

Hello Tat, this is the first day in 98 days I haven't cried hard. I mean, I'm almost afraid not to cry though. I'm afraid because it makes me feel guilty. Like, I didn't miss you today or something, but I did. I do. My eyes teared up on the way home from work but no crying. Do you think that means I'm accepting all this? I think with the acceptance has to come stronger faith. I know my faith needs to grow. I guess I was busier than normal today and not a lot of time to think. I worked almost a full day today. I actually even laughed in our sales meeting. Do you know how many people are calling me "skinny?" You would be proud, honey.

No more burliness. I thought about heaven and I want to know if you really have wings there? At the gym today, the front desk girls said you were loved by so many people. Why didn't you realize that? Why couldn't you see how important you were here? I hope you knew how much I loved you. I hope I showed you every day. I pray for a blessing of hope every day. Everything is so different. It sucks without you . . . my little misunderstood girl.

She Is Here

The rain beating heavily on the roof of the church as I prayed for you.

November 29, 2006, Wednesday • Scale: 4

Dear Kelsea Lyn, what a long, emotional day. I was awakened by Chris, our attorney. He spoke to the DOJ investigators and said they would be calling me and they did. I had to sit with them and answer their questions. I cried. They seem very sympathetic and determined. It is a blessing of hope I have been praying for. All I want is justice for you and people to know the truth. It's amazing how much stress can bring on physical pain, too. I got the worst headache during the interview. I was wiped out when I had to go to work. Susan was here, too. She's been very good to me. She made me a music CD. It scares me to think I haven't had a hard cry in a couple days. Does it mean I'm accepting this? Does it mean I'm getting used to you gone; because I don't want that. It doesn't seem right that it seems to be getting easier. I don't like it. I still miss you horribly. It all could have been prevented if she wouldn't have given you that medication. Are you with me here and I can't see you? How long till we are together again? Please help me here. I need you. XXXOOO

She Is Honored

Your investigation begins. The agents learn who you are, what you are about, and they are dedicated and determined to have justice served.

November 30, 2006, Thursday • Scale: 4

Hi Tat, better day today. I had group tonight and as always it is so very helpful.

Ken told me that with each week that passes he sees more of my spirit coming through my eyes. Another woman said it was so nice to see me smile tonight for the first time. Ken said that it is okay in the beginning to let the pain determine your day, but there comes a time that the love needs to get stronger. As I learn to live with the pain, my love for you will grow stronger. It all made sense. I just have to put it into place. The days are getting more manageable. I like that terminology more than saying "better." The hardest thing to live with is not having you physically here. I turned in all your pictures for the yearbook. You're so loved.

You're going to have your own full color page! Spoiled once again. One of these days I'm going to know my full purpose here on earth, until I get home with you. I try to honor you every day. I can't wait for your birthday and my tattoo in your honor. I love you more than the law allows. Kisses and hugs.

She Is Honored

Tonight, Ken Druck, who I admire with my heart and soul, said to me that every week he sees more of my spirit coming through my eyes and I knew.

Mark 11:24
So I tell you, whatever you ask for in prayer,
believe that you have received it, and it will be yours.

December 1, 2006, Friday • Scale: 5

Hi Sweetheart, it's crazy to have another day of no crying. I thought today about what you would want for me. I thought about you looking down on me and wanting me to be happy, laughing and loving. I understood a little more about not crying. It doesn't mean I don't miss you or think about you or still want you here. I have to remember that. It just means I'm adjusting to you being in heaven. If I am accepting these little bits at a time, I think my faith must be growing in understanding that you are okay. You're probably better off than us down here. I know you are. Digger equates living here as living in hell. So I'm okay with going a day or so without crying. Just remember, it doesn't mean I don't love or miss you. It means I am honoring you in living the life and happiness you would want me to. Colleen served Steve the divorce papers tonight. I know you're okay with it and want what's best for me. I love you.

She Is Here

Knowing Sassy and your deep love for your kitty, every kiss she gives me, every purr she purrs, every nudge of her head.

December 2, 2006, Saturday • Scale: 2

Hi Honey, it's really quiet at the cemetery right now. I have been the only one here today. You're spoiled. Its windy here, quiet and peaceful. I talked to God for awhile. He promised me He would take care of you for me till I get home there with you. Tell Him, thanks! I'm getting closer to getting your headstone.

I'm telling you, all your neighbors are going to be so jealous! I promise I'll keep it beautiful for you. I love how stubborn you're being, too, with your mound! I know as soon as your address is put in you will settle or maybe not! That would be way chill. It's getting cold, so I'll finish this at home. I miss you. . . . So, yeah, the day got harder. Chest pains tonight, loneliness, isolation, in bed early not wanting to deal with anyone or anything. I'm pissed I'm getting a divorce, honey. It's not your fault though. You just made it clearer to me. I have to learn to be okay with being alone every day and every night again. I hate being alone. I need you to be here with me, not in heaven. Help me tonight. I want to die.

She Is Honored

A visit to your grave, a beautiful glass angel holding her arms out, stuck in your grave.

December 3, 2006, Sunday • Scale: 4

Dear Kelsea Lyn, I love you with all my heart and soul. Today's message was on hope. I believe I have hope in my life. I just need more understanding. Church is usually hard because I'm supposed to find comfort there and I just am struggling. I'm still unable to sleep without taking some Trazodone. I wonder if I will ever be able to sleep soundly again. I was actually able to listen to your whole CD. Tawnia said she hasn't been able to yet. I don't think 10 minutes goes by without thinking about you. I probably think more about you now than before and I never thought that was possible. Digger loves Tawnia's boys. You know, even Brayden knows who you are. I still carry your pictures everywhere and wear your keys. I really want to get your business cards made. I want to make a difference in people's lives with their children. I want to hand them your card and have them carry it with them forever. You will be so very honored. I miss you. Hugs.

She Is Here

Today at church, Laurel told me of losing her father. She shared being somewhere one afternoon and smelling him. She quickly looked around to see him and he wasn't here but she knew he was there. . . .

While driving down the road and listening to Kelsea's' CD, an overwhelming smell of cigarettes filled the car. No one to be seen, no one around and I smiled.

December 4, 2006, Monday • Scale: 3

Hi Honey, emotional day. Why do I get so wiped out when I start my day in prayer? I mean, I start every day in prayer, but sometimes the tidal wave comes with it. I'm still getting support from a lot of people at work. Today, one guy brought me eggs and hash browns from his home because he doesn't think I eat enough because of all the weight I have lost. People don't understand how much I am working out. I mean, hon, what else do I have to do? I came home today and took a fat 2-hour nap. I've been finding myself not wanting to be very social or talk to people or meet people. I'm really trying to think that you are happy now but it's hard. You know I am going through this alone now, right? I wonder if it would be easier to have a husband through this. All I want is a man who will be able to understand my pain, comfort me the rest of my life and understand my life now. Can you help me find him? Can you use your special dust and bring him to me, soon? I love you. XOXOXO

She Is Here

Another workout, another heart rate, another day at the gym with you.

December 5, 2006, Tuesday • Scale: 4

Hello Baby doll, how was your day? Mine was manageable. Did I cry? Yes. Did I have chest pains today? Yes. Did I get sick to my stomach? Yes. But I dealt with all of them. I'm actually able to smile sometimes now. It's not a lot but it's something, right? I know what I want for Christmas. Plain and simple, I want your headstone for Christmas. I want your pad to have the chillest headstone in the neighborhood. I want to keep it clean every week I go see you and put fresh flowers there for you because you're spoiled and I love spoiling you. Will you please make your presence very obvious on Christmas? I'll be spending part of the day with you and you need to spend the other part here with us—ok? It was hard looking at some of your pictures today. That's when I got sick. I have to believe you are happy and loving life now. A guy questioned my faith tonight. I told him it has not been tested. It is still alive and growing. I love you. XOXO

She Is Honored

A girl in the bank with a 2-year-old daughter. . . . I told her of my loss and to love her daughter every single day.

December 6, 2006, Wednesday • Scale: 3

Hi Hon, well I guess it's going to be awhile before you get your perfect headstone. Apparently, they won't have the black galaxy stone for 3 months and since it has to be perfect, you're going to have to wait. I had coffee with Susan today. She helps me a lot. She also told me you were the first client Chris ever lost. He will never, ever forget you. You were so special to him. I got chest pains when I was talking to Susan today and the lump in the throat looking at your Myspace. I haven't had a tidal wave in about a week, but it hit me tonight. I'm going to come see you tomorrow so be looking for me. You know, this morning I felt good. As I drove to the gym, I honestly think I felt a little bit happy. The sun was shining, it was warm, I listened to your CD and I sang to you. Do you hear me when I sing to you? Are you dancing all around me? I isolated myself tonight in the room. I've been doing that a lot. I just don't want to be around people. I avoid some people, just because I don't want to deal with them. Do you miss me? I miss you bad. Soon.

She Is Honored

Coffee with Susan, stories of Kelsea—laughing.

December 7, 2006, Thursday • Scale: 4

Dear Kels, great group tonight! I'm going to start volunteering at the foundation, all in your honor. I'll bet you and Jenna are so happy for us. Did you like the candy cane and rose? I spent an hour with you, spoiled! I didn't feel like working today so I went home. I have been sleeping more, taking more naps. . . . I believe it's called depression. Talk about irresponsible, too. I haven't been paying my bills like I should. I guess you can say I just don't care. It was quiet at the cemetery except for the gramma that came up to me. You know how I lay with you? She thought I passed out. Can you ask your Father if someone commits suicide, if they still go to heaven? No, I'm not suicidal; I just can't remember anything about it in the bible. I can't wait to get your tattoo. I will show it proudly to everyone. Life is so different. Life will never be the same. The pain will never go away. People may think if I smile, I am okay but I'm not. I love you forever.

She Is Here

Last night, as Tawnia sat at the table with Birt, you knocked over your beautiful framed picture onto the floor.

She Is Honored

My first Jalapeño and Cream Cheese Taquito from 7-11.

December 8, 2006, Friday • Scale: 5

Hi Pumpkin, ucka Friday. I hate the weekends you know: no worries, no anxiety, no wondering. . . . I want it all back along with you. I know I have Digger to worry about but he's always home now. Come to think of it, hon, I haven't cried today. I have thought about you every hour but no tears. You're okay with that, aren't you? I know you hate me crying. At the gym, did you enjoy our conversation? I know if someone looked at me they would think I was crazy talking to myself. But I have no problem telling people I talk to you. I just wish sometimes I could hear you talking back to me. I miss your voice. I miss you telling me you love me. I just try, when I think about you and get sad, I try to picture you in heaven with your beautiful smile, so happy. Please show me somehow you're happy. We're all going to the beach tomorrow for pictures. I'm bringing your playboy bunny pillow so you will be in the pictures with us. I can't imagine the rest of my life without you. How long do I have? What do I do? Guide me, please. I love you.

She Is Here

Cardio at the gym and you were with me in the heart rate. . . . I would imagine dancing all around me, smiling.

December 9, 2006, Saturday • *Scale: 2.5*

Dear Kelsea, I'm not sure why I was drawn to go see you again today but I was. It was nice talking to you. It was nice seeing flowers from someone else there, too. It was a rough visit though. In the grocery store a guy made a comment to me about the flowers. I told him they were for you. He lost his father, dog and best friend this year. He hugged me and I truly saw his pain for me. I introduced you to 3 people today. One of them is going to go to group with me this week.

Ken is going to be proud of me. I want to help others. Just like at the cemetery, I picked up all the flower pots that had been blown over. I know you were smiling while I did that. It made you proud, hah? My heart is as big as yours. I saw you in the gym with me, too, after I prayed for Barb and her daughter. You acknowledged my prayer in the lighting up of my cell phone. Thank you. I feel like getting drunk right now. I feel like that a lot but I'm not. I promise I won't develop a drinking problem. I have to help others and I can't if I'm drunk, right? I love you.

She Is Here

What a day! I decided when I woke up to honor you every single day by introducing you to someone each day. . . .

Barb lost her daughter a few years ago. She was almost 14. I prayed you were with her daughter. I looked down at my phone and the light was on. I explained to Barb how you are with me through electronics . . . a prayer, then the light.

She Is Honored

I introduced you to Janice in the gym and a guy I saw in the store while buying you flowers. A visit to the cemetery and more flowers.

December 10, 2006, Sunday • *Scale: 2*

Hello Angel, . . . wow, did you see that major meltdown I had? I spent the day with a good friend that I really like. It was an emotional day, then it just rolled into the night. There were so many people here tonight. I couldn't deal with it all. So, I took Digger to Jimmy's to eat. We had some nice talk, but when I got home everyone was still here so I stayed in the car and listened to your CD. I think tonight was the hardest cry and biggest tidal wave that hit me yet. Did you hear my screams, too? I had the music loud and tried to cover my mouth so I didn't scare anyone. I just came straight to my room. I looked at the streetlight and thought about hanging myself from it . . . tying the rope and jumping . . . but Digger. Church was tough, too. I'm just thankful, though, for all the people praying for us. I know that is how I am able to make it through each hour, each day. The pain was great tonight, deep. I took $1^1/_2$ sleeping pills, too. I want to sleep well. So, I love you tons. Soon, the holidays will be over. Thank God. Kisses to you, my sweet little girl.

She Is Honored

Wings and Things . . . in your honor I wanted to have hot, hot wings but I hate the burn so I just thought about how much you loved wings and I smiled.

December 11, 2006, Monday • Scale: 2

Hi Sweetheart, two tough days in a row. I made a faithful, obedient decision today, then went to church to pray and I saw Steve for the first time since I moved out. It was tough but it was needed. I don't understand something. He talks about you not being able to accept his love because of your illness, but if he would have showed you love, you would have absorbed it and relished in it. All you wanted was his love. Tawnia has told me you felt as if he tolerated you and Digger and just wanted me. I'm so sorry I didn't see it earlier and provide you with a more loving stepfather. I'm even sorrier your dad wasn't here for you. I know what I'm going to get myself for Christmas: a hockey jersey with "Burly No More" on the front and "Kelsea 17" on the back. All in your honor. I just wish it was January 4th so all this anticipation of the holidays could be over. I need you to sprinkle some dust on someone for me. Can you do that please? I want someone to go through this with me who will comfort me for the rest of my life.

Again, the heart monitor on the cardio machine came on and I knew it was you and I cried. As I continued to talk to you I explained the jersey I wanted to have made and I asked you whether "Kelsea" or "Kelsea Lyn" on the back of the jersey and you told me "Kelsea." Kiss.

She Is Here

Each cardio I did today, you showed your presence. As I was doing the tread climber I thought about talking to someone about you. I thought if they asked me if you were "saved," I would answer in my mind, *She IS saved.* The heart light that was not lit the entire time lit up and I knew you were with me and I cried. As I continued to talk to you, I explained the hockey jersey I want to have made and I asked you whether "Kelsea or Kelsea Lyn" on the back and you told me "Kelsea."

December 12, 2006, Tuesday • Scale: 2

Hi Honey, how are you doing with all your new friends? All your friends here miss you terribly. I'm seeing some anger out of them now. I talked to Barb from the gym today. She's going to group with me Thursday. It's been 9 years for her and she's never truly grieved. I hope I can help her. I'm going to get your tree this weekend and bring it to you, okay? I'm working out a ton right now. Hell, I have nothing else to do. I mean, I'm in a very "I-don't-give-a-shit" phase. I feel like I am so utterly lost right now with no purpose. I feel like I'm stumbling through life. I'm not motivated at work. In the bank today, I wanted someone to come in and rob it with a gun and shoot me. I just want to die. I want January 4th here and all the holidays over. I want my tattoo. Do you forgive me for what happened? Please let me know you have forgiven me. I'm alone again. I lost my daughter, my husband and now my best friend. Why? I need you back.

Love you.

She Is Honored

In the bank and in Walmart, I shared your picture and story with 2 elderly men.

December 13, 2006, Wednesday • Scale: 2

Hi Angel, life is not good right now. It's emotional, it's lonely, it's confusing, it's vulnerable, and it's not caring, it's being so very, very lost. It's not wanting to pay bills or be around a lot of people. It's looking the other way and not wanting to talk to someone you know. It's fantasizing about death every day. It's thinking, *Maybe it's time to get on some medication.* What do you think? I'm taking a friend to group tomorrow, Barb. I'm so confused right now, Kels, I wish none of this happened and I was still in a marriage and I could still care for your every need, but I'm not. Now, I'm alone and I hate it. Is God ever going to let me be happy again? Do you know who can love and comfort me the rest of my life?

Because I really hate my life right now and it's not getting better. I can't even sleep without sleeping pills. I asked God to take me today. . . .

She Is Missed

I struggled with life today, I'm sorry. . . . I love you.

December 14, 2006, Thursday • Scale: 3

Dear Kels, at the gym today I saw a woman looking at your picture so I picked it up and handed it to her and introduced you to her. She said the picture looked like a modeling picture. You should have been a model. I met with Susan today for almost 3 hours. I love talking to her. She shared some cool stories about her aunt. Do you know her yet? She was a police officer killed in the line of duty. Can you tell her I love Susan and am thankful for her? Can you tell her Susan loves her dearly, please? I'm going to bring you your tree this weekend. I know you will love it. I'm thinking about going to work at 24 Hour Fitness. What do you think? I just think it would be better for me. Can you ask God if it would? Just another 11 days now till the next "Hell Day" is over. I still can't believe all of this. It's so choiceless; I never asked for this. I don't deserve this. At group tonight Ken said it's normal, all my day dreams of death. I'm going to go on medication. I need it. I love you.

She Is Honored

I introduced you to "Tina" in the gym today. I saw her admiring your picture. She said you look like a model. Everyone says you look like Lisa Marie Presley.

December 15, 2006, Friday • Scale: 2

My Dearest Little Girl, I love you so much. The days are harder than ever right now. I saw Dr. Johnson today and got some medication, Lexapro. I'm afraid to take it because I am afraid of not feeling all the pain. But I can't function right now. I feel like I have nothing. I cried all morning and shouldn't have been at work. I cried at the doctor's office and I had the lump in my throat today again. I have anger toward stupid people, too. Of course I'm sure it's just because of where I'm at right now, hell. Your brother is screwing up and I don't know what I will do if he gets in trouble again. I'll really lose it. Please help him, Kels. Just as you were a good kid, so is he. You two are just lost and I can't lose him, too, because I would take enough Trazodone to put me to sleep, like you passed, but mine will be intentional. I know you just wanted to go to sleep and go to school, that's what's so hard. You had no idea. Chest pains . . . I can't think because I get sick. I hate so much in life now. Will I ever have love again? I want you back. XOXOXO

She Is Missed

Yet another day struggling with life. It's so hard but you are always thought about.

December 16, 2006, Saturday • Scale: 3

Dear Kels, you amaze me sometimes. I asked if you were with us at the Christmas service and you were. You show me your presence a lot and I need it. I had to tell more people at the gym our story and I don't like it because it's like I feel unreal. I got sick to my stomach today thinking about it, chest pains, too. I can't concentrate at work. I think it's time for me to move on. What do you think? Tom came by today. He loves you so much and just can't understand this. He feels guilty like he should have been here for you more. I know you loved him, too. Did you see all the clouds and rain today? Whenever it rains, I will think of you because I knew how much you love the rain. I'm so sorry you didn't get to experience so much in life like driving, working, graduating, college, nightclubs, dancing, the love of a husband, a baby . . . so much more. Tom thinks you are looking down smiling, saying; "It's so good here, I don't miss any of that." Is it that way?

Another weekend gone and another week closer to being with you again. I love you more than the law allows and more. Good night, kiss.

She Is Here

As I sat at the computer writing to you on your Myspace, I'm asking you if you were at church with me tonight. I hear something outside the sliding glass door to the patio. I look and see red lights flashing. I reach over and turn on the patio light and there is a Tonka truck, red lights flashing back and forth on it and then it stops.

December 17, 2006, Sunday • Scale: 4

Hi Honey, I talked to Papa today. He finally called. I haven't spoken to him since they left the house before the funeral. He reads what I write to you on Myspace all the time and told me he was worried about things I write. He said, "It's been 4 months, you need to get over it and move on." Why can't people understand that when you died, I did, too? People tell me every day that I just don't look the same. Well, maybe because my heart was ripped out and life will forever be different. I want to write something for people to read and know how to help someone who's broken. I want to let people know you NEVER say, "It will get better; time heals all wounds; you need to move on; how are you; she's in a better place."

Because you'll never be here again, time doesn't bring you back, I'm not well and my head knows you're in a better place but my heart is shattered. I hope I'm better in 17 days when the holidays are over. I'm repressing my thoughts again, too. It helps me to not cry, feel sick, get chest pains, but then I can't process. I'll see you tomorrow, Angel. I love you; watch over me, okay? Kiss.

She Is Honored

I picked up your Christmas tree today to bring to you.

December 18, 2006, Monday • Scale: 4

Dear Kels, thank you for being with me all day: the TV, the IP number, the gym pop and cardio machine. You were with me all day. I know I don't talk to you enough and I'm sorry for that. It's just difficult. When I start to think about you and what has happened, I get so sick to my stomach, still. I'll bet that never goes away. I told Bobby, the cable guy, about you today and showed him your pictures. He said you were beautiful and you had my eyes. He said you looked just like me and that was a good start. He was very nice and I know you were with me. Jeanie said there were all kinds of things at your grave today . . . flowers, a tree, a poinsettia, candy cane, balloons and a glass angel. You are so loved. I can't imagine Christmas without you here. I'll try to manage the day but no promises, just be with me. I'm trying to get a new job. Can you help me there, too? I need changes in my life but I need you back more than anything. Can you somehow tell me why this happened? I can't wait for the answer. XOXOXO

She Is Here

You were with me all day. The cable guy turned the TV off trying to fix it. All of a sudden the TV comes back on. I tell him it's back on and he is surprised. He reaches over and turns it off again and says it must be possessed. I smiled. At the gym while training Nina, the bike kept pausing, then all of a sudden I heard a loud *pop* and felt something by my leg. I looked up, thinking someone threw something at my feet from upstairs. I asked Nina if she heard the pop and she said she did.

December 19, 2006, Tuesday • Scale: 3

Hi Baby doll, I had a pretty good day today till the night. I'm enjoying my workouts and getting rid of any burliness. I applied for the 24 Hour Fitness Sales position today. I need a change and a change of scenery. I think more work will be good for me. I looked pretty cute today, too, for the Open House. It's still tough, though, because everyone keeps telling me they couldn't even imagine what I'm going through and to be honest, they can't. I talked to Tom tonight and he sure loves you and is struggling and I think he's in denial still, same as me.

Barb wrote something to me and when I read it, I lost it, BAD. I didn't even realize it's only 5 days till Christmas. I'll spend it with you. I promise. I felt that lump in my throat and chest pains all day. Can you talk to God and ask Him to bless this next year for me? Can He bring me peace, joy, love, finances and someone to hold me when I cry? Can He give me good changes and ways to honor you every single day? The rest of my life is unimaginable without you. Come back.

She Is Honored

I introduced you today to 3 men at the gym. One was very upset because of what happened to you but with each introduction you were honored.

December 20, 2006, Wednesday • Scale: 4

Dear Kelsea Lyn, I had a good day today and I think because I started the day out with you at your pad. I had a good talk with you this morning. Do you think people laugh at me for the way I dress? Do you think I care?! Just like you—no! There were so many cool things left for you at your pad, so much love. Do you think people think I'm crazy, too, when they see me talking to you out loud? I really don't care though. I cried a little at your pad today when I was praying but not any more during the day. I actually had a decent day, thank you. I'm hoping to hear from 24 Hour soon, other than that I just hang out with Tom at the boxing gym. I didn't have a sick stomach, lump in my throat or chest pains today.

Someone today said, "Things will get better." When will people stop saying that and realize, NEVER will it get better because you will never come back; things are forever different. I wish I could start every day at your pad if the days were like today. Can you please show Tawnia some love? I'm not crazy and she needs more love. Resting heart rate: 49 . . . love it, I won!

She Is Honored

A beautiful Christmas tree for you . . . so many gifts for you at your pad and an hour talking to you this morning.

December 21, 2006, Thursday • Scale: 5

Hi Honey, boy are you with me or what? I can't help but to think you're with me and filling me with your spirit. I have had 2 good days. I feel like you're putting the flirt back in my step. I have been meeting people and enjoying company and smiling. I have felt a little bit of life again. The scary thing is wondering when it's going to end because I know it will. I really wish I could start each day visiting your pad. Your investigation is moving forward, too, thank God. Just remind God all I want is justice for what happened to you. I thought today about you not having any pain in your back, no bipolar, no drugs, no tears, no sorrow, no bullshit here on earth and it brought a tiny bit of peace to my heart. Richard asked me why people have the memory stickers on the back of cars. I explained it's to completely honor their children. Sometimes I do get sick when I look at it because it's reality. I'm still not there yet. I still don't know about Christmas I just know I'll be with you. I love you Angel and will see you SOON!

Honoring Me

I can't help but think about the last 2 days you have been with me: your spirit and your being and I know you are honoring me.

December 22, 2006, Friday • Scale: 2

Dear Kelsea Lyn, yet another month you have been gone from here and in heaven with your Father. It's been 4 months and I hate every second of it. This day is always hard for me each month. Work was a struggle and I lost it on the way home, crying. It was strange. As I walked into the house, it was like slow motion. I took a nap, then met with Susan. We talked for almost 3 hours! I was pretty wiped out when I was done, but it's always good to talk to her. Your brother gets so upset with me when I have a hard day missing you. He gets angry and I know it's because he feels powerless and helpless. I just felt like drinking tonight, too, so I did. I drank a beer in the shower. I called Tawnia from the bathtub for another beer. She knew I was upset then. I took my sleeping pill, too, and still didn't sleep well. Your brother's anger is getting out of control. Can you please talk to God and ask Him to bless Digger with some peace and comfort? I love you, Kelsea; I can't wait to meet you. Kisses.

She Is Honored

How can I make it on the 22nd of each month? I hate this day but beneath all the pain and sorrow is my everlasting love for you . . .

JOURNAL: THE HOLIDAY "HELL" DAYS

I am learning that I hate the approach of this day each month; it is a constant reminder of yet another month gone by without Kelsea Lyn. It's so incredibly hard to think it has already been 4 months and yet only God knows how long it will be till I am with Kelsea again.

I'm learning that whether it is 2 months, 4 months, a year or the very day . . . it is all as if it is now. The pain is still so great and the physical ailments still occur. The love has not yet taken over as I have been told it will. I believe and I hope that one day the pain will be managed and the love will shine through again and all the wonderful times I shared with Kelsea over $17^1/_2$ years will be treasured.

I will say this: the pain does not go away, you simply learn to manage it better at times. I'm going to say all of this right now because unless you lose a child, you just don't know. It's so very frustrating when people, who mean well, say things to you like; "It will get better." No. My daughter will never be here with me again so it can never get better. "Time heals all wounds." No, because in 6 years, or 10 years or 18 years, Kelsea will not be here.

There will be days that something will trigger that tidal wave of emotions and the wound will be torn open again. "You need to move forward." Please, don't tell me what I need to do because my life will NEVER be the same. I will never be that woman I was a short 124 days ago. I woke up on August 22nd and my life was changed forever: never to be that care free, light hearted, loving, spirited, compassionate, smiling, happy, kind, bounce in my walk person. My life is now simply different.

I sometimes wonder if I will have any or all of that back in me. Right now if I was to describe myself it's easy: broken, lonely, sad, empty-hearted, lost, depressed, sad and sadder.

I don't count the days as much now as I did the first 100. I'm not sure why I was counting but I was and that's okay. Someone told me to quit counting the days and I couldn't. I thought, *How can they tell me to not count?* As the 100th day approached, I got anxious. I am finding that actual holidays and anniversaries aren't the hard part; it's all the days leading up to that day. On day 100, I couldn't really function. It was just too unbelievable that it was actually 100. I hated it. After that day, though, I found myself not really keeping close track of the days anymore.

I also found myself, for the first time over the last month, making it through an entire day without crying. That was bittersweet. The day was going along and it got later in the day when I realized I hadn't cried yet. As I drove home from work I found myself feeling guilty about not crying. I sat there in the car as I drove and tried to MAKE myself cry and I couldn't. It was the strangest thing. I mean, the day wasn't special. I didn't do anything out of the ordinary; I just didn't cry. I believe I have made it two days without crying since Kelsea passed away.

The physical ailments have subsided somewhat. I don't seem to get a lump in my throat much anymore, like in the beginning. I do get the chest pains though and headaches. Whenever I begin talking about everything, my chest hurts. I know it's anxiety and a broken heart but it's something I have no control over.

Today in the store I watched a mother hugging her two little girls and loving on them all happily. I reflected back to when Kelsea was little and then flashed to finding her that morning. I instantly got sick to my stomach and my chest began to hurt. My breathing became shallow and I could feel my heart pounding so heavily. I closed my eyes and tears filled them and I did my best to not think about that morning. I don't think I will ever truly be able to repress the morning I found Kelsea.

I believe I am still in denial at times. I'm not sure when the reality of everything is going to settle in. I think I try not to think about it. It's strange how sometimes you can talk about everything, so matter of fact, yet other times you can't even begin to think about it all because you just want to throw up.

It's like my head logically knows all the clichés that we hate to hear: "She's in a better place, she's happy now, she has no more pain, she's with God, she's an angel, you'll see her again someday." But my heart is in a gazillion pieces, or has a huge hole in it, or has been ripped out of my chest, or just can't feel anymore, so I can't connect the two: logic and heart.

I did crash the hardest I have this month. There were several people at my house and things were loud and crazy. Sometimes, I just can't handle a lot of people even when it's in my own home and my family and friends. So, this one evening I told Kelsea's Godmother I had to leave and I took my son to dinner.

When we returned all the cars were still at the house and the people, too.

Digger went in the house but I didn't want to so I put in a CD of songs that we made for Kelsea . . . probably not a good idea.

I began to listen to the songs and cry. My head began to spin on the "whys" and my sobs became louder and harder. I turned up the music as loud as I could in my car and I began to scream. I screamed so loud my throat hurt and I was afraid the neighbors were going to call the cops.

Ahead of me a little way down the street was a streetlight, lighting up the street. I stared at the light out of my tearing eyes and I fantasized about hanging from it so high up in the street. I wanted to die. I eventually pulled myself together. I got out of my car and went into the house. I walked directly to my room, took 2 sleeping pills and crawled into bed.

The next several days were filled with many different fantasies of death.

While I was in the bank, I wanted someone to come into the bank with a gun and shoot me. I thought of using a gun myself in the back of my head. As I drove over a bridge, I fantasized about jumping off the bridge. While I was driving, I would look for a good place for an accident. I had a very, very dark week.

Since I have been diagnosed chemically depressed, I know the symptoms of depression and I began to get worried. I made an appointment with my doctor to see about some possible medication. I have fought it up until now because I have not wanted to mask my grief or pain with medication. But I believe there does come a time when medication MUST be used.

When Kelsea passed away I immediately began taking her Trazodone that she had been prescribed to help her sleep. Even with the medication, though, my sleep was not sound. Since Kelsea passed away, on two occasions I thought that I was tired enough to not have to take the Trazodone, but I didn't sleep at all those nights. My son asked me if I was going to take sleeping pills the rest of my life and to be honest, I really don't care if I do! I just know that medication, whether it is for my thyroid or my depression, is a blessing to have. People need to understand that just because it is for a mental health issue makes it no different than medication needed for another health issue like my thyroid. Let go of the stigma of psych med and take care of yourself first and foremost.

As for Thanksgiving . . . the sun came up and the sun went down, as it does every single day. I went out and spent a good portion of the day with Kelsea at her "pad." I have come to call it that instead of her grave because it just sounds better. So, I always talk about her pad and the neighborhood she lives in.

I am working on getting her headstone and it has to be perfect for her. I have to wait a little bit longer because they ran out of the stone I wanted and I was not going to settle for something else. So, I always tell her that it will be well worth the wait because she is going to have the prettiest stone on her block and then we laugh.

I am continuing my support group and I have also begun seeing a therapist, Susan. Susan is the woman who was helping me get Kelsea the help Kelsea needed in school. Susan has become a friend, too. I meet with her usually once a week in a quiet Starbucks setting for usually 2–3 hours. We talk about my week and she helps guide me and gives me suggestions.

I continue writing to Kelsea every night also. I had the founder of my support group tell me how wonderful and therapeutic journaling truly was for a grieving parent. He said, "Do you realize that you talk to your daughter every single day and there are people who have lost a child and have never spoken to them?" It made perfect sense to me.

In the beginning month I remember talking to Kelsea, out loud, quite a bit. It slowed down over the months but I believe that is just because I'm struggling with all of it. I do find it easy to talk to her every time I go see her at her pad. I make it out there once a week still. I usually lie with her for a bit while I cry, then I pray. I usually end up the visit just sitting there talking to her about my life.

I sometimes talk to her while I am out and about, too. I think if someone saw me and realized I was talking out loud to my dead child, they would probably think I was completely crazy! But I really don't care. If anyone really asked me I would honestly tell them I was talking to Kelsea.

It's funny how you really don't care about a lot of things that you used to be concerned with. I look at Christmas coming in a few days and I was actually thankful I wasn't participating in the holiday this year. I looked at all the people running around buying gifts, being all stressed out, and Christmas has a completely different feel now.

I realize I was hung up in that whole game once, just a short year ago.

Christmas was always a time to spoil my two children. Now, I look at it so differently. It's not about the gifts; it's about having your loved ones right there with you. It's about your children being healthy, happy, and alive. I am struggling because I still have my son to think about. I can't really forget that he is still here, alive and deserving of what he has been used to for the last 19 years. So, I plan on doing the best I can that day.

On Thanksgiving, I couldn't eat a thing. I took my son to dinner and tried to eat but couldn't, neither one of us could eat. I'm not sure what will take place in a couple days on Christmas but I am sure of one thing: the sun will come up and the sun will go down.

So, it's Christmas Eve and it wouldn't be fair not to write about it. Church was harder than it has been in awhile. I cried the entire time and just wanted Kelsea with me. Do you have any idea how hard it is to not have your child with you right now? Being blessed with her for 17 years to have her taken away? To know that God gave his only Son for us, but then took my daughter from me?

How could He do that? WHY does He do that? To me this is just another day as I said; the sun came up and it will go down in a little bit.

I don't think you can truly understand before the holidays get here what is going to happen to you emotionally: the holidays. I just keep thinking it's not going to be a big deal, just another day. Or maybe I'm just trying to convince myself of that. Well, I am here to say that I couldn't even fathom it until now.

My heart is broken, empty, dead. I hear my son's voice and I feel guilty because I just don't have anything for him right now. I can't be all happy or even act like everything is okay because it is not. He gets so angry with me because he feels powerless to help me with my pain. It's not fair to him either because he IS still here and so am I, yet I'm struggling so much.

I want to lie down and die. I want to sleep and just wake up and have this all be over. I can't even bring myself to want to wrap the few gifts I bought for him but I have to. I keep myself hidden in another room so he doesn't get upset with me. People have to understand, him included, what you go through as a parent without your child . . . the first holidays . . . the first years . . . the tidal wave you ride when you least expect it and never asked for any of this.

I'm just sick. I have no appetite. I don't want to be here, or there or anywhere. What brought on this tidal wave? I read a sentence that said look at all the wonderful creations of God: the eagles flying in the air, the ocean waves, children playing . . . and know that heaven is even more wonderful than any of those things and more wonderful than we can even imagine . . . and I know that is where Kelsea is and I believe it.

So for now, I will attempt to make it through the rest of the day. I have no guarantees of what will happen. All I know is soon I will be able to take my sleeping pill again, close my eyes and wait for the sun to come up tomorrow for yet another painful day.

MARK 14:36

"ABBA, FATHER," he said, "everything is possible for you.
Please take this cup of suffering away from me.
Yet I want your will not mine."

CHAPTER FIVE

December 23, 2006, Saturday • Scale: 3

Dear Tat, the day always starts well when I have Colleen with me at the gym. I just kind of tooled around getting things done for tomorrow, not quite sure what to expect. It was fun at the gym and sometimes lately I feel like your spirit is giving me all this charisma and I love it. It would help me out if you could hook me up with a nice man who will love me and comfort me. I did come home and just wanted to be alone. I went to my room early and fell asleep. So, I got up and took a sleeping pill and got relaxed. I have to get used to being alone I guess. I wish I had a partner right now to turn to but I don't. Kels, work your wonders up there; get that dust out for me. You know what I want, bring him to me. I'm trying to be good. Help me over the next days. I love you and miss you and need you and want you. Kisses.

She Is Honored and Missed

Your story shared, your picture, your friend Jimmy . . . stopping me in the store. He told me your picture is up in his room, a collage you made . . . he was so sand and misses you.

December 24, 2006, Sunday • Scale: 2

CHRISTMAS EVE

Wow Kels . . . how could I have known how truly hard it would be today? I went to church alone and cried the whole time. You're supposed to be here. The devotion killed me because it said no matter how wonderful things are here, it is even more wonderful in heaven and I know you are there so I broke down. To think that you are not here for Christmas tomorrow is still not a reality. The sun came up and the sun went down today. It's just another day. How is Christ's birthday in heaven though? I sat in the computer room crying. I know you hate when I cry but bear with me, please. I'll be with you tomorrow, you know. I'm trying to keep things the same for Digger but it's hard. Thank you for being in my dream last night. I didn't see your face but I felt your head against mine and you hugging me. I know it was you. Tawnia and I had a good talk about you . . . were you there with us? Please be with me all day tomorrow and give me your strength and charisma. Love you.

She Is Honored

I shared your picture with a perfect stranger in Walmart.

December 25, 2006, Monday • Scale: 2

CHRISTMAS

Dear Kelsea Lyn, Merry Christmas Sweetheart. I sit here with you at your pad and see all the love poured out to you. You have so many bouquets of flowers, windmills, an angel, a license plate: "You Are Loved," a beautiful wreath, two Christmas tree's, a poinsettia, a stuffed snowman, candy canes (one from Sees), a ceramic ornament . . . so much love. Today's been hard. I've cried almost all day. Digger and I had our Christmas in the room at 6 a.m. alone. No one else woke up till 8 am! Digger and I laughed about how our Christmas was always over by 5 am! He told me about how you used to always go jump on him on his bed Christmas morning. It's weird seeing all these people come here to the cemetery. It's like; I know they aren't visiting a child like I am. It sucks and of course no one stays and visits as long as me; you're sooooooo spoiled. As a matter of fact, you have the prettiest, most decorated pad in the neighborhood.

But, you deserve it. How is the celebration in heaven today? I'll bet it's pretty dang phenomenal. One day I'll celebrate it with you. The coolest thing is that it will be for eternity! The house was crazy today, but all the kids were blessed in abundance. All I wanted for Christmas was you, but I didn't get it. It's really warm here today and this cemetery is very decorated . . . many loved ones. Well, I'll write more tonight from home.

Well, dinner was good; lots of food. You would have loved it. It just wasn't the same without you but it makes me feel better knowing you're in heaven. I finally ate more today than I have in 4 months . . . back to the grind tomorrow. You know, every once in awhile when I think about the reality of everything, I get so sick. For awhile today, all I wanted to do was lay in bed. I mean it is always on my mind but I have learned to push it away, repress it. Help me, please. I met a guy at your pad whose little grandson was there, too. He's going to put a place in your yard for flowers for me. Thank God. You'll always be stylin! I love you with all my heart. I will be with you soon sweetheart—but no soon enough. Kisses 2 you.

She Is Honored

A card, flowers, and a bear . . . so many gifts for you at your pad . . . a wreath, more flowers . . . you're so loved.

December 26, 2006, Tuesday • Scale: 3

Hi Tat, kind of a strange day. I had a lot of chest pains today. More then I have in a long time. I guess I didn't realize how much I talked about you today but it's only because I love you so much. Tawnia put a picture of your pad on your Myspace. I didn't like it. It was really hard to look at for some reason so she put a different beautiful picture of you. Yesterday, Terry said she thinks our book will help so many people and that this one here, my memoirs, will help a whole different group of people, too. But, why did I have to lose you to help other people? Why couldn't you and I have done it together, here? The New Year is around the corner and seriously, how could it not get "better?" I hate that word. I just hope you help me. I want you to look down and be smiling at me. I want you to be so proud of me, like I was proud of you. I always bragged about you even when you were being stupid. I loved you unconditionally. I always will. Please smile down on me. I love you, Tat. Kisses.

She Is Honored

Hard day, chest pains but constantly playing your CD, singing to YOU.

December 27, 2006, Wednesday • Scale: 2

Hi Honey, boy it rained all day! Wish you were here for it . . . the day started out okay but I crashed hard. I know. I know you hate me crying and probably feel helpless from heaven. I want to make you proud to smile down on me, but you have to be patient, honey. You have to try to understand my pain, my loss, my brokenness. I lay in bed after crying for a couple hours; I was wiped out. I've had a sick stomach all day, too. I think it's nerves from the last couple days. After I trained Ruth, I got in my car to drive home. It was raining hard and I thought to myself, *This is a good day to die.* Then I thought how unfair that would be to Digger. I got more Trazodone today and I'm going to stick with that. I love all the charisma you're sending my way. Every time I turn around I'm meeting someone new. One week from today at 2 pm I get my tattoo, yippee! I hate this roller coaster I am on right now. You can let God know that, too. Group tomorrow night. Come to my dreams tonight, please, I need you. Kisses, love you more.

She Is Missed

I crashed today but only because I love you so deeply and miss you.

December 28, 2006, Thursday • Scale: 5

Hi Baby Girl, I actually had a good day. I don't think I've cried, wait . . . I did but it was just one tear. Group tonight was different. I almost felt like I ran it a little.

One of the moms lost her son to suicide; he was bipolar, too. She said at one point that nobody knows what we go through, and she's right. Having a bipolar child is difficult. When I heard her struggles with her son, my heart broke because I thought that could be you. I thought how blessed you are to be in heaven and not struggling here in hell. By the way, I dropped off the design for your tattoo at Skin FX. I can't wait. I'm planning your birthday party, too. Cupcakes, a big card, open house at night for any of your friends that want to stop by. I went to see Tommy today. He wasn't there but I talked to his secretary. I'm sure I'll see him next week; he will be so sad to hear about this. He loved you, too. I need you with me really bad. And watch over me New Year's Eve. I love you, honey, kiss.

She Is Honored

A hard workout at the gym so no more burliness . . . your picture and story always.

December 29, 2006, Friday • Scale: 5

Hi Kels, happy Friday night; wish you were here. Another good day. I'm thinking they are good days because I am not allowing myself to think about it all. I met with Susan for 5 hours today. One of my purposes? To have an annual Kelsea Phelps Bipolar Awareness Walk. I am so blessed to have Susan, a psychologist to talk to for 5 hours at no charge. Crazy! I wrote about your birthday on Myspace. I'm sure it will be nice. I have had 2 days now of no crying. I almost feel as if I am figuring out some true purpose. I quit my job today and start a new one in 2 weeks. I need a change and I think this will be good. See, it is so strange because I just thought for a split second that you are gone and I get SICK to my stomach. I'm taking the Trazodone again. So, how am I supposed to be excited about heaven when it is such a mystery? How come I haven't had any obvious signs you are with me? How about some love?! You know, not having to worry about you has opened up space inside me to become myself again . . . does that make you happy? I miss you horribly. I love you, big hug!

She Is Honored

A 5-hour talk with Susan and plans for a "Kelsea Phelps Bipolar Awareness Walk."

December 30, 2006, Saturday • Scale: 4

Hello Kelsea Lyn, another OK day . . . no tidal waves but the nights not over either. I'll be honest with you, I haven't really been allowing myself to think about you or that you're gone for the last few days. I guess that's why I haven't cried either. I got pulled over today by a deputy on the way to the gym. I was blasting Eminem and was in my Kelsea zone. I guess I blew through a stop sign. Crazy. I didn't even know because I was singing to you. He let me go. I don't like being home here alone because that's when I think too much. I thought again today that actually any day is a good day to die.

Digger has been really worried about my health lately. I'm in great shape but I guess he fears losing me now that we realize it can happen to anyone at anytime. Sudden death is the hardest . . . no preparation. I said goodnight to you and had no idea it would be my last time.

One sentence can bring on that tidal wave; then you barely have the strength to walk to the bathroom. All you want to do is go to bed or drink a beer. I'm done crying now, hard. This isn't fair. I don't understand, why you? Why me? What am I supposed to do now? Why aren't you with me? Why why why! I hate this.

She Is Missed

I struggled today, actually all week, but I talked to you today . . . did you hear me?

December 31, 2006, Sunday • Scale: 5

NEW YEAR'S EVE

Dear Kels, here it is New Year's Eve. The worst year of my entire life is about to be over. How can 2007 not be somehow better? There's that word I hate: better. Nothing will ever be "better." I loved you being at the gym with me today and I love when you answer my questions, too. I can't tell you how big a smile I had. Then, I just start talking to you; out loud because I don't really care if anyone thinks I'm crazy. I have full conversations with you! I'm going to actually do something tonight with Colleen. I haven't celebrated New Year's Eve in 20 years and I figure, why not? I know you want me to be happy and want me to do things so I am going to. Watch over me, though, and Digger. I'm planning your birthday party still. I don't know what to expect but I want you to know how proud I still am of you. You have touched so many people and have made me who I am today. Thank you. I promise to figure out God's plan for me here in your honor. It's going to be huge, Kels; I know it is. Jeanie went to church with me today. It was hard. I love you tons!!! XOXOXO

She Is Here

At the gym today, all the cardio, all the heart rates through you. You made me smile today being with me.

January 1, 2007, Monday • Scale: 3

NEW YEAR'S DAY

Happy New Year Kelsea Lyn Phelps. Of course I know there is no time in heaven, only here in hell. Hard day. I had fun talking to you at your pad. I cleaned it up a little for you too. I really do love laying with you there. I don't know why, but it's getting really hard to look at your pictures. It kills me now; I can't look without getting sick and crying. Why now? Is it because it hasn't become a reality yet to me? I bought the cake mix to make your cupcakes. I'll prepare everything tomorrow. So, I have a new year ahead of me now. Do you think this will be a good year honey? Then, how can anything be "good" without you here on earth with me? People always say, "But she's in your heart . . . blah blah blah." I don't care about that right now. You're not here with me. I can't hug you, smell you, kiss you, tickle you and hear your laugh or your sweet voice telling me you love me. I want the physical you. I want to teach you how to drive more. I want to see you walk at graduation. I want to plan your wedding and hold your baby. I want to watch you fall in love. I HATE THIS, IT'S NOT FAIR!

She Is Loved and Honored

A single rose on your pad and time alone with you there . . .

January 2, 2007, Tuesday • Scale: 4

Hi Sweetheart, well it's almost over, hah? Lot's of people writing and remembering it's your birthday tomorrow. I baked cupcakes all day for you, had some wallet-size pictures made and got a bouquet of balloons. I will be there to see you first thing in the morning. It's strange knowing you're supposed to be 18 tomorrow. Remember how nervous but excited you were to turn 18? As much as you wanted to be an adult, you were scared. Remember when you said, "I don't want to grow up!" That was less than a year ago. . . . Tawnia and I know you were messing with us and the computer tonight and you gave Greg and me all green lights. He noticed and I told him it was just you looking out for us! Please help me tomorrow. I don't know what to expect. I know your true friends will stop by. Did you see how beautiful the moon and stars were at the beach tonight? I love you tons. Be with me tomorrow. XOXOXO

She Is Honored

Cupcakes, balloons, pictures . . . all in preparation for tomorrow.

January 3, 2007, Wednesday (Kelsea's 18th Birthday) • *Scale: 6*

Dear Kelsea Lyn—Happy Birthday—the big 18! Here I sit with you at your pad . . . it's 10 am and so peaceful. The sun is shining bright, pretty scattered clouds and so warm. Once again you are so very loved and missed. Do you like the 18 pink balloons? How about that huge one? Who brought the beautiful dozen pink roses? I guess everyone knows you love pink. I took the day off of work and so did Digger. I know he's struggling, too, hon, he just doesn't show me because he's 19 and a boy. I frosted all the cupcakes first thing this morning. I woke up at 5 am and couldn't go back to sleep. Go figure. . . . I'm getting my tattoo at 2 pm today. Remember the last one I got? You were with me? I know . . . stupid one . . . but we had fun at the time. So, what's it like in heaven on your birthday? Or is that just a stupid earth thing? I have to admit today turned out wonderfully. My tattoo is amazing (ouch!). Your party was perfect. We took so many pictures and your true friends showed up here. We all laughed, told great stories about you, lit a candle, made a wish, sang you Happy Birthday, told more stories, signed your big B-Day card and genuinely had a wonderful night. I know you were with us all. It's crazy how great of a day I had. Absolutely no tidal waves. I think I was just so excited. I had the whole day planned and it was all to honor you and show my love; even your brother was here all night! I loved Josue's story about you drinking, having to pee and just letting go in your pants, then hosing you off. You were the most spontaneous, free spirited, live life to the fullest 17-year-old girl I think we all knew. You loved life, laughed and loved to make others laugh even amidst your bipolar illness and struggles. Happy Birthday, Angel. I love you to eternity and even more. Kisses and hugs.

She Is Honored

Your tattoo, your party, your friends and so many stories.

January 4, 2007, Thursday • Scale: 5

Hello Tat. Okay, so I have to say that yesterday was as perfect a day as I could have had with you being in heaven. Today I was scared. Today I could feel the tidal wave wanting to flow in and take me. I wouldn't let it. Susan explained to me all the holidays are over. I have nothing to focus on so my head is empty to be filled up again with the reality of you gone. She said a letdown is going to happen; I should plan for it. Find a safe place to allow myself to let it happen.

Then I went to group. I took Cara and Barb with me. I dropped my head and cried. I was finally able to talk and read what Digger wrote in your birthday card. . . . "Guide me on the right path." We talked about strategies to get through this time of deep despair. I'm scared honey. I'm scared to feel the excruciating pain again. All your birthday party pictures are already on Myspace; way cool. Every year I will honor you with a party. I will never forget. I'm reading through the bible again this year. I hope it will help me. Please tell me you're happy, some way, some how. I love you, kisses.

She Is Here

As I turn on the radio in the car . . . country western music. The words ring out from your song, "In the Arms of an Angel."

January 5, 2007, Friday • Scale: 3

Dear Kelsea, I know when I trust God, things will work out. They let me go at Frogs Fitness today. I loved training people there and my clients, but I just couldn't do it anymore, Kels. Then, at 24 Hour Fitness they told me to come in for paperwork. His timing, I know. Today was just an okay day, nothing really special at all. What do you think about all the kids in the house? I think they are my saving grace because they keep me busy. I've been having a few chest pains lately and Susan has noticed my finger writing. I can't look at your pictures. I can't listen to your CD except for 3 songs. I can't think about it. I wish we had the holidays still here because it gave me things to think about and focus on.

Now, there's nothing but reality. Even writing that I feel myself repressing. I believe it's a survival method. It's our way of protecting ourselves from the darkness, the dark, deep despair that I feel, the sorrow that I will live with the rest of my life, forever. I don't think people comprehend what life is when you lose a part of your heart and soul. It's empty, hollow, lonely, so very, very broken. Why am I so strong? If I wasn't', would you still be here? I'm so sorry for this . . . forgive me.

She Is Honored

Showing so proudly my tattoo, the comments of how beautiful.

January 6, 2007, Saturday • Scale: 2 Reality

Dear Kelsea Lyn, rougher day still. I saw Dane's mom at the gym. She recently heard and her eyes filled with tears and she couldn't even look at me. I hate running into or having to tell people now. It makes me ill. I've cried several times today. I'm crashing. People think I'm doing "so good," yet they don't see me so broken, crying. They have no idea of my loss, my pain, my emptiness. I don't think a person could handle seeing me that broken and in despair. It's the true me though. What my inside is, not this exterior shell I walk around with. It's crying so hard, I can't breathe. Snot clogs your nose and you can't breathe, yet it drains out of your nose as you're slobbering out of your mouth. It's getting up to get a tissue and stumbling because you're so weak, so fucking BROKEN. I wanted to come see you today. I saw Tommy. He was in shock. I came home to no one.

I can't be that alone. Not now. I couldn't call anyone. All I wanted was to be held and I have no one. I'm so vulnerable. I hate being alone. Why aren't you here? *This is not fair, this sucks.*

She Is Here

As I play your song, Eminem, and hand Colleen my card, a shock so loud and felt so strong!

January 7, 2007, Sunday • Scale: 3

Hi Tat, great news you know . . . the church is going to help me get your headstone! Soon, your pad will be finished and you'll have the nicest pad in the neighborhood. Today was an okay day. Church was hard, but seeing you is getting easier. I really do love going out to the cemetery, crazy hah? I find it so very peaceful. It's a place for me to lie with you, pray, talk to you and really hear what you say to me. I start my new job this week and I know you're going to give me some of that KCD: Kelsea Charisma Dust! I swear you have been sprinkling it on me with all the people I have been meeting. Keep it coming! I also call my morning music (on the way to the gym) my KZ: Kelsea Zone. I have to careful though I almost got a ticket the other day in the KZ. Digger and I went to dinner tonight. It was nice and I know he needs one-on-one time with me, especially now. I saw a lot of mothers/daughters out today and that was hard, really hard. I just ask, Why? My fingers have been going a million miles a minute; help it stop! I love you tons. Kiss and hug.

She Is Honored

Pastor Tony helping me with your headstone, aerial pictures taken of your pad and a visit with roses to your pad.

January 8, 2007, Monday • Scale: 3

Dear Kels, do you have any idea, honey, how difficult it was today to go pay for your headstone? I finally did it and in 90 days it will be done, perfect. I know it will almost have been a year but it will be worth it. I cried in Walmart. Why am I struggling with your pictures? I get sick if I look at them any length of time. I wish I knew how truly eternal life is . . . I have a doctor's appointment in a couple days for another mole. I figure, if it's cancer again I'm not even worried. I know that's selfish because I still need to be here for Digger. I have chest pains right now. Still, when I talk about you I get them. Our attorney called today. I need to find out where our investigation is right now. Justice is what I want, honey.

Whatever the punishment is, she should pay for all the crimes she committed. I don't know how I am going to feel the first time I see her. She took you away from me and she needs to be held accountable. Why you and not her daughter? How can she live with herself? I have spurts of anger but when is it going to really hit—all the anger? I miss you so horribly . . . despair. I love you.

She Is Honored

Your photo and my photo together on your headstone, paid in full.

January 9, 2007, Tuesday • Scale: 3

Hi Sweetheart. So, at the gym I did sooooooo much cardio and I loved it because you were with me. I was talking out loud and I know people thought I was crazy, unless they know. I love how you answer me when I ask you questions, too. I start my new job in 2 days and I'm excited. I went to the mall tonight for the first time since you went home, Victoria Secret. It was hard seeing all the young girls in the mall and in Victoria Secret. That was our store. I had bad chest pains driving through the parking lot before I went in. I doubt I'll be going back anytime soon. I met with Susan for 4 hours today. I treasure my friendship I'm building with her. We really do accomplish a lot talking. I'm really struggling right now, honey. I can't think about the reality that you're not here and in heaven. My brain just can't connect the dots. How can it already be almost 5 months??? It still seems like yesterday. I saw the El Cajon PD guy tonight. He said he told your story to some of his buddies and they all wished you a Happy Birthday. I hate all of this.

She Is Here

I enjoyed our conversation today during cardio, heart pulsing . . . giving me answers to my questions.

January 10, 2007, Wednesday • Scale: 3

Dear Kelsea, I'm tired today. I woke up at 3:30 am with Digger's alarm and couldn't fall back asleep. Head spinning on everything. I went to court and finished filing for my divorce. It will be final on June 1st. I wish he could have been better with you and Digger. I think it would have been different. I know all you wanted was to be loved. I also finally had that mole removed from my back. It was bigger than the last one that was cancerous. I am scared but I figure if it's cancer again, I'll beat it. I would probably have to laugh, too, because what else could go wrong? About the only thing left would be to lose Digger, then I would kill myself. There would be no point to life without both of you. I start my new job tomorrow at 24 Hour Fitness, can you believe it? I think I'll do well. It makes me mad to think you and I never got the chance to really work out together. We would have had a lot of fun. I wanted to take you to Vegas for your 21st birthday. Should I still plan on it? I know you'll let me know. I miss you and cried; crashed today. I love you tons.

She Is Missed

I struggled today . . . help me honor you even in my pain.

January 11, 2007, Thursday • Scale: 3

Dear Sweetheart, group was an emotional drain tonight. We talked about the guilt that goes along with losing a child to suicide. We did an exercise that helped a father realize that he was not responsible for what his son did. He realized he did show his son love. We talked about second chances and what we would do. I would have taken you shopping for your school clothes like you asked. But we all realized we don't get second chances. Ken had me show off my tattoo, purely honoring you. I cried all through group tonight. I started my new job at 24 today and I liked it. I needed a change and I think it will be good. There was a cricket in my bathroom tonight! I know why you hated them. I called Tawnia and she picked it up! Remember the hundreds of crickets we saw in Vegas? What am I supposed to do, Kels, the rest of my life without you? Will my brain ever really be able to process all of this? Would your life have been so difficult? Did God take you to save you from a hard life? Why couldn't I have helped you more? Help me.

She Is Here and Honored

A single large cricket in my bathroom . . . displaying proudly my new tattoo.

January 12, 2007, Friday • Scale: 3

Dear Kelsea, do you know what I realized? I think sometimes when a parent loses a child, they actually become closer to the child. If the child is older and doesn't live at home anymore, there are probably days that go by that the parent doesn't think about the child or talk to them. But when you pass into heaven you are thought of every single day, almost hourly. I couldn't imagine not writing to you every day. Ken said some parents never have a relationship with their child once they pass away, yet I have continued mine with you . . . that's pretty intense.

I think if I didn't write to you the loss would feel even greater. I wish more parents understood how helpful writing to their child would be to them. Hopefully, this will be a book one day where others can read about my grief, my pain, my thoughts, my stages, and my healing process. Can you help me make it all happen, Honey? Of course it's been almost 5 months now and it's still not hit me yet. My brain cannot wrap itself around this concept yet. Will it ever? Help me. I miss you.

She Is Honored and Loved

Sharing your stories with Greg . . . smiling and remembering your ways and your life.

January 13, 2007, Saturday • Scale: 3

Hi Babydoll . . . I see you got some new neighbors in your hood. I know, I cried pretty hard at your pad today. I hope you liked the bouquet of flowers. I had an okay day today. A girl at the gym heard about my tattoo for you. I showed her and her husband and they were in awe of how beautiful it really is. I told a guy at the gym, too. He saw your picture and said you were so beautiful. He lost his papa one month, his dad the next and his twin brother the next month in Iraq. All very sad but still not the loss of a child. I thought about all the trials and tribulations I have experienced. I thought about people who have been handed everything their whole life. I wondered what they would think or feel seeing me today laying on your pad, sobbing so loudly, weak . . . broken. They could not even come close to knowing what it's like to have to fight for your life, to have to lose everything, to have nothing. That's where I'm at, but I don't care. I'm a fighter. We are fighters. We'll be OK someday . . . when I'm in heaven with you again. Love you!

She Is Honored and Loved

Flowers and a visit . . . tears, prayers and talking.

She Is Here

As I lay praying in bed, I am startled by two loud knocks on what I thought was the window above my head. As I looked outside to see if Digger's truck was there and he was knocking, I realized he wasn't home. I realized the two knocks were on the wall, loud, distinct and she was here.

January 14, 2007, Sunday • Scale: 3

Hello Honey, you scared me last night with your two hard knocks on my bedroom wall and the paper flying off my desk for me and Tawnia was awesome, too.

Church was very hard today. I went alone again. I think church is so hard because I'm supposed to feel comforted, peace, trust, faith and, although I do, my heart is still shattered and empty and all I think is how you're supposed to be here with me. Sometimes I feel almost like a "marked" woman. I feel like people look at me and think, she's the one who lost her child. I hate it. I don't want them looking at me and feeling sorry for me. I can't handle, either, someone complaining to me about their life. I just want to scream and tell them to shut up. I want to say, I'll trade you lives *right now*. I don't know, Kels, I don't want my new different life. . . . I want my old life back with all my thoughts consumed by you and what's best for you. I want to pick you up at school every day. I want to teach you to drive. I WANT. I WANT. I WANT.

She Is Here

I asked you, Kels, to blow a piece of paper off the table when Tawnia and I were together. Today, while Tawnia and I sat at the dinner table, a paper ad flew off my desk onto the floor, unprovoked . . . by your breath it flew to the ground.

January 15, 2007, Monday • Scale: 4

Dear Kelsea, I love you so much. I write that and I think of where you're at and my stomach is sick. I'm still not allowing myself to process my life without you now. I still can't look at your Myspace pictures; the tidal wave comes over me then. You know they have all the stupid Valentine's stuff out now and I have to laugh at the day we were in Walmart and you looked down that aisle and said, "I HATE Valentine's Day" and you took the words right out of my mouth! You were such your mom's little girl. I thought about how when I lost my eyelashes and had to get false ones, you started wearing them, too! I know if I had to get chemotherapy, you would have shaved your head with me even though you said you wouldn't. I'm proud of who you were Kelsea. I'm proud of how strong you were, outspoken, beautiful, caring, warm hearted. I wouldn't have wanted you any other way. We struggled but you made me who I am today and I love you for that. I have to believe you're happy now . . . let me know somehow. Kisses and hugs.

She Is Honored

I spoke so highly of you today at work . . . your beauty, your strong will, your wittiness.

January 16, 2007, Tuesday • Scale: 3

Dear Kels, so where I'm at right now is this: I believe it's survival mode. I haven't allowed myself to think about you for any length of time because I can't handle it. But, then today I found myself feeling guilty as hell for not thinking about you. I think, *How can I not think about you when I miss the shit out of you but when I do I crash and I can't handle it?* It's a vicious cycle. I can still barely look at your pictures. I think what has kept me sane is writing to you every day, journaling. My new job is different . . . but I want to make you proud so I will continue trying. I saw Kathryn at the gym, you cheered with her in Pop Warner. She hugged me and said she couldn't believe it. See, just writing that made my stomach sick. I don't know what to do Kels. Is it OK for me to not think about you? When is my brain going to process this all? *American Idol* is on and *you're supposed to be here laughing with me* . . . I need to cry. I hate this. I hate this different life. I hate that God took you. Help me.

She Is Here

The heart rate at the gym.

January 17, 2007, Wednesday • Scale: 1

Hi Baby Girl, I'm so sorry I forgot your picture when I went into the gym today. I did bring a framed one for my desk. You are so beautiful. Everyone looks at this one picture of you and says they thought it was me at first. Do you know what I hate? I hate you not being here and having people tell us we look like sisters. I hate knowing I'll never be able to work out with you again. I hate knowing I won't be planning that beautiful wedding you wanted. I hate knowing you never got to go out to a bar and dance. I hate not being able to keep teaching you how to drive and taking you for your license. I hate that you didn't get to go to ECAL this year and graduate. I hate I can't go to McDonalds and get you a Big and Tasty minus the tomatoes. Tonight, I told Greg, "It's a good night to die," as we drove home. The only thing that makes me want to fight to live is your brother. How can it already be almost 5 months? How? The rest of my life? What kind of life am I supposed to have? I'm sick.

She Is Here

I'm struggling Kels, I see you at the gym with me briefly in the heart rates and then, even for a second, I know.

January 18, 2007, Thursday • Scale: 4

Dear Kelsea, did you see how long I spent with Susan again? I truly am so thankful for her. I have my own personal psychologist who spends 3–6 hours with me every Thursday! She has become a savior. We've been talking a lot about my weight and my lack of eating. I've lost 30 lbs now and I want to lose more. I just want to get skinny for you. I like the way I look. I like everyone asking me, Are you eating? Susan said she thinks because I have to go through this completely alone, it is my way of being cared for. It makes sense. We talked about the natural process of healing this loss. I don't understand how life moves forward as time goes on, but it does. It bothered me that I forgot your picture yesterday but Susan said it's my healing. I'm not crying uncontrollably anymore every day but if I allow myself to think, I will. I love you so much. I can't wait to be with you again; it's just not soon enough. Kisses.

She Is Honored

I helped an elderly man and his wife at Walmart. I put him in his car and I put all their groceries in their trunk. I did this for you Kelsea. . . . I wanted to make you proud.

January 19, 2007, Friday • Scale: 1

Dear Kelsea Lyn, roughest day in awhile, very dark. I had a horrid dream about you last night that they (the courts) were going to execute and kill you in 3 days. I panicked and kept telling everyone how wrong it was. I told them you've never been arrested or in trouble . . . and I woke up. I went and paid for the rest of your stone. While driving there, I got crushing chest pains. I got home and wrote to your Myspace. The phone rang and the doctor told me my cancer was back. I go see a specialist on Tuesday. Why, Kels, is God throwing me so much? Will you tell Him, my faith is not going to be tested? I will not turn my back on Him, so please stop. I've cried today, hard. It's been a hard day, I hate it. I walked/ran Cowles Mountain with Greg . . . he's so supportive; I don't know what I'd do without him. Please give me the strength I need to fight this melanoma. Help Him to help me. Your brother needs me and although I've wanted to die, now I know I want to live. I have too much to do here on earth. I love you.

She Is Here

You're so very funny when the heart rate hits 200 and flips so rapidly in numbers.

January 20, 2007, Saturday • Scale: 3

Hi Sweetheart, who brought you the huge poinsettia tree?! I went to your pad and it was there, so beautiful. I hope you don't mind that I brought it home and I hope you liked my bouquet of flowers and little balloon. It was hard there today. Not too many others visiting but it was cold out today. I gave Pastor Tony a thank-you card and told him about my cancer. I thought he was going to cry. My heart pounded pretty hard when I told him; I guess I'm scared. The last time this happened, you were in 4th grade and I know it affected you so I guess part of me should be or feel okay knowing at least you're not worried right now. But, I'm selfish and I'd rather you be here with me to go through it with me because we would beat if together—right? Cara called me crying tonight, missing Melissa. It's been 2+ years. It never goes away, you know. It never gets better. The pain is always there, ready to show its ugly head when we least expect it. I hate it so much. It's not reality yet. Will it ever be? I love you too much.

She Is Honored

A beautiful bouquet of flowers and a large poinsettia all at your pad.

January 21, 2007, Sunday • Scale: 2

Hi Honey, I finally spoke with Amy's mom, Melanie, today. Don't forget to tell Amy I will take care of her mom and little sister. Her mom is going to group with me on Thursday. I've never met her yet. We cried on the phone together and she was glad to finally talk to someone who understands. You know, hon, people just don't understand our pain. They see the outside of us that may seem okay but our insides are ripped apart . . . no one see's that. I haven't broken down in front of anyone since this happened because I have no one. But, you and I are the two strongest girls I've ever met and I will make it through this. I may not like it; in fact, I hate this but I have to help people so when I come home to you, we will have a mansion high on the hill. I want you to be so proud of me here. I want to make you smile all the time with my kindness to others. Yes, I know I cried today and had chest pains. I think I will shed a tear every day till we are together again. It is all for my strong love. See, I'm sick to my stomach. That's why I can't think about you now. Forgive me, please. I miss you.

She Is Missed

I struggled today with you on my mind . . .

January 22, 2007, Monday • Scale: 2

Dear Kels, I HATE this day every month . . . the 22nd. I don't understand how it is already 5 months? How it feels like it's been an eternity already. I cried doing cardio at the gym. I tried going to work and made it an hour.

For the first time since you left, all I wanted to do was lie in bed and do nothing. So, that's what I did. I came home and lay in bed from noon till about 8 pm. I know it's a combination of the day and seeing the doctor tomorrow.

Tawnia is going with me. I wish it was you who were going with me. I also wrote in my monthly journal today. I guess if I think about it, I sure write/talk to you a lot every day. I hope you like it. I can't wait to see what the other side is like. Do you ever get frustrated being here with me and me not being able to see you? I'd get pissed I think! I have had a constant chest pain today. I miss you so much. I wanted to fast today but Susan wouldn't let me. Too much pain already she said. Whatever. I love you.

She Is Here

My hands hold the cross-trainers sensor and nothing. As I finish up my half hour of cardio with one minute left I take my hands off the sensors completely. While saying, "Show me now. . . ." The heart rate shows now . . . .70, 71, and 72 for the entire minute I have left.

JOURNAL: I WANT TO LIVE

So, I made it through Christmas, New Year's and Kelsea's 18th Birthday . . . all for the first time in 17 years, without her. Firsts, are always hard, unimaginable, unwanted, choice less but such a reality. Christmas was spent completely out of tradition. For 17 years Christmas has been the most celebrated holiday I have given my children. Now, it is different. It is so very, very different. I don't think it will ever, in fact I know it will never, be the same.

My son and I woke up early. He was so excited for me to open the 3 gifts he bought me. Of course, his stocking was at his feet as always. You see, I would sneak into the kid's room and place their stockings on the foot of their beds so they would have something to keep them occupied till at least 5 a.m.!

Digger, for the first time since Kelsea went Home, shared a memory with me about her. He said Kelsea used to wake up super early every Christmas morning and jump on his bed, yelling at him to get up so they could open gifts.

He struggled as much as I did. We live with 6 other children and my kids' Godmom and Goddad. When they all began opening gifts, Digger said he didn't want to be there, so we left. We simply drove to the 7-11 around the corner and got something to drink.

I honestly can't remember what else I did that day; I just know it was uneventful. I didn't eat any Christmas dinner at home, Digger and I went out again and again I couldn't eat. We got home and I retreated back to my room, alone. Again, I took my sleeping pill and the sun went down.

New Year's was never a big holiday so it came and went and then there was Kelsea's 18th birthday on January 3rd. Ironically enough, it turned out to be the best day I have had since Kelsea passed.

I started the day writing to her on her Myspace. I went and picked up a huge bouquet of balloons to take to her pad. I went and spent a couple hours with her and decorated her pad so pretty. Then, I did it. . . . I got my tattoo. About a month and a half ago, I decided I was going to get a tattoo for her. I started looking on the internet and had an idea of what I wanted and there it was, perfect.

There are certain things I don't like. such as R. I. P. To me it is dreary. I don't really care for "In Memory Of" either. So, I came up with my own and it is simply "In Everlasting Life" because that is what Kelsea has now and I will one day, too.

I wanted a cross, wings and a halo and her dates. What I found and designed I wear proudly and each year because she loved the stars so much, I will have a little star put around it on her birthday . . . to honor her every January 3rd.

I also had "In Everlasting Life" put on her headstone. I told my best friend I wanted to start a movement in which people all get away from the "In Memory Of" and go to "In Everlasting Life." How cool would that be?

After the tattoo came her birthday party. Yes, I threw her an 18th birthday party and invited her friends. It was even better than I ever could have imagined. So many girls and her boyfriend were there. We sang her Happy Birthday and all lit a candle on a cupcake for her and made a wish. Everyone signed a huge card for Kelsea. We sat and they all told me such funny stories about the times they had with her.

Everyone brought cameras and took so many pictures and put them on her Myspace in her honor. All in all, it was as perfect as it could have been. I made copies of some of her best pictures and let all her friends take them. I didn't cry that day and what I thought was going to be such an awful struggle of a day turned out to be a "good" day.

Then, January 4th came and everything was over; no more holidays to think about or to plan for. Once again, my head became empty with idle time, idle thoughts, and a slap in the face of reality again that she was not here. It was as if all the holidays kept me occupied in some way or another and it was okay.

But, as soon as it was all over I got scared.

I felt myself slipping backwards or what I felt was backwards. I was afraid of the tidal wave that I knew was going to fall upon me. I met with Susan and we talked for 5 hours. She has been a life line to me and helps me process all this stuff going on in my head and in my life.

I have found myself over the last 3 weeks not allowing myself to think about Kelsea. If I begin to, I get sick and immediately push all thoughts out of my head. I believe it is just a survival that we must have inside us because of all the pain we feel. I think we can't live with that amount of pain forever, so at times our minds don't let us think. But then I feel guilty as hell and think, *How can I not think about her?*

I can barely look at her pictures now without getting sick. At my support group we were told, it's okay to take a break from the pain and not think about it for a couple hours at a time. It's been 3 weeks now and I wonder if I'm just in denial now? I know there are so many different stages of grief and I haven't kept track of any of them because I really don't care what they are. I just allow myself to feel what I feel, do what I do and make it through one hour at a time still.

You see, I have realized that if I don't allow myself to think about Kelsea, I won't cry and I won't have any tidal waves take me out, for the most part.

I was writing to Kelsea one night and I wrote one sentence at the end of the journal and I lost it. I found myself on the living room floor crying uncontrollably, snot pouring out of my nose, unable to breath, unable to move, alone. As I tried to get up to get some tissue I could barely walk and I thought to myself, THIS is me. This is how I feel. This is what nobody else see's or could comprehend. So emotionally drained that you have no strength to move . . . and there you are. The tidal wave just swooped you out into the water and now you're gasping for air, fighting to stay afloat, unable to catch your breath.

I don't have a problem crying in front of anyone, however, the tidal waves I ride alone. I'm afraid if someone was there with me, they would feel so utterly helpless and powerless. At that point, there is nothing they can say or do that would help and it is best to just let me be alone.

When I go to work out every day, I take a different picture of Kelsea with me and place it where ever I am so she is with me always. Many people know that and look to see which picture I have that day and others question me as to whom she is. At that time, I take the opportunity to honor Kelsea and tell them her story and about her.

Last week, for the first time I walked into the gym without her picture; I simply forgot. I began my workout (cardio) and realized she wasn't with me and I felt an extreme amount of guilt. How could I have done that? Did that mean my healing process had begun? Did I dishonor her by forgetting her picture?

I brought it up with Susan and she helped me to accept it. Yes, I was healing and that was a sign. It didn't mean I had forgotten about Kelsea; it just meant for a few moments I was living my life pain-free. I haven't forgotten it since and I won't stop taking Kelsea's picture with me to work out.

Over the last month, I have also helped 3 other mothers in their grief by taking them to my support group with me. Each has lost a daughter; one 9 years ago, one $2^1/_2$ years ago and one 3 months ago. All of them did not know about the Jenna Druck Foundation and were thankful for it, as I have been.

I have said before that I know God has a plan for me. It's things like bringing these women and introducing them to this group that makes me realize that maybe I am beginning to fulfill that purpose. It's as if God is placing me on the path of these women's lives to help them.

I'm still writing to Kelsea every day. I still go see her every week at her pad. I still get chest pains, cry, get angry and want to die at times, but life has a strange way of approaching you and telling you things.

You see, on January 19th I got a call from my doctor informing me that I had melanoma, again. I fought this when Kelsea was in the 4th grade a short 8 years ago. I went into remission but another mole on my back was checked recently and came back "malignant and aggressive."

I was sitting at the computer looking at Kelsea's Myspace, riding a small wave, crying when the phone rang and I got the news. I began crying harder and thought, *Wwhy me? How can God be throwing all these things at me right now?* I went into my room, on this grief path, and lay in bed and cried, prayed and cried some more.

The next day when I woke up I realized something. I thought about my prayers over the last 18 hours and I understood why the cancer was back; it renewed my desire to live again. You see, over the last 5 months, there have been so many times I have wanted to die. This made me realize that although I'm not afraid to die, I want to live. I have my son to live for.

I know that I will survive because I am a fighter, as was Kelsea. Just as I have survived this far in the greatest loss a person can endure, I will survive this melanoma. I'm not saying I will never ride that wave, or fall, or possibly want to die again . . . but for now I realize I must live to help.

1 PETER 5:7

Give all your worries and cares to God,
for He cares about what happens to you.

CHAPTER SIX

January 23, 2007, Tuesday • Scale: 3

Hi Honey, I hope your day was better than mine. I have been so stressed today; I didn't realize I didn't have any time to think about my pain till tonight. My cancer is a little more serious than I expected. I need a Sentinel Node scan. Please talk to your Father and ask Him to heal me, okay? I looked at a couple of your pictures tonight and cried so I quit looking. Kelsea, I'm so very sorry I didn't protect you more from what happened. I lived my life for you and your brother. I thought I was doing everything right. I was so damn close to getting you sent away and getting you help. Why didn't I check on you earlier? Why couldn't I have talked to you more that night? Why didn't anyone else tell me you took that medication? Do you know? Did you see me lying with you on your floor? Kissing you, holding you? Did you see that from heaven? My stomach is sick and nothing is easier yet. The first two years—they are like yesterday. Five months and it's not real yet . . . it's still too fresh. I can't think. I hate this. Why me?

She Is Here

Your cough medicine in the hall closet, right up front . . . where'd it come from?

January 24, 2007, Wednesday • Scale: 3

Dear Kelsea Lyn, I seriously think God has blessed me with this cancer to get my mind off the greatest loss in life, you. I think this is the least I have had you on my mind yet. I even forgot to take your picture into the gym tonight. I have struggled today with a sense of time, what day it is . . . yes honey, I'm scared. But I'm also ready to fight. I only wish you were here with me. If I have to get chemo, who is going to shave their head for me? I've had a bad lump in the throat today but it's from the stress of seeing a doctor on Monday. I got my nails done by Tawnia today. It was the first time in about 9 months. We laughed about how she would do yours and within days you had them all off and wanted them back on again! See, I just flashed on you in heaven and wonder what you're doing? I know God's not going to take me now but if He does, I'm not afraid to die. I just don't want to leave your brother yet. He needs me badly. He wouldn't make it without both of us here. Give me strength, honey, please. . . . I love you.

She Is Honored

My letters to you every single night without fail . . .

January 25, 2007, Thursday • *Scale: 3*

Hello Sweetheart, rough group tonight. I knew it was going to be, though, because of how much I'm struggling right now thinking about you. It wasn't until I was driving home talking to Colleen that I realized that it's been since your birthday I have been feeling this way. I've been unable to think about you because I get so sick to my stomach. I shared at group the whole scenario: finding you, trying to give you CPR. Ken made me realize or just reaffirmed to me that me having found you just adds another layer of hell to my already unbearable pain. He said he couldn't even fathom it. Yes, I was traumatized. I have flashbacks that I push away immediately. I cried the entire time. It sucked.

This sucks. I did tell everyone, though, that I know without a doubt you are in heaven. I will be with you again, maybe sooner that we think with this cancer. Talk to your Father . . . healing dust every morning when I wake up. . . . I ache for you, Kelsea, and still don't understand, WHY ME? Help me to understand. I love you.

She Is Here

So many tears shed at group . . . so much pain. . . .

January 26, 2007, Friday • *Scale: 3*

Hi Baby, short one . . . having to write this the next day. Can you believe how sick I was with the flu? Remember the last time I was that sick was your freshman year. It sucked. I went and got insurance through Medical today. Then, on the way home I threw up violently out the window while driving . . . attractive, hah?

I've never been so miserable. I know you would have been right here to help me out. I miss you and love you. I did get scared because when I threw up once, I started spitting a lot of blood and I thought it was my cancer and I was dying.

She Is Missed

Today, I was sicker than I have been in years with the flu. I wish you were here to care for me. . . . I know you would.

January 27, 2007, Saturday • *Scale: 2*

Dear Kelsea, another day in bed, weak and still sick. I know I got it from Jarrod. Everyone in the house is getting sick. I must admit my mind has been so preoccupied with the cancer and flu. I have barely had time to feel the pain of you not here with me. Do you think it's God's way of giving me a break from the pain? I hope I feel better by tomorrow, you know? Will you go to church with me, please? Don't forget to keep sprinkling that healing dust. I just wish I could see a year into the future to see what my new purpose is supposed to be. Who will I be helping? Because right now, I feel lost, unimportant, like I have no direction. I'm drowning in a pool. I keep getting all these trials and tribulations handed to me and I want to know, why? My faith will not fail or be tested. I love you, Kelsea, with every fiber of my body, forever into our everlasting life together. Come into my dreams so I can feel you again. I want you HERE.

She Is Missed

Again, the day was spent in bed, sick . . . too sick to think, feel, do. . . .

2 CORINTHIANS 4:18

So we fix our eyes not on what is seen, but on what is unseen. For
what is seen is temporary, but what is unseen is eternal. Amen.

January 28, 2007, Sunday • Scale: 3

Hi Sweetheart, how is your everlasting new life treating you? I can't even imagine . . . but everything in writing says it's so beautiful. We here on earth can't imagine. My mind's been really preoccupied with my cancer. I was sitting watching TV tonight when I realized that other than praying for you in church this morning, I hadn't thought about you, which meant no pain but then the guilt set in. Did you see your brother in church with me? Come to think of it, hon, I haven't cried today. Does that make you mad? Does it make you think I'm okay now?

Because I'll never be okay with any of this. Because what people don't understand is in 5 years, I won't be okay because you still won't be here with me. I know you're in my heart but it's not enough. People just don't get how much I miss you *physically*. In my heart, thoughts, la la la **doesn't count**. Any split second thought I have right now I get ill so I just can't think. If I think, I cry. I'm tired of crying but I can't stop. I love you, kisses.

She Is Missed

A lump in my throat, chest pains, a hurt back; all in church . . .

January 29, 2007, Monday • Scale: 3

Dear Kelsea, good news . . . the doctor is optimistic about my melanoma. She did tell me how lucky I am to have melanoma twice now and still be alive. She looked at me and said, "Melanoma usually kills you." That's nice, hah? So I go in for surgery soon and I should be good. I feel like I have my life back again. I felt a bit of a wave coming on today but I stopped it. I showed your picture to some girls at the doctor's office and they all know you're beautiful. It's been over 3 weeks now that I haven't allowed myself to feel this pain. Maybe it's just subsiding a bit. Maybe it's part of this "healing" process. Maybe this is what people consider getting "better?" I heard your song today, "In the Arms of an Angel," while waiting to see the doctor. I knew then you were there with me and Tawnia. What am I supposed to be doing now, honey, without you here? What is my new purpose? Am I going to love again and be able to live a complete life? I can't have another baby. I could never replace you. I want you in my car sitting next to me. I love you.

She Is Here

Waiting to see the cancer doctor in the waiting room and the music sounds, "In the Arms of an Angel" . . .

January 30, 2007, Tuesday • Scale: 3

Hi Honey, I finally worked a whole day, can you believe it? It felt very good, too. It's kind of hard right now because I find myself going through periods throughout the day when you don't consume my every thought and when I realize that I get upset and feel guilty. Is this part of the whole "healing process" because I really don't like it? I don't like that my life has begun to be functional without you here. It doesn't seem right. It's like, how? I'm just so confused and the second I allow myself to think about you, the pain floods back so I'm just not thinking about you right now, but then I feel guilty like I'm supposed to. It's a vicious cycle my head is running through. I cried tonight. I'm not crying as hard these days.

At least not every day. I still carry your picture everywhere and I wear your hockey jersey proudly, "No More Burly." I like getting skinny. I like how it feels, how I feel. . . . I still hate all of this.

She Is Missed

I'm struggling, but amidst all the pain there is no doubt how much I love you.

January 31, 2007, Wednesday • Scale: 3

Hi Babydoll, I love you more than the law allows. Thanks for the KCD today. I did well at work. I felt good at work. I know once I learn it all, I'm going to do great. Hell, between you and I they're not going to stand a chance! I decided I am going to write to Oprah, Dr. Phil and Montel and ask them to honor Tawnia for Mother's Day. Don't you think she deserves it? She has been my savior now so many times; she deserves it. I felt strong today. Not physically but emotionally. I think that working is finally helping me. It's giving me something to really focus on and to take away the focus on this pain. My surgery is February 13th . . . great, 13! I know you'll be with me. I'm really glad I have this relationship with you. I love writing to you and talking to you. Even Digger makes sure I write every night. How is he doing? I know you're with him. Please tell your Father, not to take Digger from me. I don't know how my faith would take that, too. I don't want to know. Kisses 2 u.

She Is Here

On the way to the gym, I asked you to be with me; I needed you. It's always on the cardio equipment that you show up. No heart rate, then I look down and there it is, there you are. I smile and thank you. The heart rate climbs and drops. As it gets higher, I laugh with you. I'm talking to you and in my head I say to you, "Okay, let's hit 200," and the very second I say and think 200 you're there. You amaze me.

February 1, 2007, Thursday • Scale: 3

Hi Tat, Thursdays have turned into my complete mental health day! 4 hours with Susan and 2 hours with group. I had a rough day. I found myself short-tempered and wanted to beat somebody's ass. Talking to Susan for so long today was good. I went straight to group. I didn't realize how agitated I was until Ken asked me. My leg was going 100 MPH. He asked me why I was jumping out of my skin tonight. I just told him I was tired. I was tired of losing you, going through a divorce and having cancer again. There were 3 couples there tonight and me. Alone again like always. He had 3 of the parents hug me and I knew, I lost it. Ken told them all every time they see me to hug me because I'm going to need thousands of hugs over the next couple months. I did feel better. I also learned I am going through a numb phase and it's okay. I was assured the pain will return but it's been so great, my body decided enough for now and that's why I'm not thinking about this at all. It doesn't mean I don't love you. It just means I need a break. You're not mad, are you? Please, don't be mad. I love you.

She Is Honored, Loved and Missed

4 hours with my psychologist, 2 hours with my support group, all about you.

February 2, 2007, Friday • Scale: 3

Dear Kelsea Lyn, it's so strange to go through the days now. I guess because there seems to be longer periods of time each day now that are "okay." I'll admit my thoughts aren't consumed by you now and what happened. I'm actually able to function through out the day. I can't say I feel "good" or "normal" though. I don't really feel much of anything. No real joy or happiness. The sadness and sorrow is still so very heavy but manageable right now. Probably, though, because I'm numb. At times, I'll start to think about you not here and I just don't get it. I don't understand how you've already been gone almost 6 months. How have I survived that long? I think writing to you every night keeps you here with me.

I've given up on you coming into my dreams. I bought a shirt today because it was all you! It has a skull on the front; so very you. It's my favorite shirt now. I'm working all day tomorrow so I need some KCD first thing—okay? Be with me, work with me. I love you with all my heart . . . together forever.

She Is Here

Thanks for being at the gym with me as always.

February 3, 2007, Saturday • Scale: 3

Dear Kelsea, busy day at work today. I like it though. I met a woman with breast cancer today. It's crazy the instant connection you have when you both have cancer. I've noticed my scale is stagnant since your birthday hovering at a 3. I feel like I'm on autopilot and my life has stopped in terms of my grieving loss. I don't really think I miss the pain, but part of me does. I want a hard, tidal wave cry but I can't because I won't think about you enough to bring one on. Does any of that make sense? The only time I am able to feel these days is when I am in group. I guess because I'm the safest in there. No one understands like all of us in that room; a choiceless room none of us asked to be in. It's the weekend and I am so lonely on weekends. I'm still going to be your mom, right? Will you be my best friend when I get to heaven, please? Because I feel like I got screwed there because I know we would have been best friends when you became an adult, inseparable. I hate that you're not here.

She Is Honored

Mystical, your perfume, it's all I wear now, always.

February 4, 2007, Sunday • Scale: 3

Hello Sweetheart, it was such a beautiful day outside today. It was sunny and warm. I know you didn't care for this type of weather but I liked it. When I rolled the window in the car down, turned up the radio loud, was on my way to the gym, for a brief few seconds I felt good. I was happy if that is possible. Then, again it all hits me . . . how can I feel this way with you not here? I just don't understand. I don't really like "moving forward." I don't like doing "better." Sometimes I just want to live in the pain. Every Thursday I allow myself that pain, in group. See, it's like when I start to think about you not here, I just get sick. I'm not crying every day and I guess that's a good thing. I mean just because I don't cry every day, you know that doesn't mean I don't still love you, right? My love for you grows every minute. I still can't imagine the rest of my life without you here. Will I ever be okay? I don't think life will ever truly be good again, not without you. Love you.

She Is Honored

Grief is not a weakness; it is nothing to be ashamed of. If anything, it is a badge of honor to be worn.

February 5, 2007, Monday • Scale: 3

Dear Kelsea Lyn, so at work today I kept drifting off in thought about you. I flashed on the morning of the 22nd. My heart started beating rapidly, my breath got short, my stomach got sick and my eyes filled with tears. . . . I can't do it. I can't process it still. I find myself not wanting to talk to certain people. I can't talk to anyone who knows you and I haven't talked to him yet. I can't do it. I actually worked 8 hours today. I talked to Dane's mom tonight at the gym. I tried explaining "brokenness." No one could possibly understand unless they, too, lost a child. Did you see the gerbil Sassy chased in the kitchen tonight? I'm trying to take good care of her for you. Are you with your other kitty, Pookie?

Are there animals in heaven? Kiss Poohdunk for me, too. I'm probably going to miss group this week but I know you want me happy. It doesn't mean it's all easier and I'm fine now. It means I need a break from life. I love you. XXX

She Is Missed

I'm struggling now . . . but even through the pain you are loved.

February 6, 2007, Tuesday • Scale: 3

Hi Honey, how are you? I'm not sure how I am. Still numb I think because I just won't allow myself to think. I talked to one of your friends tonight at the gym. She goes to Westhills and met you freshman year. She said you always stood up for her and you grabbed her off a counter at a party one night, threw her over your shoulder and carried her out. Girls were saying rude things about her and you didn't like it. We agreed you had the biggest heart. She also mentioned "Poison." I asked her to come see me when I'm there working and share more stories with me. Remember grinnards? I saw him at the gym and he confirmed I made the right decision in my divorce. So many changes have taken place since you went home. Some of them I like, but I would rather you be here with me. I talked to someone today and I just can't imagine the REST OF MY LIFE without you, growing old and you always being only 17. My dream? To have an annual Kelsea Phelps Bipolar Awareness Walk/Run. One day, I promise. I love you so damn much.

She Is Honored

Stories from Rochelle, your huge heart. . . .

February 7, 2007, Wednesday • Scale: 2

Hi Honey, hard day. All it took was reading one line on your Myspace and here came the wave. Lauren wrote about your freshman year, a picture taken of you. You were pretending to put your finger in a light socket and get shocked in your science class. Then I pictured you doing that, so full of life. I thought about you making everyone smile and how loved you were and I lost it. I haven't cried that hard in a month. I was so weak after. . . . I don't understand. I guess I will never understand until I am face to face with your Father upstairs. I'm going to your pad tomorrow. I didn't make it there last week and I'm so sorry. I know it was the first time I didn't come. I've been struggling. My new job is getting better though. I need your KCD every day I work. Do you like how skinny I'm getting? Another 6 pounds and I'll be as much as you weighed. How cool is that? I feel good though. No more burly, right? I need you in my dream tonight, a good one please? XOXOXO

She Is Honored

I showed your picture to everyone today, your long, beautiful hair and smile.

February 8, 2007, Thursday • Scale: 3

Dear Tatty Lyn, haven't called you that in awhile, hah? I wanted to visit you today but time just crept away. It's harder to do things now that I'm working almost full time. My life is so different now, Kels. People have left my life since you passed, yet others have come into my life, too. I would say if you were here with me right now, I would be very happy with where I'm at, but you're not. I met with Susan today. We talked about your graduation and if I will walk. Do you want me to do that for you? I can't wait to see the yearbook and your memory page. It will be bitter-sweet. Valentine's Day is coming up, too. I figured I would just celebrate it with you since we both hate that day! I'll bring you beautiful flowers, I promise. I'm still waiting for you to come into a good dream. A dream I can feel you in, see you, hug you. Will it ever happen or will I have to wait till I make it to heaven? I don't know. Kisses, XOXOXO

She Is Here and Honored

Again, cardio, you are there . . . your picture is shared and stories are told.

February 9, 2007, Friday • Scale: 2

Dear Kelsea, do you see how messed up my life is right now? I saw this movie *Pursuit of Happiness* today. If it wasn't for Tawnia, I would be living in the streets. Even with all he endured in his life in the movie, I would trade my life for his in a heartbeat. People just don't get it . . . nothing compares to losing a child, NOTHING. I've been making some poor choices in my life since you left and they all blew up in my face today. Can you help me? Can you tell your Father how sorry I am and how I need strength now more than ever? I need you to help me, too. I need KCD bad now. I need guidance. I need YOU back in my life.

This month is now 6 months. *How can it be?* I hate all this. I hate my bad decisions, you gone, nothing and no possessions, no one to love and care for me, all of it. Surgery on Tuesday. Be with me. I love you.

She Is Missed

I've had a hard, horrible day. . . .

February 10, 2007, Saturday • Scale: 3

Hi Sweetheart, how is eternal life treating you? Is everlasting life so beautiful we can't even imagine? Did God take you to save you from a horrible life here on earth or what I now call hell? I went to church tonight and I couldn't stop flashing on seeing you in your casket at your funeral. I don't know why now, but church was very emotionally difficult tonight. I know you don't have to sleep there, but I'll bet you sneak off and take little naps here and there. I bought beautiful hot pink tulips tonight for your pad tomorrow and watch out on Valentine's Day because I'm gonna decorate and spoil you that day! I'll spend it with you because it is our favorite holiday! I'm confused, honey, with my life right now. I love someone who I shouldn't right now. I was told tonight love is patient. What do you think? How patient am I supposed to be? I really need guidance here, honey. I love you so very, very much. Everlasting life . . . with you and me. Kisses.

She Is Missed

I tidal wave in church—so much pain and sorrow.

February 11, 2007, Sunday • Scale: 2

Dear Kels, rainy day and who went to your pad and sat in the rain? That's right . . . me, your loving mother. I didn't care, though, that I got drenched. I sure had a long heart-to-heart though, with your Father. Did you like the pink tulips? Wait till Valentine's Day, our fave! I told your story to a girl from the gym today. I ran into her at Walmart. I cried. Then, I just unloaded onto her my life right now. She's a Christian and is going to pray for me. Life is so crazy, Kels. I've been hanging out with a guy I met at the gym. He's 15 years younger than me but he's very nice company. I get lonely because your brother has his life. Sometimes I just can't handle all the people in the house here and I just need to be held, you know? I wish I could hug you, feel you, see your smile, hear your laugh. I will have that all when I see you again, right? Never soon enough though. I love you.

She Is Here

I now know you are with me every time I step into the gym. Cross-trainer, last 15 seconds, not touching the handles and a heart rate of 50 and I smiled.

February 12, 2007, Monday • Scale: 3

Hi Sweetheart, I had a great day at work, finally! I met a couple boys who knew you. One had some classes with you at Westhills. He told me he was so sorry for what happened. I told him you were such a good girl, my little girl. I also shared our story with a woman I signed up. I figure the more people that know my story, the more prayers we will get, right? My surgery is tomorrow. I'm not really scared. I trust that God is in control and will heal me of this cancer. I talked to Joe, a guy I met at the gym. He assured me you were in a much better place. He told me God has a plan for all of us whether it's to help someone else, show someone something. . . . I'm trying to listen to what my purpose is now. Yell it in my ear for me, okay? I miss the hell out of you. I can't believe how much we look alike. You are beautiful. Kisses and hugs.

She Is Honored

Laughing at your stubbornness, your attitude, you . . . with a boy who had you in his class at school.

February 13, 2007, Tuesday • Scale: 3

Hi Baby doll, thanks for being there with me, during my surgery. I had your pictures with me in the operating room; you were laying there with me. I've never felt so much physical pain in my life. Not even in birth! My lymph nodes under my arm are sooooo bruised and swollen and a nice scar. Just add them to all the rest, hah? At least when I get to heaven they'll all be gone, right? I told everyone I could about you today. I always try to introduce you to someone new every day. It was a long day today. You know what tomorrow is—hah? Our day. I'll see you tomorrow, too. I miss you so much, and when I die, I will have all my letters to you with me when I get to heaven. Do you read them right now already? I love you and so does Digger. Kisses.

She Is Honored

Surgery today, your pictures across my chest, everyone knowing our story.

February 14, 2007, Wednesday • Scale: 4

VALENTINE'S DAY

Hi Baby doll, so I guess this was a better day because of the holiday. I'm learning that the holidays are actually easier on me than regular days, especially today. I know I was a total brat today. I know in the past how much WE hated Valentine's Day, but today I loved it because I spent it with you. You are and will always be my Valentine. Did you like how I decorated your pad? Flowers, a card, candy, the M&M girl? I see you had more smoking buddies show up, then I found out it was your brother and George. I'm glad he finally came to see you.

He missed you. I had fun talking to you today and laughing. I made up my mind it was going to be a no crying visit and it was! I really, really enjoyed this Valentine Day and I want to thank you for it. Can you believe how much more bruised and swollen I am? I love and miss you. Everlasting life one day.

She Is Loved, Honored and Missed

Valentine's Day . . . candy, flowers, a card . . . "I hate Valentine's Day" (your infamous words). Your pad decorated, good conversation, no tears today. . . . This is our official day forever!

February 15, 2007, Thursday • Scale: 3

Dear Kels, we talked about journaling tonight in group. I think I probably journal more than anyone. I write to you every day in 3 different capacities . . . you're spoiled! I talked with Susan today, too, for 4 hours. She has been deemed one of my Angels and I call her my life coach. I think I'm still on my Kelsea vacation. Do you like it when I call you Kels? Are you still laughing at my big ass scar and stitches on my back? My back's going to look like Frankenstein! I don't care though. I'm tired of all this cancer crap. Can you tell your Father, I got the point? I'm going to live and help people. I don't want to die right now. I want to live. I want to help other parents and make you very, very proud of me. Can you believe how skinny my arms look? It's crazy. I want to be your size. I want to never be burley again. I want you in the gym with me. I want to train you but I can't and that pisses me off. Maybe in heaven? Love you tons!

She Is Honored

A silver skull and crossbones ring given to me as a gift from the girl in the bank because she knows it reminds me of you.

February 16, 2007, Friday • Scale: 2

Hi Honey, Friday night—woo woo. You know how much I don't care for the weekends. It's a time I'm supposed to be worrying about you, where you're at, who you're with and now I can't because I know you are safe in heaven. I know it's selfish but I would rather you be here and I was worrying. I saw a lot of people with set ups for the desert and I got sad because I know you should be experiencing the desert still. I know you loved to ride and I'm sorry I never got to do that with you. Can we once I get to heaven?

It's like, when I start to think about you, I instantly cry so I push those thoughts away because I don't want to feel the pain right now. Next week will be 6 months since this all went down.

How can that be? How is 2 years supposed to go by, or 10? I just can't imagine that yet. Will you help me understand *why this happened*? Please?

She Is Missed

Another day spent in pain, physical pain.

February 17, 2007, Saturday • Scale: 3

Dear Kelsea Lyn Phelps, I love your name. I love calling you "Kels." So, tonight Sassy Girl jumped up on my chest when I was lying on the couch. She cuddled on me, nuzzled her head into my neck, and licked my face, neck and arm. I told you I would love her. I felt your love coming through her to me. I know that you and I spent time together, alone tonight on the couch. I felt your love, thank you. It's really hard right now not being able to do anything, trying to rest from my surgery. I wish you were here because I know you would be taking care of me. But, I also know you would be mad at me and stressed, too, like when you were in 4th grade and I got the cancer the first time. Next week is 6 months. Do you realize it's been that long already? Are you in a better place? Is it paradise there? Do you love everyone there? Do you have a boyfriend? Do you want me happy here? Can you help me find true love here now? Can you use the Heart and Soul Dust? I miss you. XOXO

She Is Here

Sassy cuddling, licking me, loving me on my chest; so much love coming through her from you. . . .

February 18, 2007, Sunday • Scale: 3

Hi Tat, what a beautiful day at your pad. It was probably one of the most peaceful days I have spent with you. The sun was warm, a slight breeze . . . faint birds chirping and a strange scent of incense. Was it really you?

Thanks! I talked to Tawnia about the 22nd. She said I called her at 8:32 am and said, "She's gone. They couldn't wake her up." I do not remember a second of it. I thought Steve called her, not me. That is the true definition of shock. I just thought today about that and I got so sick to my stomach. I was sharing that with Tawnia. She said when she woke up today she thought about it, too. Great minds think alike. I asked her when she's going to visit you. She is struggling with it; yet I can't imagine not seeing you every week for the rest of my life!

You're in my heart and soul every day, every hour and I miss you horribly. Do you miss me, Kelsea? Do you think about me all the time? Are you watching over me? I love you so much.

She Is Honored and Loved

It was such a beautiful, peaceful day at your pad, just me and you, flowers, prayer, tears, silence, ants and conversation.

February 19, 2007, Monday • Scale: 3

Hi Baby doll, I love showing people your picture that you hate so much: your "teen magazine cover girl" picture. They all say the same thing: you are stunning. Sometimes, I was glad you didn't know how beautiful you were. You would have been dangerous. Did you see all the rain today? I'll bet there won't ever be a rainy day go by that won't be yours. Anyone who knew you knew you lived for the rain. Does it rain in heaven? Can you talk to your Father about me winning the lottery? It sure would make life a little easier. I could help so many people you know. I see the doctor in a couple days now. Am I going to have a tough fight ahead of me or is this all just a wake-up call like I think? Give me your strength, Kels; watch over me every second of every minute of every hour of every day, like I did for you. *Come into my dreams and let me feel you, please!*

She Is Missed

Too many thoughts, too much to do, not wanting to deal with this. . . .

February 20, 2007, Tuesday • Scale: 3

Dear Kelsea, I love you so much, it's killing me. I looked at your picture in my dash today and it's as if the world stopped. My breath got short and shallow, my stomach got sick, the tears filled my eyes and I pushed it all away. I talked to Laurie at the gym tonight and she looked at me square in the face with tears in her eyes and told me, "She made such an impact on so many people and she saved 45 people." I know in God's eyes that is huge, but why did He have to take YOU for everyone else? It's not fate at all. I know, though, that you and I are going to hold hands as we enter the gates to the kingdom, together. I just wish you could have fallen in love, gotten married and had a beautiful baby for us. I know you would have been the best, most loving, caring mother. I would have been so proud of you. I always was no matter what. I love you forever.

She Is Missed

I look at your pictures and my breath stops, my stomach gets ill and the tears flow.

February 21, 2007, Wednesday • Scale: 2

Dear Kels, so why did you have to give me a hematoma? I only say that, too, because it was one of your favorite words to use! You're the one who always had one! The doctor said I'm good to go; thank your Father for healing me of this cancer. My blood clot hurts like a bitch though, thanks. Bad tidal wave tonight with your Myspace. I couldn't help it. I miss the hell out of you and if I allow myself to think, I lose it. Tomorrow is already 6 months, how can it be? Time feels as if you've been gone forever, yet just yesterday. A guy at the gym said you are absolutely gorgeous and should be a model. I wish I would have been able to financially afford to get you into modeling. I'll bet your one of the prettiest girls in heaven—hah? Are there any cute boys there? Everyone loves everyone—hah? I can't even imagine. I wish I knew for sure how wonderful it was there, but I guess everyone would want to die early to be there. I love you.

She Is Honored

Introducing you to Tim, a potential new member at the gym. His own words, "She should be a model," and he didn't even know you.

February 22, 2007, Thursday • Scale: 1

My Dearest Little Girl, how am I supposed to live the rest of my life without you? It's been 6 months today and yet it already feels like I've been a lifetime without you. The pain is still as deep as if it was yesterday. How can it all be? To think 6 months and 1 day ago, I was married, living in a beautiful home with my 2 loving children and working in a job I loved. Now? I have your brother. No home, no husband, no great job . . . no color in my life. It's as if all the color in life is gone. I had a rough group. I'm tired of being strong and I hate that God took you from me. I didn't think today would be hard. I just wanted to lie in bed after I came to your pad. I had to go to the welfare office today. I met 2 angels though . . . it was humbling. I haven't been there in 15 years and there I was again. How many times is God going to strip me of everything? Tell me, please.

She Is Honored and Missed

Flowers at your pad, your jersey at group, pictures . . . pain, sorrow and anger.

CHAPTER SEVEN

February 23 & 24, 2007, Friday/Saturday • *Scale: 3*

Dear Kelsea, I'm sorry I didn't write yesterday. The day before was such a hard day that I decided to try to do something with Colleen. It was okay but hard. I couldn't go out to the bar with them, not yet still. Today, I had an okay day. I have so many of your pictures all over my desk. Last night one of the girls there learned my whole life story. She honestly looked at me and asked me how I can even function. I really don't have an answer for that, you know? I just know I'm tired or should I say, I wish God wouldn't have made me so damn strong because then maybe you would still be here with me. Do you think? I guess I just don't get it. I lived not a good life before and things were good. I had a good job, money, a home . . . then I turn to your Father and begin this obedient, faithful walk with your Father and then He does this? I haven't gotten mad at God through this. I just struggle with the why? I just hope He isn't preparing me to help one of my friends with a loss of their child like Cara did with me. I almost think of it as a pay it forward, it scares me. I don't want any of my friends to ever have to live in this hell I am now, with all this pain and emotional bullshit. The tidal waves of tears that come over you in a millisecond not ever knowing when. Someone today told me that when he hit rock bottom he realized there was only one way and it was to go up. He doesn't understand; I haven't even, I can't even get myself up off the floor yet. I have no strength. I don't want to be responsible right now. I just want to be able to walk and breathe right now. I have to remind myself to breathe. The sun keeps coming up and going down and I'm still here. Sometimes I don't want to be, but Digger needs me watching over him, honey. We need you. I love you.

She Is Loved and Missed

That's all I know right now. . . .

February 25, 2007, Sunday • Scale: 3

Hi Honey, how is everlasting life treating you? Do you like heaven? Is it as beautiful as the bible says it is? Are you loved by everyone and do you love everyone? Are you hanging out with Melissa, Brittany, Jenna and all the other kids? Do you ever think about me and your brother? Do you ever miss life here on earth? Are you with me in church every Sunday? What color is your hair and is it still so long? How is the food there? Is anyone fat or is every body perfect? Do you like not being bipolar? Does the sun ever go down or do you ever sleep? Do you really have wings? What kind of mansion are we going to have once I get there? How long do I have to be here? Do you know how much I love you? Miss you? Need you here? So much, I hate it. Kisses.

She Is Here

You were at the gym with me today, thank you.

February 26, 2007, Monday • Scale: 3

Hello Sweetness, did you see how busy I was at work today? Pretty cool, hah? It felt good and I was so busy I didn't have time to be sad. That doesn't mean I wasn't thinking of you though. How can I not when I have your pictures all over my desk? I haven't had any chest pains or lump in my throat for a while now. I do find myself, though, avoiding people at times. I see certain people and now I just drop my head and look the other way. I just am not the same happy-go-lucky, love-to-talk-to-everyone girl I used to be. I walk into church and I see how different I am; my life is . . . nothing is any "better" yet. See, when I start to think about the reality of this, my stomach gets sick. I think I'll always feel ill when I think about it. I wish God would give me a miracle and give you back to me.

Still, why? I miss you bad.

She Is Honored

"In the Arms of an Angel" played over and over and over again in my car, your song.

February 27, 2007, Tuesday • Scale: 3

Dear Kelsea Lyn, did you meet Brittany? I met her mom today off Myspace. It's been almost 2 years for her now. I believe you hang out with the children of anyone I meet here who lost their child. I can't seem to go on your Myspace these days without crying. Do you know how much I miss you? I want to talk to you more than I have been but it's so hard because I want to laugh with you and tell you how stupid my life is right now but I'm struggling. I haven't been able to write anymore in our bipolar book yet. I know though that God will open my heart up and guide me when the time is right. I just don't feel like being responsible right now. I really don't care about a lot right now. I can't even imagine my life a year from now. Where will I be and what will I be doing? I love you tons.

She Is Honored

I shared your journey with God, your dedication to the Lord, your salvation prayers, your love for Him . . . with a member at the gym.

February 28, 2007, Wednesday • Scale: 3

Hi Angel, did you see how incredibly busy I was at work tonight? It's as if all my hard work the last 6 weeks paid off. It was nice to be so busy. I felt productive. I haven't felt that in a long time. I have noticed I have been crying almost every day again . . . not bad waves but tears still the same, not of joy but of pure sorrow still. I figure I have another year and a half before I even want to be responsible. I can't even imagine where I will be in a year. Sometimes I think I'll be with Tawnia for a long time. My life is just floating right now. It's like your brother is on his own and I can do whatever I want now. I have no one to really ask anything of, no one I have to be accountable to. Part of me likes it, but more of me would rather be stressed and worried about you. I would trade this "peace" I have in my life for the turmoil with you, in a heartbeat, because I love you. Do you miss me?

She Is Missed

Thoughts of you turn to tears . . .

March 1, 2007, Thursday • Scale: 3

Dear Kels, great session with Susan tonight and, as always right now, rough group. But, Ken tells me I have to keep going. I hope you have some truth dust available . . . you know who needs it. My life is so different now with so many different people in it. I miss you so much. I would trade all the new people to have you back. You would be graduating in 3 months now. I can't believe how fast it's going. I'm sad I can't watch you walk at graduation, but I will walk for you, all in your honor. Would you like that? Do they have Carne Asada Fries in heaven? You loved them sooooo much. I used to love to watch you eat. You had my appetite! I only have about 4 lbs. to lose to be your weight, crazy hah? I want it off by my birthday. I had to remind myself to breathe tonight. I cried at group. Sometimes, I hate group because its reality of how f-up this all is. I hate it. XOXOXO

She Is Missed

A psychology appointment, parent support group and so much damn pain.

March 2, 2007, Friday • Scale: 3

Hi Baby girl, another weekend here and nothing to consume my thoughts. No wondering where you are, who you're with, what you're doing, when you'll come home, because you are home; you're with your heavenly Father and you're loving your new everlasting life. I asked you to be with me today, to show me, and you did, thank you. There's no other explanation than you when my computer screen changed to your beautiful picture. My phone kept beeping and my picture kept coming on and I knew you were with me. But I just want to be able to touch you again and hear your voice. A lifetime seems like forever till I see you again. Maybe God won't make it a lifetime. . . . I know He has plans for me here, though. My days are becoming pretty fly-by-night . . . coming and going as I please. I like some of it, but I would always trade it all for my life with you again, you know? I love you more than the law allows. Kisses.

She Is Here

My computer screen saver changed, and not by me . . .

March 3, 2007, Saturday • Scale: 3

Dear Kelsea, I saw Jessica at the mall; she works at Starbucks. She called my name and I went over to see her. She started crying and was so upset. She said she's bipolar. She said she dropped out of school because all the girls (white power) want to beat her up. She needs you so bad. She misses and loves you so much. You protected her so much. I don't understand because she is so sweet. I want to help her. Would you please be with her? I'm coming to see you tomorrow. Your dad's in town and Digger is with him tonight. Did he come see your pad? I want a puppy for my birthday. Someone to love, like Poohdunk, hah? Why is it we can't have what we really want sometimes? Do you think your Father will ever bless me with someone to love me as deeply as I love them? Can you ask Him to help me with that? I can't wait to go see you tomorrow. I love you . . . hugs.

She Is Missed

Jessica at the mall, crying in my arms, professing her love for you and deep missing of you, your protection at school . . . she needs you.

March 4, 2007, Sunday • Scale: 3

Hi Sweetheart, here I am at your pad. It's so quiet and peaceful here. I love spending this time with you. I hope you love the hot pink flowers. They actually look like the one on this page! I told our story to 2 guys at the gym today. They were very nice and said how beautiful you are, but we already know that. Both are going through a divorce, too. Crazy, hah? My life is so different now. It's like I have all this time now and nothing to be responsible for. I can come and go as I please. I like it but I would rather be tied down to you. I cried a good one here at your pad, I know. I was told today what a great attitude I have and strength. I don't want to be strong. I don't want any more trials and tribulation. I want to win the lottery! Can you talk to your Father about it? Not that money will fix all this, but it would allow me to devote myself to helping other people all the time, you know? I can't wait to hold you again and see your smile and hear your voice. I miss you horribly. Do you miss me? Hugs and kisses.

She Is Honored

I introduced you to Theo and Brad today. They know our story and told me how absolutely beautiful you are.

March 5, 2007, Monday • Scale: 3

Hi Honey, when it rains, it pours, hah? Work is starting to really pick up for me. I had 6 people sit before me today who all loved you. It was Kelsea Day at the gym! The 2 guys had been to the desert with you. I wish you would have given me more of a chance with your friends. These guys were *total* bro's and I liked them. You just kept all your friends so secluded from me it made me think they were not good but they were. I know that now.

Jessica was at the gym. She worked out with Jeanie. I love them but I still want you back. I still can't think of all the good memories yet. I still can't think about this whole tragedy. I wish I knew how long my life is going to be. I had some fleeting thoughts of death a couple days ago. I haven't had them in awhile. I haven't had chest pains in a couple months. I guess I'm healing. I don't understand healing. I don't like it. I love you tons.

She Is Here

You know how much I hate getting shocked and EVERYTHING I touched, a shock!

March 6, 2007, Tuesday • Scale: 3

Hi Kelsea Lyn, I had a dream last night, thank you. It was the closest I've been to you. I talked with you on the phone and I couldn't believe it was you. Your voice was so clear . . . "Hi Mama." I woke up still hearing you talking. The sound of your voice. I asked you if you were in heaven, "Of course I am Mama." I know you are. I try to think about what life is like for you now. If only I knew, maybe I could feel some comfort or peace in my life. It's crazy. I can't imagine not talking to you every day; I still do, but only now, you don't answer me back. Did I tell you yet? I am going to walk at graduation for you? Would you like that? I'm so proud of you because I know you would have graduated from your new school . . . with honors like in summer school. I wish you were here with me, tickling you every where. I love you.

She Is Missed

Your kitty climbing up in my lap, purring so loudly. . . . I feel your love.

March 7, 2007, Wednesday • Scale: 3

Hi Baby doll, how was your day? Mine was full. So full, not a lot of time to think, you know? Are your days full? I had a client in front of me tonight who I told about my dream the other night. He said that my subconscious was telling me that my healing process was moving forward and I was beginning to accept this all. I disagree. I do not ever foresee myself accepting your passing away. EVER. It will always be unacceptable till I reach heaven and your Father explains all of this to me. See, when I really start to think about it all, I get ill to my stomach. I had someone today ask me if the picture I was carrying with me of you, was my sister. Remember how people were starting to ask if we were sisters? I miss that. I miss you. I can't think about this—it overwhelms me.

Kisses.

She Is Honored

Again, your story and your pictures shared.

March 8, 2007, Thursday • Scale: 3

Hi Honey, how's my baby girl doing in heaven with all your new angel friends? I'll bet you hang out with all the kids of all the parents in group, hah? I'm going to come see you on Sunday again. I love visiting you on Sundays; it's so peaceful. Tawnia is struggling and missing you badly right now. Can you come into a dream for her? I've had a couple fleeting thoughts of hurting myself this last week. My finger writing is back and I've been counting. Pure anxiety, I know. I'm crying every day again, too. It really sucks to listen to parents in group talk about their struggles and hard times . . . 2 years into their grief. I think, shit, I'm only 6½ months and I have another year and a half of feeling and living with this hell and pain? How am I supposed to do it? Will I ever be able to sleep again without taking sleeping pills? I hate this new life. XOXOXOXOXOXO

She Is Missed and Honored

Group every Thursday night as hard as it is week after week after week . . .

March 9, 2007, Friday • Scale: 1

Dear Kelsea Lyn, I can't seem to go to your Myspace page without crying anymore. It's coming up on desert season I guess and your friends are missing you already. I know you will protect them all. I know you will still be there. I'm crying almost every day again. Someone said the dream I had talking to you the other night was my accepting all this and I just don't agree. I still hate the weekends. I still hate you not here. I hate that you were taken from me. I hate the pain I have to live with now. I hate having to live my life on autopilot right now. I hate being so damn irresponsible now. I hate how different life is now. I flashed on hitting a cement guardrail last night on the way home. I know God gave me a second chance now with healing my cancer. I'm trying not to have those thoughts. I just need you here with me but you can't. I hate that. Kisses.

She Is Missed Deeply

Your Myspace page . . . looking, reading, crying . . .

March 10, 2007, Saturday • Scale: 2

Hello Beautiful, if I had a dollar for every time I was told how beautiful you are, I would be rich. Another boy at the gym was wishing he had the chance to meet you. I've been having some chest pains again. Autopilot is the easiest way to describe my life right tow. I have a hard time feeling responsible, you know? More so BEING responsible. I'm trying to be able to be alone on the weekends but I have such a deep need to feel loved and it's just not happening. I feel like I have no one to love who can love me back. All the love I focused on you, I still have but I want to physically love you. I want to touch your hair, hug you, kiss your face, tell you how much I love you and hear you tell me, "I love you, too, Mama." But it's never going to happen here on earth again and I can't handle that. I can't imagine the rest of my life, but this: choiceless and I hate it all. I love and miss you, baby. Kiss.

She Is Missed
This kills.

March 11, 2007, Sunday • Scale: 3

Hi Honey, thank God the weekend's over. It was okay, nothing special. I miss you and even more on the weekends because I don't have to worry at all about you. I'd rather be worried though' knowing you would walk in the door still. I may get a little mad but I always understood and loved you. It was nice at your pad today, very quiet and peaceful. It's very strange not having to worry or be responsible for your children. Digger's doing his own thing so I am basically free to do whatever I want. But I want you here with me. I want our weekly psychology appointments with Chris. I'm sure he misses you deeply, as everyone does. I'm crying every day again and I need you here to stop my finger from writing. You were always aware when my finger would start writing in the air.

We would laugh so hard because we knew my obsessive compulsive disorder was here! Damn OCD. But now, instead of my anxiety from your bipolar behavior, now it's from you not here. I just need you, Kelsea. Will I still be your mom in heaven? Please?

She Is Honored

A single rose, a quiet hour, prayer and conversation with you at your pad.

March 12, 2007, Monday • Scale: 3

Dear Kelsea, your kitty misses you. She kisses me and wraps her arms around me and bites me like she used to with you. She chases me sometimes and attacks my legs. I loved watching you run around the house playing hide and seek with her. I loved how compassionate you were toward animals. You would have made a great veterinarian. I told your story to a coworker today and I cried for 20 minutes in his truck. I've actually began breaking down with a couple people. It's something I've not been able to do yet. I wish I had a rock to lean on during this but I don't. I have faced this loss alone. I don't want to be strong anymore. I wish I wasn't this strong right now. I want to be weak. I want to just be able to have someone hold me so I can let all this pain go. Will I ever find someone, Kels? Am I supposed to be alone the rest of my life? Help me, Kels. Give me hope. I love you.

She Is Here

Your loveable Sassy, her kisses and bites, and I feel you . . .

March 13, 2007, Tuesday • Scale: 2

Dear Kelsea Lyn Phelps, the pain is creeping back into my life, my soul, my mind. I lost it at lunch today. See, I've tried to replace my pain and hole in my heart with a male friend; now we can't be friends. He was my hope, my distraction and now he's gone and I am faced with the pain, images and reality. Digger's distraction is weed. Everyone picks one but now mine is gone. I struggled bad at work. I should have come home. All I wanted to do today was lie in bed and cry. I'm having dark thoughts, chest pains, crying, it's all coming back again. I hate this, Kels. Someone asked me today, what was wrong? I wanted to hit her. How can people ask me that question? Don't people understand just because I can walk and talk doesn't mean I'm okay? I'm broken, devastated, trying to survive and missing you. I love you.

She Is Missed

The pain is unbearable.

March 14, 2007, Wednesday • Scale: 3

Hi Sweetheart, I saw Rory at the gym tonight. He remembered me from freshman year. He said he used to tell people all the time what a good person you were. He didn't care for a lot of your friends the last year or so, but he said you always had a huge heart and were a good girl. His eyes filled with tears when I showed him your picture on my desk. I cried in the bank today and so did Dee, the teller. Do you have any idea how many people's hearts you have touched? Broken? I'm having anxiety chest pains again. I think I'm going to try to learn how to surf this summer. What do you think? If I surf, will you be out there with me every day? I'm going to come see you either Friday or Sunday. I love visiting your pad because it's so peaceful. Kels, how am I supposed to keep going the rest of my life without you? I can't even imagine it. Sometimes, I just want to be with you in heaven.

She Is Honored and Missed

Your pictures all over my work desk . . . sharing them with Rory . . . the tears in his eyes.

March 15, 2007, Thursday • Scale: 2

Dear Kelsea Lyn, do you hear our group at night? I know all you children that we have lost are all together in heaven. Do you all get together when we do? Do you all realize how much we all love you? I couldn't speak tonight at group; all I could do is cry. Ken knew without me speaking that I have had dark days since last week. Do you know how guilty I felt last night eating a French fry? It was the first time since you passed away. I ate at McDonalds and felt like I ate too much and went home and took laxatives. I learned today from Susan that I feel guilty when I experience life and have to replace it with pain out of guilt. She says I'm flirting with an eating disorder. I just like to think I'm in control. I just know my chest pains are bad right now. I thought I was moving forward but I just fell backwards into darkness again. I hate it and hate this choice less life I have to live. Love you . . .

She Is Here

Sassy jumps into my lap, snuggles so closely, nibbles and kisses my ear.

March 16, 2007, Friday • Scale: 3

Hi Sweetheart, today was better but it's Friday and I really hate the weekends. They are getting kind of better but tonight I'm home alone doing nothing and I wish and know you would be here with me if I wanted you to. We would have gone to get some fattening food like Carne Asada Fried and shared them. Then we would go to 7-11 and get sugar! Sour Patch candy, Reece's Peanut butter Cups and diet coke! Then we would sit on the couch and I would tickle you, your arms, legs (watch out for the stitches, I know), your back, then your arms again. You would get so relaxed and tired and go to sleep with me because you love me and I love you and that will never change, ever. Will you come into my dreams tonight so I can hold you and hear your voice again? My chest pains are every day again. All I do is talk about what happened and they start. I just want justice. I love you tons.

She Is Honored

Remembering good memories without the tears, dreaming of us together.

March 17, 2007, Saturday • Scale: 3

Dear Tat, well it's St. Patrick's Day. I have an opportunity to go out with some friends to an Irish Pub and I am going to go because I think you would want me to. So, I went and, in the girl's bathroom, this girl in front of me knew you. She knew Clint but hates Colette. She was really sad about what happened. It amazes me all the people I am meeting that knew you. All the lives you touched with your smile, laughter, energy and quick wittedness. I also ran into Paul.

Remember my tattoo you went with me to get: 10-16? Him? He was also very sad about my loss. Even the word "loss" doesn't come close to describing what happened in you going home. Loss is such an understatement. I am broken, sick, saddened, not whole anymore and so very, very lonely. Every drink I had was for you. Do you have any idea how much I miss you every second of every minute of every hour of every day? Forever? I love you.

She Is Missed

St. Patrick's Day. . . . Hooleys with some friends . . . in the bathroom in front of me was a girl who knew you from Clint and the desert, so sad you are gone.

March 18, 2007, Sunday • Scale: 2

Hi Kels, it was beautiful at your pad today. I know the flowers were ugly but they were St. Patrick's Day flowers. Church was harder than normal, lots of crying and questioning. I just struggle in there because I don't understand why, if God loves me so much, He would take you from me. Can you explain that to me? I'm feeling some anger coming, I think. I really hate this whole grief thing. I didn't ask for it. I didn't ask for my life to be turned upside down. I didn't ask for pain, suffering, sorrow, brokenness; I have been living with it now every day for 7 months. It's not fair. It's not right. I want to know why you were taken from a mother who devoted her life to her children. Who lived for her daughter and breathes you, Kels? I can't accept you being gone. My stomach is sick. My chest pains are real, my sadness is unbearable. Help me. . . . I love you.

She Is Honored

Green flowers, another balloon at your pad and a couple hours with you at your pad as always. . . .

March 19, 2007, Monday • Scale: 2

Hi Honey, I can tell summer is coming now and I don't want it to. I'm afraid for August to get here. I am going to be such a wreck. Kelsea, I hate all this. I hate seeing mothers walking around with their daughters because you're not supposed to be gone. You're supposed to be here at Tawnia's with me and Digger. I'm supposed to be planning your graduation. I'm supposed to be helping you get your driver's license and get a job. I know Hooters would have hired you, too. I'm supposed to be saving my money because you would have gotten straight A's at ECAL. We're supposed to still be seeing Chris and Usha. I miss watching you play with your kitty. I miss your annoying loud music and watching you straighten your beautiful hair. I miss the hell out of every fiber of your being. This wasn't supposed to happen. I'm supposed to still be taking care of my baby girl. Disbelief is what I feel. I hate this. I love you.

She Is Honored and Loved

A picture of you with me wherever I go.

March 20, 2007, Tuesday • Scale: 3

Dear Kels, I've had training at work the last couple days and pretty busy, you know? But when I got home I went on your Myspace and a wave came over me. I think, because all your friends always profess their love to you and how much they miss you. You see, just writing that sentence made me sick because when I write it, it's reality, I guess. I spoke to Geeni today and the ball is going to start rolling. The investigation is over and now all I can do is pray for justice in your passing. Again, my life is so different now, but I have to have faith that I am here with Tawnia for a reason. Did you see her Myspace name: Missin' my lil' girl. I want her to have another baby, a girl. I guess I want another girl to be able to love because you are the only girl I ever allowed myself to love, ever.

Why did God have to take you from me when I fought so hard for you and us? WHY?

She Is Missed

Francesca wants to visit your pad . . . bring you flowers and show you respect.

March 21, 2007, Wednesday • Scale: 3

Hi Sweetheart, well in class today 3 of the young guys I worked with saw your picture and wanted me to hook you up with them. Do you have any idea how many guys would have loved the opportunity to know you? So many . . . I found out that a boy named Zach passed away. Katie from Granite Hills had it on her Myspace. He was 17, too. I want to go to his funeral for his mom and dad. I want to help them if I can. They probably have no idea that they are beginning a journey into hell. How different their lives will be now, how empty and painful. I hope they have more children because they become the reason to live, like your brother. I wonder how he is doing in his grief. I get so wrapped up in my own that I forget he lost his little sister and how much he loves you. His life, also, is forever changed. All our lives will NEVER be the same. I'm pissed. I love you.

She Is Honored

Three guys all admiring your picture at work . . . all wanting to meet you.

March 22, 2007, Thursday • Scale: 3

Dear Kelsea, it's been 7 months today and I can't believe I have made it without you for this long and yet it's so short. It feels like I haven't seen you in a million years but the pain is as deep as the first day. I am beginning to think this pain will never go away. Susan went to group with me tonight. She understands now why it is difficult for me to go and yet how I need to be there. She talked about the "heaviness" of the group and she is right; all the parents' hearts are so very, very heavy now. But, how can that be when they are so empty and broken into a million pieces? I had chest pains all through group tonight for some reason. I also cried most of the time. I'm not listening to music still while I drive now either. Crazy. I don't really know why; I just don't feel like it. My birthday is next week and the way I look at that is I will celebrate being 1 year closer to being with you again. It is still not soon enough but your brother needs me more than ever now. I love you and miss you terribly. Kisses.

She Is Honored

Susan at group tonight speaking such kind words about who you are . . .

JOURNAL: DISTRACTIONS TO TIDAL WAVES

Yes, it has now been 2 months since I have been able to sit down and put my thoughts in place. A month ago, I hit the 6-month anniversary. That's a strange word to use for something like this. Anniversaries are generally something to celebrate, to live for and to cherish as each one rolls by. But for the anniversary of the death of your child, each and every month is simply hell. After Kelsea's 18th birthday party, things got really good. It's as if after January 3rd I decided to go on vacation, vacation from my grief. I chose to not think about her anymore or what had happened. I chose to push it all deep down into my being and just not think about it. So, I was able to function (autopilot) each day and people got to see a mere glimpse of who I used to be.

I could go to work and concentrate for longer periods at a time. I could talk to people about Kelsea and share good memories. I could talk at my support group and participate in the discussions. I was able to breathe.

This went on for about 5–6 weeks. All this time though I felt a deep sense of denial. I felt as if I was able to push everything down and away because I didn't believe any of this really happened. I felt guilty for not thinking about Kelsea. I thought, *How can you do that?*

But I learned from Susan that it was my body's way of protecting me.

She helped me to accept this little vacation I was taking and made me realize that it wouldn't last. Taking that vacation was my body's way of realizing I couldn't live with this overwhelming amount of pain for the rest of my life because I would die.

I knew the 22nd of February was approaching and I honestly did not think it would have been any different than the other days I had been experiencing. I was so very, very wrong. It fell on a Thursday, my day off. I woke up crying. I felt such heaviness in my heart and I didn't want to. I went to the gym, wore my headphones so I wouldn't have to talk to anyone. Then I went to her pad and spent the majority of the day with her. I brought her beautiful flowers, I prayed, I cried, I talked to her, I lay with her.

I have found that bereaved parents are so very different when it comes to what to do once your child has passed away. Many people believe in burial; many chose to have their child cremated. Many of us visit our children at the cemetery and many keep their child close to them in a beautiful urn.

I chose to bury my baby girl. She is laid to rest in a beautiful, peaceful, quiet cemetery and I can proudly say I will be there with her one day. It is a double plot; the stone is complete with a beautiful picture of us both on it, arms around each other. She called me Jesus Freak and I called her Tat. Across the bottom, the stone simply says, "I love you more than the law allows." I believe she has begun the journey into her everlasting life and so that is the header: "In Everlasting Life." So, I spent the 6-month anniversary at her pad.

Unfortunately, Susan was out of town that day and weekend. So, I went to my support group with no prior help for the day. As I drove down to group, my heart was heavy. I had functioned somewhat during the day but wanted to lay in bed and not deal with life.

I walked into the room and for the first time at group, I saw Elyn. She had come by my home within the first couple weeks of losing Kelsea and brought me some comfort. She had lost her young son a few years earlier and knew my pain, my sorrow, my hell.

I saw her and I broke down. She wrapped her arms tightly around me and held me while I cried and expressed the fact it was 6 months, today. I was weak. I sat next to her as she held my hand the entire 2 hours. I couldn't speak that night; I didn't want to speak that night. I listened and cried and left when it was all over. I got home, crawled in bed and realized the sun had come up and the sun had gone down and I was still here.

Over the next several weeks, I found those waves coming more frequently. I found myself thinking about this whole thing that had happened to me. I found myself experiencing chest pains again. I found myself pulling away from what had been my distraction for the last 4 months.

See, I learned that I had actually been developing a pretty good technique over the last several months. When the bad thoughts would start to creep in, I could replace them with thoughts of my distraction. My distraction became a man. A man that within the first 2 months became a huge part of my support through this hell. This man had been in my life 15 years ago and there he was again. It felt like fate. It felt like he was placed there a short few months before Kelsea passed away, to be here for me when she was gone.

So, our friendship developed again. He called and checked on me, tried to make me laugh at times, held me when I needed a hug. I was vulnerable.

The more time I spent with him, the more he held me, the more I forgot about my pain. I found that the second I began to think about Kelsea, I replaced it with day dreams of this man and being with him. It helped, a lot.

Susan would talk me through this emerging relationship. She understood the distraction he had become. She also helped me understand that bereaved parents usually find some type of distraction, whether a man, alcohol, drugs, spending money, gambling, T.V., the list goes on . . . and I chose a man, a man that was emotionally unavailable at the time.

Then the day came when it all had to end and I began to grieve yet another loss. I had now lost the person who had become my best friend through this, too. What was so frustrating is that I knew in my heart that if I had not lost my daughter, I would not have become involved with him. He would have remained my friend and not become my best friend.

This brings me back to where I have been the last few weeks, broken. I understand people don't know sometimes how to react or what to say to a bereaved parent, especially when they feel so powerless. But I have found myself getting angry when people who know me and what has happened, ask me what is wrong when I am having a difficult day.

I feel like saying, "Hello. My daughter?" But, because I have had some days of autopilot that have been better than other days, when they see the true brokenness in me they question what is wrong.

I know I am all over the place right now. My thoughts are scattered and random. I have had thoughts of dying again. I've had thoughts of running my car into a cement divider. Thoughts of just wanting to be with Kelsea in heaven NOW. I still can't sleep at night without my sleeping pills. I have tried and my mind runs a million miles an hour and spins and I toss and turn and can't sleep or function the next day.

My son and I have been arguing a lot. I know it is his anger toward this whole loss and he is taking it out on me, the closest thing to him. I am so enthralled in my own grief that I have forgotten he is grieving, too. He has found several distractions. All are detrimental to his well-being, but I cannot seem to get him to understand that. I fear for his safety. I fear he is spiraling out of control and I can't stop him. He needs counseling yet refuses it. I fear I am going to lose him, too.

Then, there is the "flirting with an eating disorder" piece. The easiest way for me to describe my eating regimen is simply that I had no control over my daughter's death. I have complete control over what the scale says when I step on it each morning. I want to weigh what my daughter weighed. This is not the disorder though.

You see, one night I went out to eat with a friend, Dennis, to McDonalds. I actually drove through on my way to go see him and got a double cheeseburger. I didn't know we were going to go to McDonalds for him once I got to his work.

So, we drove over there and I decided to get a Filet-O-Fish. Now, I had eaten 2 sandwiches.

Dennis had french fries and I found myself picking at them, too. As I ate a couple fries, I looked at him and told him, "This is the first time I have eaten fries since Kelsea passed away." Now, to the ordinary person that would be no big deal. However to me, someone who had not savored a french fry in over 7 months, it was a huge ordeal.

After I had eaten the french fries, I felt so incredibly guilty. I felt guilty for eating 2 sandwiches. I had not eaten that much at one time in over 7 months. I felt fat. Dennis didn't know what was going through my head but I did. As soon as I got home I went into my room and took several laxatives. I wanted all that food out of me as quickly as possible.

Herein lay the eating disorder . . . it's called bulimia. I was bulimic in college and got very good at throwing up my food each time I ate. But I had no idea the whole binge-purge thing counted when you took laxatives. Purging did not only have to be throwing up. I also learned from Susan that there was more to this than just eating french fries and feeling fat.

It's very hard right now to do certain things, eat certain foods, actually anything that ties me to Kelsea. Kelsea and I used to go to 7-11 every morning before I took her to summer school and get coffee. I have yet to be able to go into 7-11 for coffee. I don't know if I ever will.

I have been told that my behavior is as follows: if I do anything that shows any kind of joy, happiness or life, the next thing I do is something to punish myself. It's because I do not believe I deserve happiness so I will sabotage myself by eating french fries and then immediately take laxatives to purge myself of that joy.

I've been told it's ridiculous that I want to weigh what my daughter weighed because I am not a 17-year-old girl. But I don't care at this point which brings me to not caring. I have found myself slipping more and more into debt. For the first time in my life, I have been overdrawn in my bank account by almost $300.00. I have gone to the store for a necessity and gotten things, not only do I not need but I have no money for. At least I am aware of this, though, and I am hoping to get a handle on it all.

It was 7 months and two days when this next wave or actually Tsunami reared its ugly head. My support group happened to fall on March 22nd, the 7 month. Susan went with me to group that night after we had met for about 3 hours beforehand. Group was tough and I felt a wave coming on.

Friday the wave was still building; I could feel it. At the gym I had my head phones on and couldn't look at anyone and didn't want to talk to anyone. I sat on the lifecycle and cried while pedaling. I made it through the day and into Saturday.

At work that day, I looked at Kelsea's beautiful picture on my desk and the tsunami took me out. I realized for the first time that Kelsea was GONE. My brain kept repeating that and absorbing it. My eyes filled with tears and I couldn't move. I couldn't breathe. My chest hurt. Seven months later I realized this was real. I could not function or think and I knew it was time for me to go home and that's what I did.

Once home, I retreated to my room and began the uncontrollable sobbing. The loud noises one makes when they are distraught and so broken. My thoughts raced and I thought about the sleeping pills I had. I wanted to take them and just go to sleep. As I cried, barely able to speak I picked up my phone and realized I had to reach out. For the first time since this tragedy took place, I knew I needed to talk to someone through this wave of destruction.

See, I had not done that yet. I always rode this wave alone, being strong. It would eventually calm down and I would be okay. Not this time though. I knew this time was going to be different. I scrolled through my phone and called a friend. No answer. I scrolled and called another, only to receive his voice message. I left none. I called another and he answered. He became my angel.

I met this guy at work when I sold him a gym membership a couple months ago. He was traveling back and forth from coast to coast taking care of business and we became friends. It was strange, though, because although I had called him 2–3 times prior I had always gotten his voice mail. I thought I would just try, though, and he picked up the phone.

He could hear immediately in my voice that I was not doing well. He offered to come over and I accepted. I gave him directions and I waited for him in the front yard. As he walked up, he wrapped his arms around me and I broke. I cried harder and longer than I had ever. He consoled me. I vented to him, I explained things to him, and I eventually laughed with him. He spent 2 hours with me and he probably doesn't realize he saved my life. He left and I went into my house, took my one sleeping pill, prayed and thanked God for sending him to me, and I went to sleep.

Yes, the last several weeks have been constant waves rolling in, better known as "dark days." I feel as if I have taken 1,000 steps backward and am right back where I was when this first happened. Some hours are darker than others and all I can do is remember to try to breathe. Remembering that the sun will come up and the sun will go down and I will be one day closer to being with Kelsea Lyn again.

Proverbs 3:5
Trust in the Lord with all your heart,
do not depend on your own understanding.

CHAPTER EIGHT

March 23, 2007, Friday • Scale: 3

Hi Little Girl, so were you with me at the gym today or what?! 20 minutes of cardio on the bike with no sensors for my heart rate and there you were the whole time. I gotta tell you though; the pin on the leg curl machine was awesome! I know you pulled it out when I wasn't looking, thanks. The days have been kinda harder than before and I don't understand this whole grief thing.

Susan called me today, I think to double-check on me because last night's group was rough and she knew I would struggle today. It's like even though I knew you were with me in the gym today, I had a small wave come over me midafternoon.

Luckily, I was kept busy in the evening though. Dinner with Richard was nice. It's hard to believe we have been friends for 14 years now. Isn't Joe's dog, Jake, cool, too? He reminds me of when we had Bo. I wish we could go back to that time and I could change things and protect you better, then maybe you would be with me. I love and miss you.

She Is Here

The pin on the leg machine taken out as the weight stack flies up, and it wasn't by me . . .

March 24, 2007, Saturday • Scale: 0.5

Dear Kelsea Lyn, this had been one of the darkest days I have had yet. I've been fighting off a tidal wave but I couldn't anymore. At work I looked at your picture on my desk and for the first time, my brain told me, "She's gone," and I felt it. I started crying and went home. It took 7 months and 2 days for it to hit me. It's like it's just happened again. The pain is unbearable. I cried so hard in my room and I thought about just taking a bunch of sleeping pills and going to sleep. For the first time, though, I picked up the phone and knew I had to reach out to someone. I kept calling people and no one would answer, then God sent me an Angel—Jon. He answered his phone, heard my pain and came to the house. I haven't cried that hard in someone's arms, ever. He let me talk and just listened. The pain today, chest pains, crying and this tidal wave were so damn real; I hate all this. I want you here. I want answers about why God had to take a child that was so loved by her mother, a mother who lived for her daughter, a mother who would have died for her daughter. Will this pain go away? I can't do this.

She Is Missed

The worst tidal wave yet, the darkest day I've had . . .

March 25, 2007, Sunday • Scale: 3

Hi Sweetness, it was a beautiful day outside today. Sunny days are bittersweet. I love that weather but it is a reminder of August 22nd. Sorry I only brought a single rose to your pad today but I'm broke. I'm struggling financially and I'm not sure what I'm going to do. Funny thing is I really don't care. I know that's bad but it's the truth. Church was rough, too. I can safely say that all days are rough right now. I got angry out at your pad. Did you hear me yelling at your Father up there? I think I'm getting to the anger state little by little. I wanted to scream at your pad. I kicked the ground, sorry. I love lying out there on my back under the sun. It clears my head. I know I haven't talked to you a lot lately but you know it's not because I don't love you; it's because I'm *struggling*. I want you back here right now. I want to be your mother right now. I want our old life back, every bit of it, now. I love you.

She Is Honored

A single rose at your pad on our weekly visit.

March 26, 2007, Monday • Scale: 3

Dear Kels, well today was not too rough but I was really busy all day. Work was crazy, hah? Thanks for the KCD . . . did you see how cute that little girl was whose mom I signed up? She held my hand and walked with me everywhere. Have I mentioned how loveable your Sassy Girl has been? Do you miss your kitty? I promise to take care of her forever. Digger went to the gym tonight. It was nice having him there. Do you have any idea how much I was looking forward to you and I going to the gym and working out together? It makes me sick to think I'll never have that. Another thing? Prom. You didn't even get to experience your Senior Prom and that pisses me off. You would have been stunning. You are beautiful. I'm going to walk for you at graduation—okay? One year closer tomorrow to being with you. . . . I love you. XOXOXO

She Is Missed

I miss you, need you, love you, want you back . . .

March 27, 2007, Tuesday • Scale: 3

Hi Honey, it's my birthday and I wish you were here to celebrate it with me. The best way I can look at my birthday is to think of it as me being one year closer to being with you again. My days have been a bit better but I feel like I am almost going on vacation again. I have to, though, because I can't continue living in that dark pain. Tomorrow is Hollister Rand at group. I hope you're going to be there to talk to me. She is supposed to teach us to "reconnect" with all the children we have lost. I'm excited because I know you'll be there. Tawnia made me dinner tonight and they all sang Happy Birthday . . . we're you with us? Did you see me partying with Hawaii? I had your picture up against the beer bottle! You were there with me, hah? Kelsea, I love you and will be sorry the rest of my life that I couldn't protect you from what happened. Please forgive me.

She Is Missed

One year closer to being with you, Happy Birthday to me.

March 28, 2007, Wednesday • Scale: 3

Dear Kels, so I was hoping you would have showed up tonight for the psychic. I should have been in the front row. I was a little bummed. I thought she would have talked to me. I have group tomorrow, too. I did pretty well today until I read your Myspace comment from a friend about what a great friend you were. See, I'm starting to struggle right now. If I allowed my self to, I could completely lose it. Do you feel as if I honor you somehow, everyday? I want to make those business cards still. I have a lump in my throat tonight and it's been awhile since I felt that. I feel, honey, like my life is spinning out of control. All I want is to be loved. I know Digger loves me, but I want to feel the love from you and I can't right now. Help me, please. Help me feel again. I love you.

She Is Missed

Group tonight. . . . Hollister Rand, the psychic, where were you tonight?

March 29, 2007, Thursday • Scale: 3

Hi Honey. Mental health Thursday, hah? They are such bitter/sweet double-edge sword days. I love meeting with Susan; she truly is a savior. She helps me with my spinning out of control life. I'm kind of in a self destructive mode with my distractions. I need to stop the distractions. I'm just hurting myself. I couldn't talk at group tonight. I haven't been able to talk for about 3 weeks now. I asked Ken at the end if I could call him if I wanted to hurt myself. He wants to sit down with me and come up with a plan of action. Susan called me at high risk last Saturday during my tsunami. I hate that feeling, the waves, the feeling of having no control. . . . Tawnia said she needs your help with the boys. I've had chest pains and a lump bad today. Susan says I'm hanging onto something. It's called pain and suffering. I hate it. Kisses and hugs.

She Is Here

There is no doubt; every time I step into the gym . . . you are with me in your heart rate games.

March 30, 2007, Friday • Scale: 3

Dear Kelsea Lyn, today was better than the last few. My chest pains are beginning to worry me though. I've had a lot lately and I don't know why. It was beautiful at your pad today, so quiet and peaceful. It warmed my heart to see the cigarette someone left for you in your honor. Your stone should be here soon.

I'm not sure how I'm going to feel then. I promise I will keep it perfect for you though. I think I'm going to Magic Mountain on Sunday. I've never been. Will you go with me? Be with me the whole day, please? I feel like I am stumbling through my life right now in the dark. Will you be my light? The one who guides me with your Father in the direction I'm supposed to go? I want to be happy one day again. The days have been dark for awhile now. I hate this roller coaster of life and emotions. I hate it all but I love you. XOXOXO

She Is Honored

A visit to your pad, a single rose and an unsmoked cigarette.

March 31, 2007, Saturday • Scale: 3

Hi Baby Girl, still a better day, thank God because those dark days were really getting to me. I need to go to the doctor because my chest pains are all the time now. Work is going better. I really like it there but it's because of Hawaii. He's become my best friend, Kels. I nicknamed him Hawaii because that's where he is from. He holds my hand when the darkness begins to come over me. He talks me through the hard times and I wish he could have met you. He would have loved you and your fiery spirit. He is helping me to see life again and he is bringing color back into my life some days. He wants me to be successful at work and helps me. Can you thank your Father for blessing me with him and ask Him to bless Hawaii? Please? I still miss you every second of every minute of every hour of every day. Do you ever think about me and Digger? I still hate this. Kisses.

She Is So Missed

April 1, 2007, Sunday • Scale: 3

Dear Kelsea, church today was probably the easiest it has been since you went home. I had a sense of peace about me and I think it's because of Hawaii. I still cried for you, missing you, but it was just easier. I trained a couple girls today at the gym and it felt good. I get so sad, though, knowing I will never have the opportunity for us to work out together. I loved when you would go in the gym with me; you were so much my daughter and I was always so proud to say that. I tried going to Hawaii's friends' house with his kids and it was hard. He's so lucky to have all his children and family but I don't think people understand why I can't handle social events now. I wanted to just go home. I looked at the pictures on your Myspace for the first time in months and it brought me so much sorrow and pain. I haven't been sleeping well. Will I ever? I love you.

She Is Honored

Your picture in the gym; being told how gorgeous you are . . .

April 2, 2007, Monday • Scale: 3

Hi Sweetheart, I stopped a wave today. I still cried but I stopped the tidal in the wave. I met yet another boy who knew you tonight at the gym. My new Assistant Manager also said you were so beautiful. My question is still, Why did God only give you to me for only 17 years? What kind of purpose does it serve to bless someone with such a beautiful child only to take her away? See, I'm getting pissed just trying to answer that question. My mind spins and searches for answers that no one can answer for me. No matter how strong my faith is in God; He hasn't told me yet, why? Work is getting better. I do like my new job but I hate my new different life. I would go back to being stressed in a heart beat to have you back in my life, alive again. What is everlasting life all about? Do you like it? Tell me.

She Is Honored

"She's so beautiful, she's with the Angels now . . ." simply stated by a friend.

April 3, 2007, Tuesday • Scale: 3

Dear Kelsea Lyn, did you see how busy I was at work tonight? Crazy, hah? Garrett and Robert came in to join. I really do like them and I wish I could have met more of your friends that you hung with. I'm doing some training, too, and I like it. I picked up Hawaii's daughter and drove her to the gym. She was telling me about going to Magic Mountain and it was strange listening to her talk because all I could think about was it being you. This weekend is the Easter Celebration at church. I know when I see all the Angels in the show, I am going to think about you and how much you wanted to do that and now you are a real Angel, the real thing in heaven with your Father. Call me selfish but I want you back with me in this place called hell. . . . I miss you and love you tons.

She Is Missed Every Day

Not a second goes by that Kelsea is not on my mind . . . till we meet again.

April 4, 2007, Wednesday • Scale: 3

Hi Honey, I cried at work tonight. You see, I began listening to Hawaii talk about his family to another guy. He has 5 children and I got both jealous and envious. You and Digger have been my whole family for 14 years and I accepted that whole heartedly. But, now my family feels in-complete. I don't know if I can belong to someone else's family. I struggle still, being in social environments. I just don't know. Work is getting busy. I still long for us working out together.

Tonight a mom signed her young daughter up and they were so excited to do it together. I'll never forget walking on the treadmill with you or you complaining about sweating in aerobics class in high school! I got you out of class, though, didn't I? I always did what I thought was best for you. I hope you believe that. I hope you never forget how much I love you. Kisses and hugs.

She Is Honored

I shared your pictures with some members at the gym . . . as always I was told how beautiful you are.

April 5, 2007, Thursday • Scale: 3

Dear Kelsea Lyn, I finally talked at group tonight. It's been a few weeks since I have been able to. I think it's Hawaii that's brought some peace into my life here lately that allowed me to open up again. I even had a lady come up to me after group and tell me how good it was to hear me talk. I also met with Susan and I love her so much for guiding me down this journey through hell. She helps me so much in all areas of my life and I trust her so much. She gave me such a nice Easter card. I hope I can make it through the service on Sunday. Digger's going with me but you're supposed to be there, too. Will you please be with me and help me that day? I'll come see you at your pad, of course. Do you want an Easter basket still? It's been $7^1/_2$ months now and I still love you more with each day that passes. Do you miss me like I miss you? I love you.

She Is Here

Cardio at the gym, no matter what I did, treadmill, life cycle, and cross-trainer, you were there.

April 6, 2007, Friday • Scale: 3

Hi Kels, happy Friday, hah? I would give anything to get a 3 am phone call to pick up your drunk butt wherever you were. I'm just glad you trusted me enough to know you could call me no matter what happened. Not all parents can say their child trusted them enough to call. Digger had to leave work early today. He called me and said he was struggling at work and just having a hard time. I understood. I know he struggles but I forget sometimes because I'm so caught up in my own pain. I'm sure he has dark hours and dark days like I do. I got out all your pictures tonight and looked at how absolutely beautiful you are. You have such a smile in all the pictures. You seem so happy in the pictures and yet I know how much pain you lived with and I'm sorry I couldn't help you more. I tried my hardest you know. I miss you more than life itself. Kisses to you. XOX

She Is Here

"Suds in the Bucket. . . ." Sara Evans on the radio singing your favorite song.

April 7, 2007, Saturday • Scale: 3

Dear Kelsea Lyn, a friend of yours from Kansas wrote to you on Myspace today and it started a wave . . . when I think about the other people, thinking about you being gone, it makes me sick for them. It's crazy I know. Tomorrow is Easter.

This is the first year in 19 years I haven't gotten Easter baskets. It's like I've just forgotten that whole side of tomorrow. Digger and I will go to church and then I'll come spend the day with you, okay? You know Hawaii? I am so thankful he's in my life and it's hard to think if I didn't lose you, he wouldn't be in my life. You brought us and put us on the same path. Do you like him? Do you think he is good for me? I know he is good to me. A couple times now he has mentioned he feels like you were his daughter. He feels that close to you because of my love for you and that warms my heart. He has brought some life back into me.

Thank your Father for me, please. I love you tons.

She Is Here

The cross in my car on my mirror; wrapped up high, then it's swinging again. You put it up and you took it down.

April 8, 2007, Sunday • Scale: 3

EASTER

Hi Baby doll, Happy Easter . . . do you celebrate Easter in heaven? You've got to do something for Jesus's resurrection. We had a big dinner here with ham and everything. You should have been here. Church was not too hard because they didn't have the angels in the celebration show. I did cry, though, at your pad. It was beautiful seeing others visiting you. The two little bunnies on a stick were cute. It was cold out there today. I finally got a pink ribbon on the tree I have deemed your tree; next will be the pink wind chime. It was nice having your brother here all day. Who did bring those other flowers to you? Things are a little easier right now because of Hawaii. It's like I finally have someone to hold my hand through this dark journey. I think I wouldn't be where I am today without his help. I owe it to you . . . are you happy for me finally? I love you.

She Is Honored

So many bouquets of flowers at your pad and more people visiting you.

April 9, 2007, Monday • Scale: 3

Dear Kelsea, I am beginning to realize that although things are not getting better, life is getting easier. I also know, though, that it will be short-lived until another simple trigger happens and brings on a wave. I think since I have begun making better choices in my life and not falling so much things are a little easier. It helps too, though, when I know you are with me, like in the gym today. I felt a cold breeze all around me and I wasn't by an air conditioner! It's like you were blowing on me and dancing all around me as if to say, here I am Mama! I didn't cry today now that I think about it. It's a double-edged sword, though, because part of me feels so guilty that life was easier today because I am afraid still to accept that you're gone. I love you so much. Kisses.

She Is Here

So I'm doing cardio and I feel a cool breeze on my back. I look up for the air-conditioner vents and there are none. I proceed to feel a cool breeze periodically all around me. Then, on the radio today, everytime I listened was one of your songs.

April 10, 2007, Tuesday • Scale: 3

Hi Tat, I feel like I'm jumping on the not-think-about-it train again. I'm scared, though, because when I got off of that train on February 22nd, it led into several dark weeks. Am I going to be spending the rest of my life getting on and off this train? The only refuge I have is that now I have Hawaii to pick me up, dust me off and let me feel the pain, yet comfort me. Someone mentioned the Prom the other day. I wish I could go there for you. I wish you were experiencing Prom and graduation. Why would God take those away from you and me? What glory can there possibly be in your not being here with me? I took 2 Trazodone tonight because I'm tired and need the rest because exhaustion is grief's worst enemy, right? When can I be with you? NEVER soon enough.

She Is Here

As I write on the computer, Sassy jumps into my lap ever so lovingly and I feel you.

April 11, 2007, Wednesday • Scale: 3

Dear Kelsea Lyn, I find myself during the day realizing that you're not here with me. I don't understand how my brain functions and how I just wake up every day and function, then all of a sudden I remember you're gone and it tears me apart. I finally got a call from Geeni F. and she said that on Monday charges should be filed. I know that nothing will ever bring you back, but she needs to be held responsible for what she did to you and me and Digger. I can only pray and trust that justice will prevail. I'm thinking your stone for your pad should be here soon. I promise to keep it beautiful for you . . . after all it will be both our pad one day. I only have 2 pounds to go to till I'm at your weight. I think I'm going to go for an extra 5 pounds, too. I like the way I look. You would be proud. I miss you always, kisses.

She Is Here

I'm struggling again . . . but there you are in the gym with me. I wear my heart rate monitor and my heart rate DOES NOT show! All I see is a beating heart-shaped icon on the machine and I laughed.

April 12, 2007, Thursday • Scale: 3

Dear Kelsea Lyn, you are so funny with a 204 heart rate on the cardio machine! I'm only 2 pounds away still and I didn't realize I weigh the same as I did in high school. That's awesome! I met with Susan and it's always good, although I cried today. I do think I'm pulling my life together a little bit, though, now that I've gotten rid of all my distractions. Although Susan seems to think my weight loss is a distraction and control issue for me. I do agree, but I had no control over my loss with you and this, I do. I know you understand. Did you see how much I confessed at group? Ken said I look like I have life in me for the first time. . . . I know it's Hawaii. I know you want me happy and loved. I'm thinking he may be the one to do that for me. Do you hear him when he talks to you? Do you want me with him? I know you will guide me on this journey. I'll miss you forever . . . be with your brother.

She Is Here and She Is Missed

There is no doubt . . . you are at the gym with me with a 204 heart rate, which makes me laugh and group makes me cry . . .

April 13, 2007, Friday • Scale: 2

Dear Kels, how am I supposed to keep going on in my life when I think of your being gone? Everyone says, "She would want you to be happy," but it means nothing to me. *Nothing.* Will there come a day when I will be able to accept all this? I went to Hawaii's house today and lay down to nap. As I prayed, I cried and it hit hard. He came in the room and just lay with me while I cried. I told him, this is me broken. I don't think too many people get to experience that first hand. I wouldn't wish this journey in hell on anyone. I don't want to have to help any of my friends with a loss; it scares me . . . you know, like Cara did for me. I've been getting pretty run-down lately but I think it's from losing weight. I don't care though. I think all the parents at group last night agreed that we all just don't give a shit anymore about so many things. All we want is our children back again . . . is that too much to ask for?

She Is Honored

I bought Ice Breakers candy today . . . in the grocery line . . . like you always grabbed. . . .

April 14, 2007, Saturday • Scale: 3

Hi Sweetheart, I did well at work today. I sold a good membership with training. It was nice but it's funny because on the other hand I don't even care. What do you think about me being a bartender? I'm thinking about doing that. Tell me if I should and I will listen. I still feel like I'm on auto-pilot. I am able to function every day and do daily normal tasks but it's so mundane. I mean, it's really a chore to have to pay my bills one day a month.

It's hard for me to be responsible. You know I was good before at taking care of business, but now, I just get up and do. By the way, do you have to have me get a shock every time I touch something? I went to a Mexican restaurant and looked at the Carne Asada Fries and I got sad. We were so bad . . . chowing down on those fattening, yummy fries together! I want that back. I'll never eat fries again. I love you.

She Is Here

As I touched a girl at work, a shock! I jump and laughed and I share our story of hating being shocked.

April 15, 2007, Sunday • Scale: 3

Dear Kels, sorry I couldn't lie with you today at your pad, but the ground was soaked. It's cute all the little stuffed animals you have there. It warms my heart to see not only the animals I leave for you but new ones, too. Did you like the pretty rose I brought? Your stone should be here soon . . . bitter-sweet it will be. I cried 3 times today: at church, with Hawaii and at your pad. That's never going to change is it? Hawaii keeps telling me how good I'm doing and that it's okay to be happy and still know the sadness is there, too. I wonder if people see the joy yet deep sadness in my eyes. Sometimes I hate people looking at me and wondering how I am making it . . . how strong I am. . . . I wish I wasn't strong so you were still here. Would you have truly struggled through life if your Father hadn't brought you home? Am I being selfish for wanting you here, thinking I could have taken care of you? Are you better off in heaven or here with me? I want answers. Kisses 2 you.

She Is Here

Always with me in the gym . . .

April 16, 2007, Monday • Scale: 3

Hi Little Girl, you know you will always be my little girl forever. I had to drive by the house today and around your old stomping ground and I can't do that anymore. I got sick. I didn't cry today, though. . . . I'm finding some peace in my life. I'm finding and feeling love again. I feel like I'm getting "life" back in me.

It's like I have someone in my life now who accepts me broken, sad, crying . . . the thing is, honey, I never would have met him. Are you happy for me? Is this man the one you want me to spend my life with? I wish you could tell me, "Yes, Mama, he's good for you, he makes you happy, and you have my blessings and my Father's." There was a college school shooting today. So many children lost . . . take them into heaven and welcome them all, please. A journey of hell is awaiting their parents. Kisses.

She Is Honored

City High, the group we listened to . . . Carmel, the song about you . . . Myspace . . . remind me of you.

April 17, 2007, Tuesday • Scale: 3

Dear Kels, I had to go to the doctor straight from the gym; I thought I was having a heart attack. My chest was so tight. But my heart is perfect besides being so broken and empty. It's stress and my chest is just having spasms. Were you there with me? Are you with me all the time or do I have to share you? There's a girl at work who brings in her little girl who's about 2 years old. She gives me a hug all the time. Her little hug today was so tight and long. I closed my eyes and I felt you. I cried. I look at young mothers with baby girls and I think, *Are they going to lose her? Does she have any idea?* When you were a baby, never in my life did I ever think I would be writing in a journal to you in heaven every night. I still get sick when I think about this so I just don't. All of a sudden I think, she's gone, and I push it away. Is it denial? Is it forever? I love you.

She Is Missed

My heart aches and my soul is full of sorrow.

April 18, 2007, Wednesday • Scale: 3

Hi Baby doll, so at work today I shared our story with so many people. I had the nurse from your grade school recognize me. I told her what happened to you and she wept at my desk. I was so busy at work that a wave hit me when I got home. I miss you so much at times I just can't deal with it. Hawaii came over and I laid in his lap and cried. He lets me ride the wave as long as I have to, then he picks me up. I met Garret's Aunt Ashley today. She told me you used to go to her house a lot. I like her Kelsea, and I wish I could have been more a part of that side of your life. Maybe I could have done more and this would not have happened. Maybe you would still be here if I would have done things differently. Am I selfish for wanting you here or was God selfish for wanting you with Him? I just don't know. I know I love you. Hugs.

She Is Missed

So many tears shed today from people in your past.

April 19, 2007, Thursday • Scale: 3

Dear Kels, so I was at group tonight, eyes closed and tears flowing. Sometimes I wonder if I should even go to group because that's the night I feel the most pain all week. But, Ken tells me I *need* to keep showing up; so I will. I had a trigger tonight. . . . I flashed on you asking me to take you clothes shopping for school and I said no because I knew Steve didn't think you deserved them. So, to save hearing him bitch at me, I told you no for that day and we would go the next when he went out of town. I got really angry then at myself for not taking you because you would have been with me that night and I could have saved your life. Because you would have been with ME. You would still be here if I would have just done what I wanted to, not what I thought Steve wanted . . . triggers for the rest of my life. I hate them. I hate this. I hate you're gone. I love you.

She Is Here

It was strange . . . as I lay on my stomach taking a nap, I felt something underneath me, pushing on my legs alternating up to my stomach. A gentle feel, almost like a heartbeat. I lay motionless, not wanting to disturb the rhythm or the feeling, all the while trying to figure out if I was imagining this feeling or if it was real . . . it was real and I knew and I felt you.

April 20, 2007, Friday • Scale: 3

420: KELSEA'S DAY

Hi Precious, so today was 4-20-(07), did it make you smile? I have your little red box you made with 420 all over it and it makes me smile. I will never forget the day you explained to me what 420 stood for. Doobie Time, the 4th letter of the alphabet, D, and the 20th letter of the alphabet, T, compliments of Bob Marley! I wish you could tell me that you put Hawaii in my life and that you're happy he is in my life. I struggle with the happiness he brings me and the pain from missing you because I wouldn't have both of you. Is this the path your Father wants? Was His plan to bless me with you to bring Hawaii into my life? I'm confused. Why couldn't God have blessed me with BOTH of you in my life? At the same time?

We could have been a family, a real family with a man who would have loved you and your brother. I'm sorry I made a poor choice in Steve. If only he could have loved you unconditionally, it may have been different. If only your dad would have showed you more love, this may not have happened. So many people failed you and I'm so sorry for that. Do you forgive me? Please forgive me. Kiss.

She Is Honored

420: Deemed Kelsea's Day.

April 21, 2007, Saturday • Scale: 3

Hi Sweetheart, so tomorrow will be 8 months and I don't know what to expect. I know I'll be coming to see you for sure. I'm not sure why lately, but the last few days I have been telling so many people our story. Everyone asks me how I'm able to function and I don't know how to answer. I met a woman today whose daughter was murdered 8 years ago in Mexico. She's going to group with me Thursday. It's times like that when I see my purpose in part of this loss, but I just wish I could have helped people with you by my side. I met a girl whose uncle was bipolar and he killed himself, and I wonder how difficult our lives truly would have been with your illness. Is that why God brought you home? To save you from a tormented, painful life? Would I not have been able to help you enough? You know I would have died for you or why couldn't we have all gone together? You, me and Digger? I love you forever.

She Is Honored

I find myself sharing the tragedy of your loss with so many people that sit before me now at work.

April 22, 2007, Sunday • Scale: 3

Dear Kelsea Lyn Phelps, so hard to believe it's been 8 months. In church today the message was about having peace in your life even amongst trials and tribulations. I just don't feel it yet. I enjoyed my visit with you at your pad although I got chest pains driving there. Out there I have to admit it's very peaceful. I took Digger out to dinner tonight. I actually was able to make him laugh. I know I need to spend more time with him. I hope you are with him and watching over him all the time; he needs you. My life now, Kels, is beginning to feel like I am actually living again. Some moments I am able to feel my good emotions again. I am feeling love again toward Hawaii. It's not scary at all; it's what you would want for me, to be happy and taken care of finally. Thank you, Kelsea, for Hawaii. I only wish you were here with us.

She Is Here

As I walked into the house my phone began playing all 3 downloaded songs, unprovoked. As I shut the phone the time said 2:22 . . . as I drove to your pad, "Suds in the Bucket," and both times I knew.

JOURNAL: A VACATION

It feels like forever has passed, yet it's only been another month. It has been a month, though, of vacation. It's been a month of putting my grief, my thoughts, my sorrow on a back burner. It has been a month of my slow distraction becoming spinning, hard, out of control . . . a distraction that became not only from one man but many.

My intimacy stayed with one man but my attention and time began to be spread out to several male friends. I found myself going from visiting with one, right to another, to another. Finally, one weekend I felt as if my life was spinning completely out of control.

I called Susan and spoke to her about it. I felt better and knew what had to be done and that was simply to stop seeing all of them. It was time for me to put away that bottle, push the food away from my plate, throw away that bag of weed, stop going to the casino, stop shopping, stop throwing myself into my work.

You see, in group I learned that all of those things are distractions of various types that bereaved parents all do. Mine was men. I found myself just hanging out with them all the time because it took my mind off the fact that I no longer had my daughter, that she was gone. Once I was able to open my eyes to the damage I was creating toward myself, I was able to refocus on my grief. Grief is something I am learning I will do for the rest of my life until I take my very last breath.

Over the last month, I can say that for the first time I have felt some comfort that has come in the form of a best friend, I call him Hawaii. He was brought into my life only by my daughter's passing. He started working at the gym the same day I did.

He had seen Kelsea's Myspace page and was touched by it. Over the last 4 months I have talked to him about my distractions, my pain, my sorrow, my story. He listened without passing judgment and made me feel safe. When I finally told him Kelsea's story, he understood me better and the true tragedy of it all hit him.

For the first several months I had to go through this alone. I have my pseudo family and they are so loving, but it's hard to lose a child and not have someone to hold you every night you want to cry. It's hard to go through this when you have no one to tell you it's okay even when it's not.

I will never forget the night Hawaii came over to my house and I had been looking at Kelsea's Myspace page and crying. I heard him come in the house and I walked into the living room. He could see immediately I had been crying, set his things down on the table and said, "Come here." He sat on the couch, I crawled up into his lap and curled up like an infant and cried for I don't know how long. All he did was hold me and that's all I needed. That's all any of us really need at any given moment. We need someone to unconditionally open their arms to us even though they feel powerless because no one can fix what we feel at that very moment.

I know that most marriages do not survive the loss of a child. All the books I have read say that even the strongest of marriages struggle. All I can say is if this happens to a couple, remember how very differently men and woman grieve. Remember there is no length of time for anything and everyone's lengths are so different. Don't give up on each other and don't turn away from each other. Let each other cry, get angry, get quiet and just let your presence for each other be known.

I think it has been the support of Hawaii that has allowed me to feel some small pieces of life over the last month again. When I am with him, as I said, I feel so very safe and protected. I have been able to smile and sometimes laugh. He keeps telling me how happy I am now and I have to constantly remind him that I am only that way with him. Yet, it brings hope to hear his words.

When it comes to being in the real world, with real people and real events, I'm still on autopilot. It's funny, Hawaii told me one day that when he first saw and met me at work, he thought I was "fake." I took offense to that at first and couldn't understand that at all. But, as we talked more I realized what he meant. He would see me talking to people and smiling and laughing and he said it just seemed fake. He was absolutely right. That's not me, happy and laughing; that's the autopilot in me that goes through the motions every day.

The autopilot wakes up every morning, gets cleaned up, ready for work, works for 8 hours, eats meals periodically, talks to people, works out, goes home, gets cleaned up and goes to bed just to wake up the next morning and do it all over again, with my eyes closed, not feeling anything or seeing any real color around me. It's the me that is simply surviving each day and trying to do it to the best of my ability. Sometimes I am successful and sometimes I'm not. But, I will say if he wants to call me fake for that, then I accept that description.

I think and I have learned that one cannot live in such deep grief for extended periods of time. I believe it is our mind and bodies way of protecting us when it pushes grief away from the table. Sometimes I think, *Okay, this is good because I haven't been crying every single day and my thoughts have not all been dark.*

But, then the guilt slips in as to how can I be feeling this way? How can I not be feeling utter sadness and sickness? How can I be driving down the road, blasting Eminem with the window down, feeling the warm sun on my shoulder and feel "good" when my daughter is gone? How the hell can I do that???

Then I get pissed at myself for having fleeting moments of normalcy. It's such a vicious cycle, this grief thing. It's all the phases hitting you over and over again, at different times, and not ever knowing which one's going to rear its ugly head.

It's like I lived my whole life, 43 years, without ever losing anyone or even thinking about death. I just float through life doing this and doing that, going here, going there. First you're a kid, then you're in college, then you get married. You decide to have some kids and have one boy and one girl, perfect. They are 15 months apart and close growing up. So close in fact, my parents tell me one day, "Your kids are too close." How could that be? I always asked myself.

Then I get a divorce and spend the next 14 years raising my children alone. I live my life for my children and every decision I ever make is in their best interest. I struggle sometimes working 2 jobs so they can play football and cheer or so they can do gymnastics and play baseball.

I go to all their school functions and never miss a sporting event they are involved in. I fight for them in school because they are special education students for mental health reasons and I fight for their rights and fight for them to be understood. They weren't bad kids; they were challenging children.

I finally get my son graduated from high school and know I am so close to seeing my daughter graduate, too. I'm still living my life, more so for my daughter now, only to have her taken away from me? Only to go into her room to wake her up for school and I can't? I try but I just can't wake her up.

I flash on that morning and I think that is why I go for long periods of time without thinking about this all. Whenever I start to think, that's what comes into my head and I *can't* do it. Susan wants me to see a psychologist and receive Eye Movement Desensitization and Reprocessing therapy, EMDR. This is a type of therapy that helps me to process that morning. It will help me to be able to deal better with what happened that morning and the trauma I live with.

In my group there are so many different types of deaths to our children. Some have died of cancers, accidents, suicides, murder. I find myself trying to figure out what category Kelsea's passing would fall under. I wonder if it would have been better to have not been the one to find her. Would it have been better to not have been the one trying to save her? Someone told me that I should be thankful that Kelsea was home. She said, "Kelsea came home to her family where she was loved. She went to sleep in her own bed where she felt safe . . . and she woke up with her Father in Heaven. She came home to go Home."

I guess what kills me is how unfair it was that she came home and just went to sleep in anticipation of going to her new school the next morning to start her senior year. She had no idea that when she went to sleep she wasn't going to wake up. How unfair is that? Do you have any idea how hard that is for me? To know she trusted she was going to wake up the next day? It's tearing me apart to think how unfair it all is.

I'm still visiting her pad every Sunday. It's our time. I did have chest pains driving there on this 8-month day and I cried hard but I have to go. I can't imagine right now not going and laying with her for awhile, talking to her and praying to her Father. I know her headstone will be arriving soon and I'm scared. I don't know how I am going to handle it finally being there. Will it be a total reality hit and wipe me out or will I finally be happy that it's there? I just don't know.

I do know that I do not believe in anniversaries of death. Personally, I don't understand why anyone would want to even acknowledge that day. I'm already feeling the anxiety of the one year day and I still have 4 months to go. I foresee myself not even able to get out of bed. I see myself not wanting to have to deal with anyone or anything. Maybe it won't be that hard but I don't see how it truly couldn't.

As I sit here writing, the tears are pouring down my face. My head hurts, my heart hurts. But I look out the sliding glass door and once again, the sun is going down, another day has passed and I am still breathing.

2 CORINTHIANS 12:9
Each time he said, "My gracious favor is all you need.
My power works best in your weakness."
So now I am glad to boast about my weaknesses,
so that the power of Christ may work through me.

CHAPTER NINE

April 23, 2007, Monday • Scale: 3

Dear Kelsea, I hope you like this new journal. I thought the front was so perfect for you. I've had a lump in my throat most of the day. Tawnia and I talked tonight about how she cannot eat and doesn't think she will ever again be able to eat hot wings. Me? I will never eat french fries or drink 7-11 coffee. But she said she puts Franks Hot Sauce on everything and never did before. I guess for me, the fries are linked to the Carne Asada Fries we shared and the cheddar cheese fries from Jack in the Box, too. Work has been picking up and that's good but I get exhausted. I'm busting my butt in cardio and not eating enough and I felt it today. I just want to weigh what you did. I know I can do it. I read a blog on Myspace and it killed me. I wish I knew what heaven was really like. Have you met Jesus? Have you met God? Can you ask Them to guide me through the rest of my life so I can be with you in everlasting life? How long do I have to wait? I love you more than life itself. Kisses and hugs.

She Is Missed

I missed you today, where were you?

April 24, 2007, Tuesday • Scale: 2

Hi Sweetheart, rough day. I had to take half the day off of work. I was doing well at work but it's not good enough. I'm not a sales person, I'm a people person.

Then I got the call from Geeni and a warrant is being issued. It's finally coming to fruition . . . justice. I'm not sure how I'm going to feel the first time I see the person responsible for your death. I've had a lump still in my throat and a head ache for 3 days now. It's like just when you're feeling okay or having a few good days, WHAM! Darkness comes over you and you're just screwed, you know? I cried so hard today for a long time. Honestly, this has been such a hard emotional day, from work, and to the call to Hawaii. Sometimes, hon, he says things to me that no one has ever said to me in my life and I don't understand and it hurts, but he's still a good man. I wish you were still here to meet him. I know he would have loved you and you would have liked him. Give me strength, please, and tell your Father I need a blessing of hope. Kisses.

She Is Honored and Missed

The call . . . an arrest warrant . . . deep sorrow . . .

April 25, 2007, Wednesday • Scale: 3

Dear Kelsea Lyn, I love you with all my heart and soul. I miss you with every fiber of my being . . . will it ever get easier for me? One of your friends from the gym tonight promised me you were in a "better" place. She sounded like she really knew what she was saying. I just don't know. I want to trust in it all, you know? I meet with the district attorney tomorrow. I'm not scared at all. I am trying to prepare myself, though, for a trial if it goes that way. I thought about seeing Laura Wion for the first time. I don't know if I'll even be able to look at any of them. I haven't cried today, first time in awhile, too. I found out graduation is soon. I want to walk your graduation in your honor. Would you like that? I'm scared to get the yearbook, though, and see your entire page dedicated to you. I'll bet you're happy about that though. I saw Brandon (Lakeside) at the gym. I'm going to the river with them this season. Do you mind? I'll go in your honor. Tell Melissa, Brittany and Jenna I said hello . . . and hug them for their moms, too.

Kisses.

She Is Missed

Your friend at the gym who misses you—she promised me you're in a better place . . .

April 26, 2007, Thursday • Scale: 3

Dear Kelsea, it's finally here, justice. I met with the D. A. today and I am pleased with what we talked about. Most important is that Laura Wion cannot do this to another mother or family. I know it will not bring you back but people must be held accountable for their actions. I trust God will assure that for me. I didn't go to group tonight. Ken wasn't going to be there so I just didn't feel like it. So, what do you think about me being a bartender? Would you be proud of me if I did? I swear every drink I poured I would think of you. I wish I could have been able to share a drink with you on your 21st birthday. I think I still will. I told Hawaii the next time I get married it will be on April 20th . . . 420 all in your and Digger's honor! I will never forget you educating me on that number. I hope you realize that no matter how mad I ever got at things you did, I always loved you. I describe you to people as a girl that just blew where the wind went . . . a true free spirit. Now, you are truly free . . . till we meet again. I love you.

She Is Loved and Honored

So many comments, such loving comments left on your Myspace.

April 27, 2007, Friday • Scale: 3

ARREST MADE

My Dearest Little Girl, it finally came to fruition . . . the beginning of justice in an arrest. It's so surreal, though, because there was a press release on the news and an article online. I wasn't really sure or didn't think how I would feel and it's taken my feet out from under me. Thank God Susan is coming to be with me. We're going to see a movie I think. I tried calling your dad and he did call me back. I couldn't even imagine the way he feels. I know tonight I feel completely broken again. Please talk to your heavenly Father and ask Him to give me the strength I need for what lays ahead of me, okay? I think it's hitting me hard, too, because Hawaii has not been here today for me and I feel alone again. Tawnia is having a difficult time, too, right now. This is so unfair, Kelsea. Laura Wion has no idea how bad she ruined my and Digger's life. She changed us forever and she had no right to do that. I want her punished the same as she punished us. I hate this pain. I love you.

She Is Here

Last night Tawnia thought about the water park on July 4th and wondered if she would be able to go without you . . . today Brayden out of the blue questioned Tawnia about the big water park.

April 28, 2007, Saturday • Scale: 3

Hi Honey, it's surreal still. It was on the news again this morning. I find myself telling everyone she's finally in jail. A few members at the gym approached me and said they knew it was about you. I know I have a road ahead of me. I found this methadone organization I am going to contact. Methadone and bipolar teens are what I am going to pursue. I'm supposed to work tomorrow so I don't know how I will get to see you, probably right after church. Hawaii is going with me to Sonrise. I'm excited about it. I usually spend Saturday nights with Hawaii. You really would have liked him. He would have made us feel like a family and you could have been a part of his big family. I know that's all you ever really wanted, to be a family with a dad and to feel loved and respected. I'm so sorry I never provided you with that. I'm sorry I didn't do better for you. I tried my hardest but it wasn't enough. I love you. Kisses.

She Is Missed, Loved, Needed . . . Always.

April 29, 2007, Sunday • Scale: 3

Dear Tat, church was good. With Hawaii there I felt better and church wasn't as hard as it usually is. I'm sorry I only got a few minutes with you today but I brought the dozen pink roses in celebration of Laura Wion being in jail. I had to work today and I hated it. I can't work full time. I get exhausted and then the tidal waves roll in. They are letting me take off to go to court tomorrow. I will be there every second she steps into court. Susan will be with me, too. I'm a little scared because I don't know what I will do when I see her for the first time. I came home after work and a wave rolled in . . . all the emotions I am feeling and no one to hold me right now. Tawnia saw my pain tonight. She kept trying to get me to laugh with Jarrod. I love her and hope I can repay her one day for what she's done for me and

Digger. I'm such an emotional wreck right now. I don't want to blow it with Hawaii, you know? Help me, honey to do the right things. Bless me with some KCD. . . . I love you with all my heart and miss you, too.

She Is Missed

Cantankerous was said to me today and I laughed because you loved using that word, and then the sorrow rolls in. . . .

April 30, 2007, Monday • Scale: 3

Dear Kelsea Lyn, so I went to court today and it was surreal. As I held your picture in my hand, stroking it, I got angry that I even had to be there. Tawnia and Susan were with me. I didn't get to see Laura Wion and the rest of her family was not there either. I will promise you this: I will be there every second. It will be another week now. I see so many of your friends at the gym now and they all miss you so much. I think Mallory should be getting ready to have her baby. I know you would have been such a wonderful mother to your children. But I won't have the opportunity to see and that makes me mad. She took away, no she ripped out of my life, so many things I was supposed to experience with you. My life, Digger's life . . . they have been changed forever and I just don't see how any of it can be for the better. Am I missing something, honey? Can you tell me what to do now? I need you. I love you.

She Is Here

Stopped at a light, cigarette smoke smell, no one around.

May 1, 2007, Tuesday • Scale: 3

Dear Kels, I'm tired tonight, really tired. Tonight at the gym, Hawaii was talking to his daughter about her going to Prom; it was tough. I know you would have been going to your Prom. You would have been so beautiful. I told them how Digger wanted you to be in a Prom dress and how you looked like a Barbie. I can do all things through Christ who strengthens me . . . I got the coolest license plate holder today from Jayme. I will keep it forever. Adam asked me what I'm going to do with your bedroom furniture.

I told him I'm keeping it. I'll bring it with me wherever I go. I know that sounds silly but I don't care. I would like to have a quilt made out of your clothes. I guess I should try to start looking for someone to do that. I still struggle with having to be responsible although I do think I'm getting better. I'll bet you are smiling so big at all the attention you're getting now, but you're still supposed to be here being loved by me. Hugs and Kisses.

She Is Honored by All

A newspaper article . . . the truth . . . will be told.

May 2, 2007, Wednesday • Scale: 3

Hi Honey, I think I screwed up at work tonight but I don't care. I talked to Susan about it and she was right; I'm not a sales person. I'm too honest. I believe in giving someone the absolute best deal available to them and not making money for myself or the company. You and me, our hearts are too big, I think. At least I have a job interview tomorrow. I need some of your KCD tomorrow, okay? I know you're smiling thinking, oh my gosh, mom . . . you're a bartender! Did you ever think I would do that? I sure didn't but Hawaii has faith in me that I can do it and I trust him. I've told so many people what's going on and I can see you in heaven, smiling at all the attention you're getting. I will make this so public so you will save many, many lives. I think I am beginning to get a glimpse of the impact this is going to have on lives but it doesn't make it any easier. The waves still come and will continue until we are face to face again and I can't wait. I love you, kisses.

She Is Honored

Telling your story, letting everyone know how public I want this to be.

May 3, 2007, Thursday • Scale: 3

Dear Kels, I got the call today that your address stone is ready. I just do not know how I am going to handle it all, you know? So, at group tonight I finally spoke. A lot of parents saw the news and knew it was us. I felt myself telling the story and getting angry and happy. Angry about what happened yet happy she is in custody. I'm glad she can't see her family. I'm glad she has no freedom. I'm glad it's all going to come out, the truth about what happened. I said in group that I'm pissed and I'm going to enjoy every second of anger I feel right now. I've been floating through all this for 8 months and now that an arrest was made and it's all starting, I'm finding anger in it. I still don't think I've gotten angry with God though. I trust in His justice. I know He has a plan for me; help me find it, honey. Talk to me and guide me in your honor. . . . I love you, kisses and hugs.

She Is Honored

Group, I talked a lot about what's going on, all the while having your picture with me clutched tightly in my hand.

May 4, 2007, Friday • Scale: 3

Hi Honey, I forgot to tell you, I got the job! Can you believe I am going to be a bartender? I'm glad I get to quit 24 Hour Fitness, you know? My heart's not there. I paid for your stone to be placed today and for a cup so I can keep flowers at your pad. I'm glad Susan was with me today. So, what do you think about me and Hawaii? I only wish you could have met him. I guess I can't say that enough, can I? He's a good man, Kels. Probably the finest man I have ever been with and I have to thank you for bringing him into my life. Are you happy for me? Is this who you want me to be with? Your stone should be put at your pad next week. Crazy how it's happening at the same time as court is starting. Was that your Fathers plan? Can you ask Him to give me strength through this and somehow understanding? Ken told me I give strength in group to other parents.

I don't know how, but I'm thankful if I am. I love you.

She Is Here

From the second I stepped on the cross-trainer you were there, 30 full minutes.

May 5, 2007, Saturday • Scale: 3

Hi Honey, Happy Cinco De Mayo! I know how much you love this holiday . . . it's our little secret! I hope you liked the flowers I brought to your pad. They were fiesta flowers . . . hahaha! It was a hard visit though. I went to work today and I had to leave. I just can't handle the pressure, honey, of sales at work. I just don't care. Everyone else working sales there runs when a new guest comes in and I pretend I am on the phone when actually I'm talking to a dial tone. So, instead I came to see you. It was nice out there today. I went to a party tonight with Hawaii. If he wasn't with me, I wouldn't have gone. You know, I can do things in life if I'm with him. I'm so thankful for him. You will meet him in heaven one day. I just wish it could have been here on earth. I'm on a bit of a vacation again, I think; I don't know. You're supposed to be graduating in a month. I'm sorry you are not . . . forgive me.

She Is Honored

A trip to your pad, so peaceful.

May 6, 2007, Sunday • Scale: 2

Dear Tat, do you like my new dog, Griff? Hawaii got him for us today. He says Griff will be good therapy for me. I'll admit I spent the whole day with just me and the dog and it was peaceful. I walked him just about all day long! I miss you, Kelsea. I miss you every hour of every day. I miss your smile, your laugh, your smell. I miss tickling you and watching *Deal or No Deal* with you. I miss taking you to 7-11 for coffee. I miss sharing french fries with you. I miss your mood swings and sleeping with you at night. I miss our messy bedroom. I miss your dirty dishes all over the place and watching you eat hot wings. I miss you trying to be tall with your big black sandals and I miss buying you Sour Patch candy. I miss you calling me Mama and telling me you love me. I miss you smoking cigarettes on the porch. It's not fair. I HATE THIS.

She Is Missed

A dog named Griff . . . therapy for me I am told because I miss you painfully.

May 7, 2007, Monday • Scale: 3

Dear Kels, so do you like Griff? Would you have liked him or does he slobber too much? Did you see him chase Sassy today? I quit 24 Hours today and it felt good because like at Frogs, it was getting harder and harder to even walk in there. So, I spent the day with Griff and he does help occupy my mind and that's good because we have court in the morning. I'm anxious to see her plea. Just tell your Father I'm asking for justice. I can't help but think that you are supposed to still be here with me and Digger. There's so much in life you're supposed to be experiencing and you won't and that pisses me off. It pisses me off that I won't be able to help you plan your wedding and pick out a dress or laugh at you when you're pregnant and love the babies you were supposed to have and live in the same town so we see each other every week. But it's all been torn away from me and I don't understand, why me??? I love you.

She Is Missed

My mind's on vacation because the pain still runs so deep.

May 8, 2007, Tuesday • Scale: 3

ARRAIGNMENT

Hi Sweetheart, do you have any idea how mad I got in court today when I heard the words, "not guilty to all counts?" I mean, I knew in my head that would happen but to actually hear that made me want to RAGE. I just shook my head, honey, in disbelief. How can she say that? Then the cameras in the courtroom and the interviews after? My head was so blank when they asked the questions. I'm just thankful Susan was with me. All I can remember is saying I want justice for what happened and that you should be here with me. I still struggle with that piece, the understanding of why this had to happen. A girl at court said that I am going to be a voice through this. Well, why couldn't I have that voice with you next to me? We would have been so powerful together. We would have been a team and now we can't and that pisses me off. I will always love you. Kisses.

She Is Honored

An arraignment with the media.

May 9, 2007, Wednesday • Scale: 3

Hi Baby, thanks for being with me and sprinkling that KCD on me! Do you think I did okay my first day on the job? Can you believe how many tips I got? I did enjoy myself and I think I will be good as time goes on. Did you see how quick and witty I was a couple times? I know that's you helping me, or did I bless you with your quick wits? I love telling the story to people about the border patrol to your left and the Mexicans to your right. Remember? You are so damn funny, or your, "What? You want shellfish?" It makes me sad to think you will not be able to experience going to a nightclub and dancing. I don't know where you got your soul for dancing but you did not dance like a white girl! Can you forgive me for not protecting you more from this? Did I give you too much freedom and trust in God too much? Do you think I was a good mom? Please let me know somehow.

She Is Missed

Today and forever.

May 10, 2007, Thursday • Scale: 3

Dear Kelsea Lyn, I'm struggling today. I felt like Hawaii was slipping away from me. You know me . . . the phone is our life line and he doesn't get it. I can't blame him, though, because he's never had to be a single parent like me nor had challenging children. Anyways, I miss you terribly. Susan and I had lunch today with Hawaii. I have to say, they are my 2 favorite people since all this has taken place. I don't know where I would be without them. I couldn't go to group tonight. I just really didn't feel like dealing with it tonight. I think because of court and TV, I just couldn't do it. I had a pretty emotionally draining day between Hawaii and Richard. I thought I was going to have a heart attack at Hawaii's. My heart never beat so hard or fast but your Father gave me the wisdom to keep my mouth shut. Thank Him for me. I miss you and love you.

She Is Honored and Missed

Your story told, the arrest, the news and my sharing of anger.

May 11, 2007, Friday • Scale: 3

Hi Hon, happy stupid Friday, hah? You know I still don't like this day. Today I was driving down the street listening to country music and it's crazy how all of a sudden your brain realizes *you're gone.* Then, I get an intense feeling of guilt for enjoying the music and the sun. Then, the sadness and pain that you're not here with me hits. Kels, what is heaven like? Do you have a body and still look like your beautiful self? Do you really have wings like an angel? I'm afraid to go to your pad right now. I'm afraid your stone is going to be there and I don't know how I'll handle it. Will it be hard for me? Please be with me that day, okay? I'm opening at work tomorrow. Help me do well. Are you proud of me for being a bartender? I remember you wanted to work at Hooters when you turned 18. You would have been great at it. I just know it. I was always proud of you no matter what you did. I love you.

She Is Loved

So many comments left on your Myspace; so many friends still writing you.

May 12, 2007, Saturday • Scale: 3

Hi Honey, what a day at work, hah? I'll bet you would have liked to be a bartender because you get a lot of attention and can be a smart ass at the same time. Of course, I forgot my keys to open the bar and had to run home! Susan came in today and it was nice to have her there. I have one problem with the job though, I don't like seeing people leave the bar drunk, then get in their cars and drive. But honey, how could I stop that? Maybe I should just say a quickie prayer for them as they leave for your Father to protect them and get them home safely? So, tomorrow is Mother's Day. Digger is going to church with me, then going to take me to breakfast. I wish you were there with us. Why did God take you, Kelsea? Here come the tears. Here comes the sick stomach and confusion and complete and utter sadness. I love you so much. Kisses.

She Is Honored

I shared your picture with everyone at work today, loving my new job.

May 13, 2007, Sunday • Scale: 2

MOTHER'S DAY

Dear Kels, you're supposed to be here with me and Digger, going to breakfast. Do you celebrate Mother's Day in heaven? Do you all celebrate for all of us still here? Do you all know how terribly missed you are? So I went to your pad and saw your stone placed . . . do you have any idea how mad I was that it was WRONG? I mean, they had the names on the wrong side of the picture and everything was wrong! How could they have messed it up??? I didn't even want to stay but I did. Do you like Griff? Did you see how he just stands there over me? Don't worry, I haven't forgotten about Sassy. She's just so independent now and loves catching mice! Do you see how much fun I am having at work? I only hope it stays that way. Hawaii stopped by and surprised me. We've kind of been distant the last week or so. I hate it but accept it as your Father's will. I love you.

She Is Missed, Loved and Honored

Happy Mother's Day to me . . . your address placed; such a perfect beautiful stone (even though it was wrong).

May 14, 2007, Monday • Scale: 3

Hi Honey, how is heaven treating you? I saw Adolfo and Elda at your pad yesterday. She just kept telling me you are in a better place but how does someone truly know that? I thought about you so much today and just kept getting so sick to my stomach and had to push it out of my head. I still don't think it's a complete reality to me yet. Maybe when it is, it will go hand in hand with acceptance? And to be honest I just don't see that happening, honey; know what I mean? I saw Katie at the gym, she sure loves me. I wish I knew her relationship with you. Were you guys close? Oh, they are going to fix your stone for me. Thank God, I can't have anything less than perfect for us to spend our everlasting life together. I look forward to us together again. I know I have things to do here first though. Help me with them, please? I love you.

She Is Here

Cardio with Okalani . . . the heart rate appears on her machine and she says, "See, Kelsea's messing with me."

May 15, 2007, Tuesday • Scale: 2

Dear Kelsea Lyn, so the days are getting harder again. Is this what I have to look forward to the rest of my life, Kels? I've been crying all day and I screamed so loud in my car my throat hurt. I feel anger creeping in more frequently now. I'm still praying all the time but it's still here. I lost my phone today and I didn't care at all. Every time I look at a picture now, it hurts but I can't stop. Do you know what it's like to cry so hard and no one is around to see it? It's like the pain is so deep that no one can even fathom it. I know you hate me crying but I just can't help it. Today, Hawaii kissed my back, your tattoo. He does that a lot you know. It's so incredibly bitter sweet . . . bitter because you are gone, sweet because I love him, and he brings me happiness. God, Kels, why couldn't you have been here so he could have known you? The yearbook will be out soon and I'm scared to look at the reality of it. I hate this. I hate everything about this but I love you more every second of every day. Kiss.

She Is Missed

I've cried all day today, thoughts of you constantly running through my head.

May 16, 2007, Wednesday • Scale: 3

Dear Kels, hi Sweetheart. Do you see how hard life is for me again? It's like I'm driving down the damn road and WHAM, I realize you're not here and it just knocks me on my butt. My life is so different now. I've lost 2 jobs now since you left. A big part of it is that I simply can't concentrate enough or care enough for the jobs I had. My new job is pretty much a no brainer. It's kind of cool because I can introduce you to people there and share our story. I actually have fun there. It's no stress. I talk to people and can be a smart ass with your quick wits coming through! I hope you're in heaven watching me at work and I am putting a smile on your face. Give me the witty comments and some KCD every shift I work, okay? I love you with all my heart and soul. I miss you so much, Kels. Hugs and Kisses.

She Is Missed

Sometimes I struggle because I see no signs; I know they are there but the pain is too deep to see. . . .

May 17, 2007, Thursday • Scale: 3

Hi Honey, great night last night at work, hah? I really do love that job. I hope I just get better at it. I'm so thankful Hawaii helped me with this. I couldn't meet with Susan today and I really wanted to because things have been rough the last few days with crying a lot. The only solace I have had has been staying with Hawaii at night this week. Tonight at group, Ken wasn't there. I was leery at first because we just had group with no one running it. I talked more tonight than in awhile. Group is hard because it's so damn sad but I know I have to keep going, either to help someone else or to hear something to help me. But, it ran late tonight and I found myself just wanting to get out of there. I had enough tears and sadness and I ran out of there. I just wanted to get home to Hawaii. It's so hard to see new parents, too, with fresh losses because I remember that pain and I don't wish it on *anyone*. I love you.

She Is Missed

I look at your picture and such sadness overcomes me. . . .

May 18, 2007, Friday • Scale: 3

Hi Baby, did you hear all the nice things Hawaii said about if you were here with us? I believe he could have made such a difference in your life. He talks with this love for you when all he knows is my love for you. I talked to a girl at the gym that goes to Sonrise. She said what a blessing it was to have 45 salvations the day of your funeral. She said she had not been able to bring 45 people to the Lord and she's almost 50 years old. Then, on your Myspace, Chelsea wrote about how at Grossmont College one of the

Criminal Justice classes talked about you and the case. Do you realize what an impact you have had in the world? But you know what? I would rather you still be here with me and your brother than to have touched people. I know that's probably pretty selfish but it's the truth. I want you back here now. I don't want to have to write to you. How long do I have left here in this hell? I love you.

She Is Honored and Here

I shared our story at the gym and chills ran through me constantly. . . . I heard a song on the radio and chills ran through me again. . . .

May 19, 2007, Saturday • Scale: 3

Dear Kelsea Lyn, how has your weekend been so far? I know there is no time in heaven, but do you still know it's the weekend here? What do you think you would be doing right now? Desert season is over and river is coming but I know you don't care for river season. How is Melissa? Are you 2 best friends in heaven? Do you see how many things have happened since you went home?

The memorial in the yearbook is going to be so surreal. I'm a little scared. I'm going to ask Lauren to have people sign it for you. I'm a little bummed I can't walk in your graduation for you but I don't know how well I would have held it all together. It's hard to believe you left on the second day of your senior year and now you would be graduating in a couple weeks. You would have gone to Prom, too. I wonder with whom? Maybe Jeanie? I would go to that for you, too, if I could. I would do anything in the world for you. I would have died for you. Did He take you because your life would have been hard? I would have helped you. I love you.

She Is Missed

A huge cricket or roach in the back room of the bar, dead laying upside down, yet still I get the chills and smile at how much you would have jumped.

May 20, 2007, Sunday • Scale: 3

Hi Sweetheart, it was nice visiting you today at your pad. Do you like it when I bring Griff with me? I do like your stone but I will love it when it is perfect and done right. I'm still having a hard time, honey. But I'm also not really allowing myself to process this again. I did talk to a woman at the gym and I got a huge lump in my throat. I also felt the chills run through me again. Is that you touching me? Remember when we heard the song about the girl in the wheelchair having wings and flying away? Remember how we both totally got the chills then? Do you know how much I miss not being able to do things with you? I miss you not sitting in my car with me and listening to the radio so loud that the car next to us at the stop light rolls their window up! I miss not buying you Black and Milds. I miss the hell out of you. I love you.

She Is Honored, Missed and Loved

A visit to your pad, every week without fail.

May 21, 2007, Monday • Scale: 3

Dear Kelsea Lyn, I love you more than the law allows. I'm watching *Deal or No Deal* and you're supposed to be next to me. Why aren't you? Why did God have to take you from me so damn soon? Doesn't He know the pain and hell that I have to live with now? The constant reality that hits me as I drive down the road and realize you're gone? The heartache I feel and the envy I feel of mothers with their teenage daughters? The questions I have when I see mothers with little daughters, wondering if they realize they could lose them one day without any notice. The anger I feel at times when I can't help it? All the questions as to WHY? All the tears I cry when I know how much you hated to see me cry? I know in my heart you would want me to be happy. I just want you to be a physical part of my happiness. I want to hold you and kiss you and play with your hair. I hate all of this!

She Is Honored

You and your case discussed in a college criminal justice class, such an impact.

May 22, 2007, Tuesday • Scale: 3

Hi Honey, it's hard to believe it's been 9 months today. I wish you were pregnant because you would be having a baby in that amount of time. It's crazy how I equate times to the time you have been gone. I'm seeing Chris tomorrow. I have to sign some release papers for your attorney. I'm excited because I miss him. I'll never forget the first time you saw him and how happy you were that your doctor was so hot. He loved and cared about you just like everyone else. I only wish you would have realized how loved you were. I know you knew how much I loved you. Remember when you asked me if I would lose an arm for you? I would have lost my life for you, honey. You and your brother were my life. You know I lived every day for you and fought so much for you and what was right. Do you know I can't get myself to get any coffee from 7-11? Or eat french fries? I'll wait to get to heaven and we can have them together, okay? I love you.

Kisses.

She Is Missed

Still meeting with Susan every week to help me deal.

JOURNAL: ARRESTING ANGER

Finally, an arrest. It's been a little over 8 months after the loss of one of the most precious things in my life and justice is now beginning to rear its head.

It was the end of April when I got the call that I was to meet with the district attorney and the investigator. I showed up at the Department of Justice building in downtown San Diego not knowing what to expect. Over the next hour, everything that I had been praying for was coming—true justice.

As I sat there talking and listening to everything that was going to be happening, it was surreal. An arrest warrant was being issued and within a couple days the woman responsible for killing my daughter would be in jail. No matter how you look at the scenario of what happened, the circumstances, the facts, the underlying truth of the matter is she handed my daughter the pills that killed her.

It was the next morning at about 9 am that I got the call: "She's in custody." I felt good, I felt some peace and I felt justice. Within an hour, the phone was ringing and the news of her arrest hit the internet and that night the television stations. Then, came the anger. For the first time in 8 months I actually felt some anger. I don't think it was a bad anger though. It was completely directed for the first time to Laura Wion. For 8 months I did not allow myself to even think about her but now I had no choice because the next phase of this journey was beginning.

People would ask me how I was able to not go over and confront her or call her. It was simple; I did not want to jeopardize anything for the criminal case I knew would take place. So I laid low, never talking to anyone about it, the facts, the names, anything. It's funny because I couldn't even tell you what she looked like and didn't even recognize her when I saw her in court for the first time. The brain is such a powerful thing and I probably didn't WANT to remember what she looked like.

The arraignment went well. The news was requesting to be in the courtroom and was there waiting. Again, so surreal. I was sitting there with Susan as she held my hand. Laura Wion's husband was sitting right behind me and when I realized that, I raged inside. I was so pissed I couldn't believe he was right there.

The attorneys met with the judge in the judge's chambers before even coming before the court. I have had a feeling for awhile that this was going to potentially be a public event but I had no idea the extent of coverage it would have.

As the judge spoke about the media's request, he asked if the defense had any objections and of course they did. It was beautiful when the judge said that the court recognizes objection . . . overruled, and the cameras went on. Our first victory.

As her attorney stood before the court, I listened carefully to every word spoken. I knew in my head that he had to give a not guilty plea but to have actually heard him say, "Not guilty on all counts" made me rage again.

I thought, *How can you say that? How can you plea not guilty when she did this?* I was crying, holding Susan's hand, and basically unable to move. Her attorney requested bail be lowered and it was granted, but that had no bearing on me. I knew she could not afford even the lower bail so I knew she would remain in custody.

It was a quick court appearance and as we walked out of the courtroom, the media was there immediately. I spoke to Kelsea's attorney about what will be happening next and then to the news. I had one of Kelsea's many beautiful photos clutched in my hand the entire time and the news first shot Kelsea's picture.

Then, they hooked me up, turned the camera on and began the questions. I was unable to speak. My head was completely blank without a single thought or word to answer the reporter. I looked over to Susan for an answer and she looked at me and said, "It's okay." I began to talk, the entire time looking over the reporter's head directly at Susan.

My heart was hurting, my thoughts were now racing and I knew I had to be careful about what I said. A few questions were asked that I refused to answer because I simply did not want to jeopardize the entire case. I do remember one of the first questions asked; "How did you feel when you saw her (Laura) for the first time?" I told the reporter that I couldn't even look at her, and I couldn't. Not once did I look at her or even want to see her. It was bad enough that I had her husband right behind me.

I will say this, if you find yourself in a position of having to speak to the media, find solace in knowing you are not alone. But more important, you are your child's voice. Try to imagine the questions you may have to answer and practice the answer in your head. It will be one of the hardest things you will ever endure as a parent, but you will feel peace in knowing you are honoring your child, still.

Next came the newspaper reporter. He asked me more questions that I could not answer. It was all surreal. I knew that this was going to be big but I had no idea HOW big. I believe, though, that it is all part of God's plan in helping people through Kelsea's loss. A purpose I must find. I have to say loss because death is so final, so harsh and so real.

I know this is just the beginning of yet another journey. A journey no parent should ever have to go through, yet we have no choice. The loss of a child has got to be one of the most choiceless events to ever take place in a person's life. It is not a choice I would wish even on my worst enemy.

As I write that, I think about whether or not Laura is a part of that and I guess if I am being honest, I would say that I do wish she had to experience the hell I will live in for the rest of my life. Hopefully, one day I will feel differently but it is too soon, too fresh, too open-wounded to think any different.

I would have to say over the last month, not much has changed as far as getting "better." I still attend group but I am finding it harder and harder to go lately. I know it is because a lot of times I just repress my thoughts about all this. Then, when I walk into that room with other bereaved parents, it is such a double-edged sword. Everyone tells me I need to continue going and so I do. If I had my way, I wouldn't go. I guess it's in case someone says something that will help me or I may say something to help bring peace to another parent.

I remember one night everyone seemed to be laughing, joking, smiling and I thought to myself, *How?* I was definitely not in the same place they all were. The facilitator mentioned the energy in the room. I brought it to his attention, though, that everyone who was smiling had a lot more time between their loss and mine. He was very understanding and respected those of us with such fresh losses.

I've found it very difficult lately, too, seeing mothers walking around with their teenage daughters. I see mothers carrying around their toddlers, loving on them all happy and I find myself wondering if they even know that their little girl could be taken away from them in an instant.

You don't know when, or how, or why, but it happens. I never in my life ever thought I would lose one of my children, yet I sit here now writing every month on the 22nd my journey. I write a love letter to my daughter still every single night. I write to her on her memorial Myspace page and read the struggles of some of her friends when they write to her, still.

It's crazy, too, the comparisons you make and think of at different times.

Kelsea passed away on the first evening of her senior year. Now, she is supposed to be graduating from high school in another week. I can't even believe an entire school year has passed. She is supposed to be going to Prom. She is supposed to be walking with her high school class at graduation and going to the parties. She is supposed to be starting fashion design school and working at Hooters. Yes, she always wanted to work at Hooters once she turned 18 and she was so stunningly beautiful that I know she would have gotten the job.

She is supposed to be testing to get her driver's license. She is supposed to be living her life as a young adult and she's not. And I have a lump in my throat and tears rolling down my face as I think about all that she is not going to be able to experience.

I have anger for Laura Wion. She took it all away from Kelsea and me. I want justice here on earth because Laura Wion will have to pay the price when she goes before God on judgment day. I pray for the maximum sentence in this and my hopes are that something positive comes out of this.

I'm thinking that, if anything, other parents are going to see the devastation Laura Wion has caused in so many people's lives and the punishment she is going to receive and will think twice about handing another person's child ANY type of medication.

I have also learned that the local junior college is discussing Kelsea's case already. The criminal justice classes will be following this closely and Kelsea will be a tool in their learning. But, to be honest I would rather have her here with me than to help all the people she has helped and is yet to help. I know it is the selfishness in me, but it is also the truth.

I miss her so much, it pains me daily. I have had thoughts over the last couple days again of simply wanting to die. I have laid in bed with my eyes closed, listening to the airplanes flying over the house and just thinking how easy it would be if one of them would just hit the house. This would all be over, all the pain, suffering and yearning.

I am so fresh into this loss and all I keep hearing is the first couple years are as if it just happened and it holds true so far. I spoke to someone in the gym today who lost his 5-month-old son several years ago. Again, he reiterated to me "the first 2 years." He looked at Kelsea's picture and he made the comment that losing a child is horrible, but to lose someone as beautiful as Kelsea is tragic.

As I spoke to him about everything going on, I felt okay. All it took, though, was me saying, "She's supposed to be here," and my eyes filled with tears, my lip started quivering and he knew. He stepped off the cross-trainer and wrapped his arms around me tightly as I stood there in the middle of the gym sobbing. It was another wave that hit and it was big but he was there to hold me as I rode it. He knew how I felt and he knew there was nothing he could say to me. I thanked him.

Next to him on another cross-trainer was a woman who looked at me and asked if it was me she saw on the news. I said yes and she immediately told me how sorry she was for me. After my wave passed, she got off her cross-trainer and hugged me. She again apologized to me and said if I ever needed a hug in the gym, just ask her. I told her that whenever she sees me, to hug me because I won't seek it out, but I welcome it. She smiled and said she would.

I also lost another job this month. I lasted 4 months at the gym I was at when Kelsea passed away and had to leave. I could not handle all the members constantly asking me, "How are you?" I walked out one day and knew I had to find another gym.

I thought it would be better to get into a different environment where not everyone knew what happened. I started doing sales and struggled. I still didn't care. They wanted me to work more hours and my brain simply could not handle it and it shut off. I went in one day as I did at my other gym and just quit. I knew that with the trial coming up and court dates and all the emotions that went along with it all, I would be no good as an employee and that was not fair to my boss or me.

Currently, I am bartending at a little sports bar. It is no pressure and all I do is pour drinks and talk to people. Yes, I tell them about my daughter sometimes. I keep her picture on the bar behind me when I go to work so everyone can see Kelsea, but mostly I have it there so she is with me always.

I brought Kelsea the most beautiful pink angel wind chime the other day when I went to her pad. I hung it on the small tree they recently planted right by her. It's perfect, just like she was.

Mother's day . . . was not as difficult as you would have thought. I would assume because I still have my son and we went to breakfast together and celebrated. It is always nice to do something with him one-on-one. I have found periodically because I am so wrapped up in my pain that I forget he is grieving, too. So, I make an effort at times for us to spend some alone time together. He is going to be 20 soon and has his own life, but he also lost his only baby sister.

I think it's so very important to remember your living children. I know that it is difficult at times and they can easily be forgotten. It's important to recognize they grieve, too. I find it difficult right now to talk about Kelsea with Digger but it is so important. It gives me an opportunity to see where Digger is in his grief so I can get him the help he may need. There are support groups designated for children and young adults who lose their sibling and I encourage parents to seek this out if needed.

It took several months to get Kelsea's headstone delivered but it was finally ready. It came the week before Mother's Day. I was a bit scared, though, at how I would feel seeing it placed. Would it be a reality and hit me hard or would I find solace in it? I went on that Sunday (Mother's Day) to see her and as I drove up I saw it had been placed. I call it her address stone because, once again, headstone to me is too final and sad sounding.

It is a double plot and I will lay with her one day. When I realized they screwed it up, I was furious and didn't even want to stay with her. The stone was beautiful and, when it is done correctly, will be perfect for us. I walked the neighborhood and no one had the stone she had, absolutely no one. That made me happy to know her pad is not like anyone else's around. I call where she is at the neighborhood she lives in because, to me, cemetery is too final. Spoiled again!

A lot has happened over this last month and I know there is a lot more to come. I know I am crying every day again and I don't care. I don't care where I am, who I am with or anything. I am happy about the media coverage because I know Kelsea would have loved the attention. She has an entire memorial page dedicated to her in the yearbook that I am afraid to look at when it comes out.

Several pictures and a couple poems she wrote will be in there. Again, she would have loved the attention.

I also think about it being 9 months now and how if Kelsea was pregnant she would be having a baby in that amount of time. I would give anything for her to have been pregnant and having a baby. But, that is just another thing I have been robbed of in life, watching my daughter marry and have a family. She wanted children so badly. She always used to talk about how strict she was going to be with her kids and how she was going to give them all cell phones with a GPS in them so she knew where they were at all times!

She talked about being rich and having a huge home to live in with a man who would love her so much. That's all she ever really wanted, to be loved, and it's all been taken away from her, me, and her brother . . . it's not fair and it's not right.

So I close this month with all the feelings of the prior months but adding anger to it. If the truth be told, I am happy Laura Wion is in jail and unable to see her family. I am happy she lives in a little room and is told when to do everything. It brings me some peace to know that the wheel of justice has begun turning.

My faith in God is strong enough, too, to know that justice will prevail. I will continue my fight each and every day to walk, talk, function, focus and breathe through this new life.

I will continue waking up each morning that my eyes open up, knowing I have yet another day to live but finding some solace in knowing I am also a day closer to being with Kelsea again.

JEREMIAH 30:17
I will give you back your health and heal your wounds,
says the Lord.

CHAPTER TEN

May 23, 2007, Wednesday • Scale: 2

Dear Kels, were you with me when I went to see Chris? He said he felt you there with us. He said you were more than just a client, that he really cared about you but we both already knew that. I did a lot today for your case, you know. All your medical records will be released now. I've been crying a lot again and the lump in the throat is here. I did get your pink angel wind chime, though, from Dennis. It will be beautiful. Do you see what's happening with Hawaii and I? I just don't get it. Can you talk to your Father and ask Him to help Hawaii forgive himself? He is such a good man but continues to beat himself up. I wish he would realize all I want is to love him. He helps give me hope in my life, Kels, and some joy. He helps me grieve my loss and lets me cry in his arms. I can't think of life without him now but I may have no choice like I had no choice in you leaving. All I can do is pray for strength in both my losses and trust in your Father's will. I love you, little girl. Thanks for listening to me. Kisses.

She Is Honored

A visit with Chris, a trip to Dr. Torchia, a call to Dr. Johnson—all to further your case.

May 24, 2007, Thursday • Scale: 3

Dear Kelsea Lyn, I hope you love the wind chime. It was beautiful out at your pad today. I know I cried hard and prayed harder. I really did enjoy talking to you today. I know I haven't really talked to you lately but sometimes it's really hard. I do know you listened, though, because "Jesus Take the Wheel" was on the radio as soon as I got in the car, thank you. I also went and got more information for Geeni, your investigator. I've actually been doing a lot for your case the last couple days. I do not really like my life right now. I guess I'm just tired of the trials and tribulation God hands me. Is He ever going to bless me with a man who can love me equally? I'm really questioning it. I mean, I know I'm not perfect, hon, but I'm not bad either. Why do people find love so difficult when it's so easy? Maybe that's one good thing you will never have to deal with; a broken heart from a boy. Thank you for listening to me whine. . . . I love you more than the law allows. Kisses.

She Is Here

A pink angel wind chime at your pad, the radio turns off, then back on by itself and "Jesus Take the Wheel" is beginning. . . . I look at the clock and it says 2:22.

May 25, 2007, Friday • *Scale: 3*

Hi Honey, well tonight I had to work at the bar, my first weekend night. It was pretty busy but I think I did okay. You gave me some great witty comments, didn't you? Thanks for the KCD! I'm not used to being up so late though. By the way, I saw Hawaii at the gym and I didn't think I would. My stomach flipped. He quit his job working at the gym, too. We did talk though and I felt better. I understood what he said to me. Then he stopped by work and that's all I want, to love him. I just don't understand why God has put so much on my plate. Why I have been handed so many trials and tribulations. Why do I have to be so strong? One person a day at least tells me how "strong" I am when they hear about what has happened. If I wasn't strong though, I would be dead. I have to care for your brother still and fulfill whatever God's plan is for me. What is it? Kisses and love . . .

She Is Missed

I love you, need you, want you. . . .

May 26, 2007, Saturday • Scale: 3

Hi Hon, busy night last night but slow night tonight . . . oh, well. What's cool about my new job is being able to dress the way I do. I only wish you could have been here to come in and hang out with me. I knew it would have been a few years, but still. I would have taken you to Vegas on your 21st birthday too. I'll bet you would be working at Hooters as soon as you graduated which should have been June 8, 2006. Lauren is going to take your yearbook around and get it signed. I took a nap today. I'm not used to being up so late. But as I got to work, I thought to myself, *I love this job and that's a good thing right now.* I miss you with all my heart. I love you, kisses.

She Is Missed

Stunning, you are.

May 27, 2007, Sunday • Scale: 3

Dear Kelsea, it was such a sunny beautiful day today and I struggle with that because it reminds me of summer and August. I love the weather but then I feel guilty for enjoying it. Church today was on memorials and not forgetting the ones we have lost. I just can't see me doing anything or wanting to even get out of bed on the 22nd of August. It's a day I never want to remember. It's still 3 months away and yet I am dreading it already. I had chest pains today at the end of the day. Hawaii and I went to his best friends for a BBQ. It was fun. I got to talk about you a lot. Do you hear me when I talk about you? You know I talked about you all the time even when you were being stupid. I always loved you no matter what you did, purely unconditional love. I still love you unconditionally. Will I still be your mom in heaven? Do you still look at me as your mom? I miss you being my daughter. I love you tons.

She Is Missed

I look at your pictures and feel such sadness.

May 28, 2007, Monday • Scale: 3

Dear Tat, did you like everyone being at your pad today? I was so surprised to see Tawnia and the kids . . . they ate lunch with you, did you like it? I also had a woman come over to me who said she could tell I was in "deep grief" because of the way I was laying with you like I always do. She was right and it was nice to have someone acknowledge that. I got some sun out there, too. The flowers looked beautiful and I'll bet Steve brought the 2 American flags. It was Memorial Day and I wanted to recognize that with you. You may not have been in the military but you and I definitely fought our own wars. I would have fought every day of my life for you. I'm going to fight this case and win for you, too.

THAT I promise. I wish you were here right now because then I wouldn't be worried about Hawaii because I wouldn't know him. Please watch over him right now and bring him home. Kisses.

She Is Honored

Lunch at your pad with me, Tawnia, Cheyenne, Brayden, Peyton and JT.

May 29, 2007, Tuesday • Scale: 3

Dear Kelsea Lyn, I've had chest pains a lot today and I'm not really sure why. I haven't cried today though . . . at least not yet. It's so hard for me to be going through the day just doing what life hands me and all of a sudden this bullshit that I'm living hits me, the thought that you're not here. How can that be? I can't even tell you how different my life is now. I have so many people telling me that they don't understand how I am able to function and be standing the way I do . . . how strong I really am. Can you ask your Father why He made me so strong? Can you tell Him I would rather be weak and have you here with me . . . that I am selfish and would rather just have you here and have my old miserable life back because, even through all our turmoil, I still loved you and your brother. You know the 2 of you were first before anyone and everything. I love you.

She Is Here

Hawaii's phone talking with no buttons being pushed.

May 30, 2007, Wednesday • Scale: 3

Hi Honey, did you see how much sun I am getting? I haven't had this much color in a long time. Remember how much you loved the beach? We lived there! No matter how cold it was, you always played in the water. Did you know Cory? I know he is with you, Melissa, Jenna, Zach, Brittany . . . why does God take you children from us? I met 2 guys at the bar who lost a son each. Why does God bless us with you, and then take you away? What possible purpose does that serve other than to put us parents in such a place of hell? I'm not sure what happened at work tonight but I felt a little down. It was a busy night and I did well and met some good people but I just wasn't myself. Did you run out of that KCD? I hope you find more by Saturday. I'm getting pretty good though at faking doing shots. You know, I'm not a drinker . . . besides I don't want to get fat. No more burly. I love you, kisses.

She Is Missed

2 men at the bar, both have lost a son . . . from all 3 of us, you are all missed.

May 31, 2007, Thursday • Scale: 1

My Dearest Kelsea Lyn, I knew I felt this wave coming on last night. I've spent the day in bed, crying. I went to see the civil attorney today. Maybe that set it off. I cried in the car, at home and I thought about taking a bunch of sleeping pills and the news reporting, "Kelsea's mom is dead." Then I thought your brother would kill himself, then we would all be gone. Instead, to punish myself, I took some laxatives. I have felt fat lately and out of control with my eating, even though I haven't gained any weight. Susan helped me understand I wanted to punish myself. My divorce is final tomorrow and even though I wanted it, I am grieving that loss, too. I just want my life back. I feel like I have no purpose now and I feel lost. I couldn't even go to group tonight because I'm in a dark place right now and I can't handle more sadness tonight. I wouldn't be safe driving.

We have court tomorrow. I just want to take my Trazodone and go to sleep so this day will be over. I hate this pain and sorrow. I hate going through it alone. Why me? I love you.

She Is So Missed

A tidal wave rolls in as darkness sets.

June 1, 2007, Friday • Scale: 2

Dear Kelsea Lyn Phelps, yet another dark day. Of course having to go to court in the morning doesn't help. I can't believe what Laura Wion is trying to do. She's concerned about things when she took you away from me? I don't know how she can live with herself. How can someone kill someone else's child and live with that? She was laughing with her attorney. Thank God Susan was with me, she kept telling me to breathe. It's crazy how you actually slow your breathing down so much you have to be told to breathe. I have to go back on Monday again to court. I just want justice for you, honey. I've been really confused with Hawaii lately and I get sad because he brings me peace and hope and sometimes I just don't know what he wants or doesn't want. Can you sprinkle some of your LD (Love Dust) on him for me? Please? I know God's blessed me with him because God took you but what do I do now? Guide me baby girl in what you want for me. I love you.

She Is Honored

A court day. . . . I will always be there every second through this court hell.

June 2, 2007, Saturday • Scale: 3

Dear Kels, did you see the 2 nice guys I met at work? They invited me and your brother to the river with their families. It would be fun but, to be honest, I'm a little scared because of Melissa. Should I go? Today was a little better but I worked all day and my mind was pretty busy. Someone on Myspace told me your yearbook is out with your pictures and 2 beautiful poems you wrote. You had your mama's talent when it came to writing. I am going to finish our bipolar book eventually. It's just hard to concentrate on that or anything for that matter right now. It's hard to believe a year ago I was driving you to ECAL for summer school every morning and stopping for our 7-11 coffee. It's not fair, Kelsea Lyn. See, whenever I start to think about this, I get sick still and just want to push it all away, but I can't because this is real and I hate it all. I really hate it all. I want you here with me. I want my little girl back. I love you so much.

She Is Honored

Your picture posted so proudly at the bar for everyone to see.

June 3, 2007, Sunday • Scale: 3

Dear Kels, can you believe who pulled up to your pad when I was visiting you today, Paul? Remember the day you went with me to get that tattoo for him on my ankle? I know, you think I'm stupid! But, you were with me and I will never forget that. It was beautiful out at your pad and I got some good sun. Can you believe how butt-white my legs are? I love spending that quiet time with you, even with all the tears. Did you see the nice leather book that Lauren from church bought me? She knows I have a picture of you at all times and she wanted me to have that. She is a good woman and ask your Father to bless her, please. I worked tonight and that guy dropped me a $50.00 tip! I still can't believe that. I do love my job right now. I don't know, hon, where my life is going or what I'll be doing in a year but I don't really care right now either. I just want to be able to keep breathing and have strength. I love you.

She Is Honored

A visit to your pad and a surprise visitor who asked to sit with me and we talk about you.

June 4, 2007, Monday • Scale: 2

Hi Honey, rough, rough day I know. I don't know if I will be able to handle a trial. Today in court her attorney tried to make you sound like a horrible child. It made me so upset that all I wanted to do was yell at her, "You killed my daughter!" All they kept talking about was her health. Who cares about her health? She killed you, she needs to go to prison for what she did and deal with the reality that she took the life of an innocent 17-year-old girl. I was wiped out when I walked out of there. I came home and slept. I've been doing that a lot lately . . . staying in bed.

I still can't sleep if I don't take my Trazodone. Do you see how much Hawaii supports me when I'm grieving? He just held me while I sobbed today, hard. We had a nice dinner at this house and I know he's only in my life because you are not. I know God blessed me with him for taking you from me. I love you so much, Kelsea Lyn. Are you happy for me? Kisses and hugs.

She Is Honored

Yet another day in court, all in support of you and justice.

June 5, 2007, Tuesday • Scale: 3

Hi Sweetheart, it's hard to believe you are supposed to be graduating from high school in a few days. Why did God have to take that away from me? I know you would have made it and I would have owed you $500.00 for straight A's. Colleen pointed something out to me today. She said you got straight A's in summer school, you had a good boyfriend, you were home that night, your toxicology report was clean, you were in therapy regularly . . . you were on such a good path again. This whole court process is going to be hard. If ever I had to keep my mouth shut, it's going to have to be now. I worked an extra shift tonight. Did you see how busy I was? The people there truly are compassionate to what happened to us. I've gotten so many numbers to people who just want to listen to me. I don't want to talk, though, most of the time. I would never reach out to them, I don't think. I don't know, hon; I just wish I had all my old life back with you and all our drama. There was nothing you could have ever done to diminish my love for you, it's still unconditional. Kisses.

She Is Missed

I ask for you to be with me . . . where are you?

June 6, 2007, Wednesday • Scale: 3

Hi Honey, I had to baby sit early this morning for Tawnia. I realized all the patience God blessed me with for you and Digger is gone. I had a baby that wouldn't stop crying and I got frustrated and struggled with that. I always loved babies. They never cried around me. I remember being told I had the patience of Job. Not anymore. I also find myself looking away from people because I just don't want to talk to them. I always had a smile and a hello for everyone and that's all gone. Why would God take you and all those good qualities away from me? I've been spending a lot of time with Hawaii again. Is he my blessing from God? He does bring me peace when I need it and gives me hope for a future.

He holds me when I need to cry, like today. I only wish I could have you both here physically with me. Do you like him? I know he loves you . . . just like me.

She Is Honored

18 kisses on my Kelsea Lyn tattoo from Hawaii . . .

June 7, 2007, Thursday • Scale: 2

Dear Kelsea, I don't think a day will ever go by now that I won't tell you I love you always. I went to Westhills and got the picture back that I used for your senior picture. You are so beautiful. I made copies at Walmart and shared it at group tonight. There was a woman tonight who found her daughter, like I did. It was crazy to be able to identify with someone at even a deeper level. We exchanged phone numbers. We talked tonight at group about tomorrow. I don't know what to expect. I hope a wave doesn't come over me knowing you should be graduating. I'm going to spend the day with you though. I would have if you were still here so I will tomorrow. I spent most of the day crying. Hawaii's daughter graduated tonight. He's very blessed to have his family. I only wish I still had my whole family, you, me and Digger . . . that was our family. I love you.

She Is Missed

Tears sporadically all day long, sorrow and sadness.

June 8, 2007, Friday • Scale: 3

GRADUATION DAY

Dear Kelsea Lyn Phelps . . . congratulations on graduating from high school; there is no doubt in my mind that you would have pulled it all together and did it. I guess I'll have to find something to do with the $500.00 I would have owed you. I hope you love the roses I brought. I know it was a pretty generic balloon but you got the picture. I have to admit the red roses look beautiful. I'm so glad I got the water cup placed at your pad to keep all the flowers fresh. It's a beautiful day out here right now and I'm getting some good sun and color. I know you hated laying out with me but now you don't have a choice! I hope you watch over all your friends today and tonight. Protect them, honey, from any harm, okay? No other parents need to enter into hell with me.

Hawaii has had a few dreams about you. It warms my heart when he tells me them. You are always lying in bed with both of us just talking away. We have your senior picture in a beautiful frame on his wall unit. Did you like the letter I wrote to him from you? I know that's what you would have said to him. You realize, once again you are spoiled. Do you ever see any-one spend as much time at other pads as I do??? People come and go but nooooooooooo! Not your mama. She loves spending time with you, always. Back to dreams . . . why don't you come into mine? I've only had dreams where I couldn't find you and I was panicking. I just need you to come visit me so I can feel you, hug you, touch and smell you.

If I could change one thing it would be that I would have taken you shopping for school clothes, shopping like you wanted to and I wouldn't have worried about Steve getting mad. You would have been with me then that afternoon and wouldn't have gone to Jamie's house. You wouldn't have been given those pills and I wouldn't be sitting at the cemetery with you. I would be proud of you graduating and I would be looking forward to your next endeavor at fashion design school. But, I can't go back. This is a final choice that God took upon Himself, for what reason I don't know. I know I love you, miss you and need you every single day of my life. XXXOOO

She Is Here and Honored

The phone rings as I'm placing a dozen roses and balloon on your pad, it's unknown caller ID. . . . I say hello and I hear nothing and it's gone. Meowing cats, so loud like they're right here and they're not . . . spending the day with you.

June 9, 2007, Saturday • Scale: 3

Hi Honey, what a great night we had last night, hah? I put your picture up high in the bar for everyone to see. Do you see how sunburned my legs got? Oooops! I'm actually getting some good color and it feels good. Can you believe, too, how much I made in tips? I'm pretty tired, though, today. You know, I wish you were here so I could talk to you about what Hawaii did right now. It's times like now I wish I was with you so I don't have to deal with life's crap. I can't imagine life with nothing but hope, joy and love. This world really does suck. I'm really getting tired of trials and tribulation. Can you talk to your Father and ask him to just bless me with hope, joy and love? All I want in life, Kels, is to be able to love unconditionally. To pass the love I gave you onto someone else. Its times like right now I'm just tired and want to stay in bed and sleep. Help me through this one, Kels. I love you.

She Is Missed

I need you today; my head is spinning.

June 10, 2007, Sunday • Scale: 3

Hi Sweetheart, I'm not sure who the woman was in church today who held me while I cried, but ask your Father to bless her for me. It was beautiful at your pad today again. It's so peaceful out there. Did you see the bishop who came back to see me after he left? He wasn't really sure what drew him to turn and come back to me, but I shared our story with him. Do you have an idea how much I miss you? How much I miss touching you? Seeing you smile? Watching you put your makeup on and straighten your hair? Change your clothes a 100 times a day? How much I miss your messy room? Having to buy you Black and Mild cigarettes? Watching you look for re-fries? I miss our closeness. I miss taking you to school and picking you up. People ask me every day, how are you standing? Honestly, honey, I don't know. I wish I wasn't so damn strong so maybe you would still be here with me. I hate being strong. I love you so much . . . kisses.

She Is Missed, Honored and Loved

Lunch at your pad with you.

June 11, 2007, Monday • Scale: 2

Dear Kelsea, I hated today. I hate drama, turmoil, frustrations and mistrust. I know you saw what happened today with Hawaii. I believe your Father brought us together but what is He trying to teach us right now? Communication? Trust? Why the trials right now? Haven't I had to deal with enough emotional distraught? I couldn't even imagine you having to go through what I did. You would have probably knocked her out. I don't know why God has graced me with so much patience, understanding and forgiveness. I just don't want to be made a fool right now. I need guidance in this relationship and wisdom. What's that saying, "Once, shame on you; twice, shame on me?" But, I know you see how much I love him. He's good to me. I just wish he trusted me more. I've been through a lot of bullshit in my life and have experience . . . trials and tribulation is what has made me who I am today. I love you.

She Is Missed

So much turmoil, so much confusion, I needed to talk to you today.

June 12, 2007, Tuesday • Scale: 3

Hi Sweetheart, I enjoyed my visit with you today even though I wrote in my journal to Hawaii. It's like when I have turmoil in my life, I just come visit you and it all calms me down. It's so peaceful at your pad. I know, the back of my legs got sunburned again. Tawnia saw it and said, "Boy, Kelsea would be pissed at you!" I never knew how much my tanning upset you. I knew it was because of my cancer. Hey, just think how much sooner we would be together! But that would not be fair to your brother. He needs me and I need him. I hope, I TRUST, that you are with him all the time. Is he a good gambler? I know he loves going up to Barona Casino. He goes with Ryan all the time. Remember when you had to sneak away with Ryan so Digger wouldn't know? He had such a crush on you. So many boys loved you and you never knew it . . . thank God. I love you.

She Is Honored, Missed and Loved

A trip to your pad, a good talk and a good cry.

June 13, 2007, Wednesday • Scale: 3

Dear Tat, have I told you lately how much I love you? I think actually I tell you that every day still. It was another beautiful day today and I washed Hawaii's car so I could get more sun. It looked perfect. I sure wish Tawnia could have given you her red Ranger. You would have looked so damn cute in that truck, all tricked out. You know she was going to give you that for your 18th birthday.

Tawnia loves you so much but you knew that. Work tonight was okay. It was pretty slow . . . no freaks at least. I really do love that job and I show your picture so proudly. So many guys ask who you are and want to get hooked up. You would be dangerous the older you got, with your beauty and heart. I miss you more than life and I want you back. Kisses.

She Is Here

As I sit at the computer, static through the radio . . . it's not turned on and I haven't touched it.

June 14, 2007, Thursday • Scale: 2

Dear Kelsea, good day with Susan. I haven't met with her for 4 hours in a long time. She is such a blessing in my life as my life coach. She said a lot of things to make me think about what's going on in my life. I think she was the devil's advocate today. Group sucked like always. I really hate going to it these days, but I don't really have a choice. I guess one day I might hear something that will help me or give me some peace. It's just so damn sad there that I guess I don't feel like dealing with the pain because I've gotten good at masking it to people. The funny thing is it *never* goes away, ever. I cried in the gym through my workout today. It just hits you whenever the hell it feels like rearing its ugly head. I hate that this is my life now. I want my old, miserable life back with you in it and all our fights. I love you.

She Is Honored

Every week I make it to group as painful as it is . . . it is to honor you.

June 15, 2007, Friday • Scale: 3

Hi Sweetness, another Friday without you. I don't think there will ever be another Friday I won't long for that 3 am phone call from you. I would trade everything in my life right now to have you back. I truly believe no matter how tough your bipolar illness would have been, I would have been right by your side fighting for you. I see homeless people and know they probably suffer from some type of mental illness. I think I would not have let that ever happen to you. I would have died trying to save you, just like losing all my eye lashes from the stress you caused me. I would lose all the hair on my body from stress to still have you here. Like you asked me one day, yes, I would have lost an arm for you. I would have given my life for you. Can you see how much I love you? Do you know how much I miss you? This still isn't real. I love you so much.

She Is Honored

I couldn't stop telling stories about you today to Okalani and we laughed.

June 16, 2007, Saturday • Scale: 3

Hi Baby girl, I miss you. I went to the beach today with Hawaii. Remember how I used to take you and Digger every week? You could go in the water no matter how cold it was. I guess that explains your love of winter and the rain. I'm actually watching *Ice Age* right now. Do they have Disney movies in heaven?

Do you remember anything about your life here on earth? They say that once you get to heaven you don't remember your life here. I was told once, too, that heaven is such a beautiful place that we can't know how wonderful it is because, if we did know how glorious heaven was, we would all be checking out just to get there. It made sense to me actually. Tomorrow is Father's Day and I feel bad for your dad. I know he is going to struggle. I know he's grieving horribly and I hope you are with him, too. I love you, Kelsea Lyn. Kisses.

She Is Loved

Ice Age on TV, your favorite movie. . . . I watched it for you.

June 17, 2007, Sunday • Scale: 2

Dear Kels, I know . . . I missed church today. Please, tell your Father I am sorry but I got called into work. Work was okay. I don't think I have worked there one day that I haven't told someone our story. Today, though, I had chest pains.

Kelsea Lyn, I hate crying. I hate thinking about this whole thing because I get sick. Digger and I went to dinner tonight and you are supposed to be there with us. I feel like I am just burying everything right now. All my feelings, pain . . . it's like right in front of me, but I just don't want to touch it or feel it or see it. But, I don't have a choice because it's in my face, it's real and I can't do a damn thing to change it. I still don't understand why God would bless me with you to take you only 17 years later. See, I just lost it. I hate this. I flash on finding you. Why?

All you wanted to do was go to sleep. You didn't know you wouldn't wake up. THIS KILLS ME. Help me. I love you.

She Is Missed

Stopping my thoughts, pain and sorrow . . .

June 18, 2007, Monday • Scale: 3

Hi Honey. . . . I needed that sleep last night. I've been getting run-down and I remember what Ken said, "Exhaustion is grief's worst enemy." I took a couple good sleeping pills. If I try to sleep without them, I still can't; my head just spins. I wonder sometimes if I'll have to take them the rest of my life. I worked an extra shift tonight. There are so many guys I meet at work that look at your picture, hear me talk about how funny you are, how caring and they all say they would have loved to know you, date you, even marry you! I did have that freak though. Did you see how quick and witty I was about that other guy being my husband? I know that you were helping me. Of course, I know you got your quick wits from me and your huge heart and beautiful eyes. We looked so much alike, I can see it now. I love you.

She Is So Beautiful and Honored

Your story told over and over and over again at work. A guy looks at your picture and tells me he would have married you . . . a clean-cut guy.

June 19, 2007, Tuesday • Scale: 3

Dear Kelsea Lyn, can you believe still all your friends who are still profess-ing their love to you on Myspace? It brought on such a wave today. I haven't cried that hard in awhile. I'm so thankful, though, that Hawaii knows what to do when I ride these waves of pain. I was literally weak after crying. I know how much you hate me crying, but how can I stop? The hole in my heart will never be filled again. You will never be replaced and I can only try to imagine what your relationship will be when I get to heaven. Will I be able to resume the job of being your mama? I hate the fact you cannot get married and have a baby like you wanted so badly to do. You would have been a great mother and wife. I would have been proud of you. I'm still proud of you, always. Your beauty is still stunning. I can see your beautiful wings . . . I love you, Kels.

She Is Missed and Honored

Reading your Myspace comments from your friends still, and a huge wave of pain and sorrow rolls in.

June 20, 2007, Wednesday • Scale: 3

Hi Tat, did you see how well court went for Tawnia? I know you are with her there. I was pooped today from being up with Digger last night. Thank you for watching over him, Kels. I know you kept his truck from hitting that wall. 2 different people mentioned to me that you were there with him. Between that and my prayers, I think he will get through this "child' stage. Do you see how well things are going with Hawaii? I'm happy with him, I just will always wish you could have met him. You would have loved him, honey. I've kind of found myself on another vacation. It's strange how your mind is able to know when the grief is too much and the pain needs to go away or you just want to die. I'm going to take the good sleeping pills tonight because I need the rest. Your Trazodone works okay. I'm up to 100 mg now. Remember how bad that knocked you out? Did you see the poem I wrote for Hawaii's birthday gift? I think he'll like it. You brought us together and I love you for that, but I hate that you are gone. I hate writing that. It makes me sick. I love you.

She Is Here

I ask you to be with me today. I hear several little "beeps" from no where, no explanation. The treadmill, I hold onto the heart rate monitor and get nothing. The second I let it go . . . 161 pops up and proceeds to descend all the way down to 42, making me laugh, and I trusted.

June 21, 2007, Thursday • Scale: 3

Dear Kelsea Lyn, there was a woman at group tonight; her daughter was just like you but 3 years older. She was bipolar, non-medicated, dropped out of school, self-medicating. . . . I know you were in school and doing well though. It hit home so hard I lost it. I read your poems and showed the yearbook. I told the mother that I write you a letter every night. A few people thought that was really special. It is. Ken even said we want to publish it at the end of a year. That would be cool, but I shouldn't have to be writing you a letter every night. Sometimes I get tired of everyone talking about your "purpose' while you were here, all the people whose lives you affected. It's just my selfishness that doesn't care about any of that and there's a part of me that would be miserable again to have you here. I would live in turmoil to be able to help you. I would live with stress and worry to have you here with me because I want to think I would have helped you through all of it. You and me, little girl. Now, I have none of it. I want I, I want you. I love you.

She Is Honored

The yearbook pictures and poems I shared at group.

June 22, 2007, Friday • Scale: 2

Dear Kels, here I lay at your pad in the beautiful sun and warmth. There is a new neighbor in your neighborhood and my heart goes out to all the people. My pain is as deep as theirs, still. I don't know if they lost a child but a loss is a loss and it hurts so much. I wish we didn't ever have to experience the pain of loss. I wish we all knew exactly what happens once we leave earth but we don't. I know I have my faith and I'll see you in heaven. I see you waiting for me to hold my hand as we enter the Kingdom. But all of those images do not make any of this pain and sorrows go away. At least not yet. I wonder sometimes if the pain stops. I think about how 10 months ago today, my life vanished as I knew it.

Just overnight I went from a life to a living hell. Again, I ask myself how I have the strength to walk, talk and breathe. What is it, Kels, that keeps me moving and able to live? Is it you? Ken said the first way to honor our children is to live.

Why does it not feel like I'm honoring you that way? This pain sucks. I shouldn't have to be writing to you. I should be talking to you. I miss you.

She Is Honored, Missed and Loved

Flowers, Propel water, journaling, crying . . . all on the 22nd of this 10th month in which I have learned to hate.

JOURNAL: WHO'S THE VICTIM?

Ten months. I just can't comprehend that my beautiful little girl has been physically out of my life for 10 months now. I haven't been able to hear her voice, see her smile, watch her laugh, touch her hair, smell her, hug her or tell her how much I love her.

I don't think anyone can even fathom the loss of a child unless you live it.

You are robbed of so much of your life when your child is gone. If you think about the simplest things in life, saying good morning each day, saying good night at the end of the day, watching your once little girl put makeup on so perfectly as you sit in amazement at how she learned to do that. If you think about life without your child, you think about hell.

Over the last month so much has come about in this court case story. I made the decision that no matter what amount of time it took that I would be in a courtroom. I would be there. If I walked in the courtroom just to hear the judge say, "Continued," I would be there. Kelsea's attorney sees my conviction in this and I have always fought for Kelsea. This would be no different. If anything, this is even more of a fight, all in her honor.

So, over the last month I have had to deal with several court days. Laura Wion, who took my daughter's life, seems to be experiencing medical problems while in custody. She apparently lost a significant amount of weight. She experienced symptoms of withdrawal the same as a heroin addict experiences when they are trying to kick the drug.

I have a clear understanding of this because of my 10 years as a deputy.

I have seen many women kick heroine and methadone when they came into custody and were unable to take the drugs.

I had to go to court for a bail review. Her attorney made many claims of insufficient care while in custody. I will say this about being in custody especially when you are a high profile case; the care is good. The sheriff's department covers their tracks and had Wion evaluated at a reputable hospital by their pain management unit. She was found to be overmedicated by this unit and her medication was adjusted accordingly.

This adjustment led to her withdrawals. If I am being honest, I think to myself, *So what?* She took the life of my daughter and here I am sitting in court listening to her attorney talk about the concern of his client's health. What about the health of my child? What about the fact that my daughter was bipolar and this woman knew that.

I found myself raging while sitting in the courtroom having to listen to this trivial bullshit about the health of a woman addicted to pain medication. The bail had been reduced but not significantly. I looked at Susan at one point and told her that I didn't know if I could handle this. I have already made up my mind that, if this goes all the way to trial, I am not too proud to know I will have to take some type of medication to help me through the hard court days.

Then, yet another court day. Once again, we were sitting in this courtroom discussing the health of this woman. It's as if the death of my daughter wasn't even a topic. How could that be? Why were we sitting here in court talking about nothing but this woman's health? What I did learn was her weight loss was a lie.

Originally, her attorney stated she had lost approximately 10 pounds over the month she was in custody. It was beautiful when the sheriff's department had a witness from the medical staff that said he wanted to clear one thing up first and foremost. This woman had actually put 1 pound on since she came into custody.

When it was all said and done, the judge this time around decided to let Wion out of custody and released to her home. There were stipulations made to her release. One was that no minors could be present in her home. I was upset that she was being released, but I was also told by my attorney that it really meant nothing. I have to trust in this as part of the justice that will prevail.

I will say Laura Wion would not even look at me in court. When the judge said he was releasing her, her husband began to cry. I just thought to myself, *Shut up. How could he be crying? He didn't lose his 17-year-old daughter. His life had only been affected for the last month having to live without his wife. How would he feel never being able to see her, touch her, and feel her again?*

The premise behind her being released was that she was costing the county too much money in medical expenses. She had seen the nursing staff over 100 times, the physician approximately 23 times and the psychiatrist 3 times in a 30-day period. That does not include her trip to the pain management unit or trip to the emergency room when she began having seizures.

Yes, I understand the judge's decision and reasoning behind the release, but I do not have to like it. I would rather she remained in custody. Now, I have over a month before my next trip to court to hear if she is going to try to plea out. Kelsea's attorney, Chris, told me he doesn't foresee coming to any type of agreement with Wion's attorney and believes it will be going to pretrial the first part of August.

Graduation came and went and it all happened without Kelsea. You see, everything in life continues on as if nothing happened when you're not directly involved. Originally, I wanted to walk in Kelsea's honor but I was told I couldn't. Under normal circumstances, I would have fought that decision but honestly, I didn't have the energy. So, instead on June 8, 2007, I brought my daughter a beautiful bouquet of red roses and a graduation balloon. I sat with her a good portion of the day out at her pad and I did the usual: I laid down with her first and cried, then I got on my knees and prayed, then I sat up and talked to her.

The day was not as hard as I thought it would be. I still got to spend it with my daughter and I find going out to her pad so very peaceful. Since she has passed away, I have been out to see her once a week, sometimes twice. My visits vary in length but I am always there longer than anyone else and that makes me smile. I always talk to her and tell her how spoiled she still is by me being there so long.

One day, I was writing in my journal to her and I saw a woman sitting with whomever she lost. This woman was there as long as I was and I saw her writing also. When I was getting ready to leave she was, too. I walked over to her and asked who she was visiting and she told me her mother. Her mother had passed away 3 months ago and they were just recently able to bury her.

I showed her Kelsea's picture and told her I lost my daughter. We briefly discussed how Kelsea passed away. This woman proceeded to open her heart up to me and tell me about her children and how they were addicted to drugs. I gave her a hug. She told me she was just talking to her mom and I told her to never stop because her mom hears everything she is saying and I hugged her again. I knew Kelsea was looking down on me smiling, saying to all her friends up in heaven, "See, there goes my mom again, being nice."

Kelsea used to ask me all the time, "Mom, why do you have to be so damn nice to everybody?" She always sounded annoyed by it but I know deep down inside her huge heart, she loved the fact her mom was so kind to people. There have been times I have gone out to her pad and all the flowers and plants in the pots all around the cemetery had been blown over by the wind. I would go and stand each of them back up and straighten them out before I left and I just knew Kelsea was smiling and laughing, and that made me smile.

I have started a new routine when I leave her pad. There is a song on the CD made for her funeral that I play for her now, "In the Arms of an Angel." I open the door to my car and turn it up so loud that all her neighbors can hear it, too. I sit with her and sing to her and I kiss her when it's over and tell her good-bye.

I recently read in a book about a father who went to visit his daughter at her pad (grave) every Sunday for the last 16 years. I see myself there one day, too.

I think I have found myself again taking a vacation from the pain this last month. When I say that, it simply means I don't allow myself to think about her being gone. There isn't a day that goes by, or even an hour, that I do not think about my daughter, but it's a fleeting thought that does not allow me to enter into the torture chamber or jump on that wave. Because the truth is if I was to allow myself to think about her being gone, I still get sick to my stomach and the crying comes on strong.

I've found myself driving down the road and here comes this thought, Kelsea's gone. How can it be? Why? Then the lump in the throat . . . the tears, pain, sorrow. A person can only handle so much of that at once and so I push the thoughts away and try to switch my thinking to something else. For the most part, I am able to do that but at times I still find myself riding that wave. The man who came into my life 6 months ago is still here for me, the one whose lap I crawled into like an infant and cried.

I will say that this man has become such a large part of what I believe to be some of my healing. He has been a blessing in my life since Kelsea has gone home and I am eternally grateful for that. But, if the truth be known, I would give anything or anyone to have Kelsea back.

I have to wonder why every morning I'm still breathing. I guess it's the same reason the sun comes up and goes down every day because that's just the way it is right now until I'm with Kelsea again.

1 THESSALONIAN 3:4
*Even while we were with you, we warned you that troubles
would soon come and they did, as you well know.*

CHAPTER ELEVEN

June 23, 2007, Saturday • Scale: 3

Hi Honey, crazy busy last night at work. I didn't share our story with any-one though. I could have but I just didn't feel like it. That's the first time, now that I think about it, I didn't feel like sharing. It's hot out today and all I'm going to do is lie around. You know I don't have too many days I do that. I'm not even going to go to the gym. Kels, would your life have been a living hell with your bipolar illness? I wish you could have helped me understand more how much pain you lived in every day. The emotional pain inside your head must have been horrible and I'm sorry I couldn't have helped you more. I tried to do my best for you all the time. We didn't fight really at all and when we did, I understood it was your illness. I guess that's a blessing. But why would God take you from me? I am a mom who lived her life for her children and every decision made was for them. I just don't get it yet. I hate this feeling, this loss, and this emptiness. I love you.

She Is Missed

Thoughts of you every hour of this day . . .

June 24, 2007, Sunday • Scale: 4

Dear Kels, can you believe your brother went to church with me today? I am on a mission to save him, honey. He's going down a path of destruction. I don't think I could survive and live if God took him from me, too. I know I couldn't. The beach was nice today. I went off alone and thought about the times I would bring you and Digger to the beach. I looked around at how beautiful everything was and I cried. I miss you so much that words can't even describe it. It's like, if I start to think about the reality of this whole thing I get sick and could easily ride a wave. So, instead my brain just takes these vacations from it. I'm on one now, I think. I still think about you every hour of the day but I won't let myself go into that torture chamber; it's too painful and it creeps up on its own without me opening that door myself. Do you see how good Hawaii and I are doing? He brings me peace and makes me smile and I thank you for that. I love you. XOXO

She Is Honored and Missed

A quiet moment taken away at the beach . . . watching all the children play in the bay and remembering our times spent at the beach as tears roll down my face.

June 25, 2007, Monday • Scale: 4

Hi Sweetheart, did you enjoy our visit? I like going out to your pad to see you because it's so peaceful. I know, I still cry, pray and cry some more. Do you like the song I play for you now before I leave, "In the Arms of an Angel." I have to tell you, Kels, I'm struggling, feeling guilty. I feel guilty because I am so happy with Hawaii. I've been thinking that all the trials I have lived through brought me the happiness I feel now. Don't get me wrong, honey, I would give ANYTHING to have you here with me. I would lose all my eyelashes again just to be able to see that smile of yours or get that call that you're on your way to the desert or that 3 am call that you're drunk at 7-11. Maybe I'm crazy for wanting that stress back but I love you unconditionally and all the hard times come with your smile, your hot wings, your quick wits and attitude! I miss the hell out of you. Do you miss me? I love you. Kisses.

She Is Honored

More flowers at your pad, reading a book, praying and talking to you aloud.

June 26, 2007, Tuesday • Scale: 4

Hi Honey, it was rough today. I was with Hawaii at his daughter's house. She has a little girl, a baby. One of her friends came over and she had 2 beautiful little girls. I watched them loving on the little girls and it hurt. I don't get jealous, I'm envious. I wonder why and I think about how I used to throw you around, tickle you, love on you. I was afraid she was going to ask me if I had any children and I just didn't want to deal with it. Thank God she didn't. I have to say, I was really busy today and didn't have a lot of time to think about how sad my life is without you. That's a good thing sometimes though. I always wake up thinking of you and go to sleep thinking of you and I don't ever see that changing. If I even remotely begin to think about that morning my stomach gets so ill.

That's when I start repeating, "I can do all things through Christ who strengthens me." I believe that. I love you. Kiss.

She Is Missed

I always have thoughts of you every single day.

June 27, 2007, Wednesday • Scale: 3

Dear Tat, have I thanked you for bringing Hawaii into my life? My only regret is that the 2 of you did not get to physically meet. I tell him about you all the time so he kind of knows you. I hope you hear me when I talk to you about him. He's a good man and cares about your brother. Does your Father ever get tired up there of hearing me cry when I pray? I know I lost it today in the room. Tawnia saw my bloodshot eyes and I told her I just had a moment. Her response was, I better get used to them because they never go away, and she's right. I think I will cry every day for the rest of my earthly days, some days harder than other days. Do you enjoy my letters I write to you every night? I hope so because I love writing to you. This is the hardest journey and trial a person will ever endure. I hate it. I don't want and didn't ask for this journey but I am powerless in what has happened and I hate it all, but I love you. Kiss.

She Is Missed

A quiet moment alone in my room, with prayer and tears for you.

June 28, 2007, Thursday • Scale: 4

Dear Kelsea Lyn, wow . . . did you see what a mental health day today was? Thank God for Susan. She has become such a trusted friend to me and savior. She helps me to realize that although I do not want to go to group, I have to. It's like tonight, this new mom spoke directly to me and said, she is a sponge for other people's feelings and she said she felt my pain from the second I walked in as she cried for me. Her loss was only 2 weeks ago. I don't think they realize that all week I take a vacation from the pain but every Thursday I allow myself to go to that place and feel. It's safe at group. It sucks but it's safe. That's how Susan explained it and it made sense. I also feel like I'm growing apart from your brother. He's angry with me and I think it's because I spend so much time with Hawaii, but I have to start cutting the strings, right? Can you please watch over him for me and guide him? I miss you more than life itself and learned that this pain gets "softer." When? I love you.

She Is Honored

Group, reading your poems out loud.

June 29, 2007, Friday • Scale: 1

Dear Kelsea Lyn, today was one of the hardest days since you went home to heaven. Today, I learned how truly *raw* my grief can become when faced with adversity. It's like all that needs to happen is one event to send me tumbling into hell again with the pain, a place I don't ever wish anyone would have to go, yet there I was. You know how much I love children and Hawaii? Well, to have one of his children judge me without knowing how much I fought for you and your brother, it just took me down. I'm struggling to get back up again and to breathe. It's like I didn't realize how close I am to the bottom of this pit. No one understands, not even Hawaii on this one. All I wanted tonight was for him to love on me because I miss you and need you and I just wanted comfort. Please, talk to your Father for me and ask Him to bless me with guidance, wisdom and the right words when I speak. I can't handle this new "normal" life I am supposed to live. I want you back. I hate all this . . . kisses and loves.

She Is Missed

Such a hard day, I needed you so badly.

June 30, 2007, Saturday • Scale: 3

Hi Honey, do you like the red, white and blue flowers? It was really hot out at your pad today. I think I was the only one there today. We had a big birthday party today. A year ago, you were there playing so innocently on the slip and slide. Remember, you asked Tawnia if you could live with her for awhile to get yourself together before you started school? You were getting so mad at this one little boy who kept cutting in line and being mean to everyone. It's times like that, watching you, that I saw the little girl in you who really was a child. I know you were struggling in life but for a few hours you seemed like a normal girl.

Would your life have been terribly hard? I had begun to worry about you and your bipolar illness. We talk a lot in group about having a bipolar child. Unless you have a bipolar child, Kels, you just can't understand. It's the same as people unable to understand the loss of a child. I'm sorry you were so sick and I couldn't help you more. I love you, Kels.

She Is Honored

Always a visit to your pad, this time red, white and blue flowers to help you celebrate the 4th of July.

July 1, 2007, Sunday • Scale: 3

Hi Honey, okay so a couple things happened at work tonight; I know you were there with me. First, it was pretty cool when you pushed the shot glass off of the shelf behind the bar. Someone said, "Who did that?" I said, that was my daughter!

Then a bit later, over in the corner . . . were you pissed??? Or were you just really wanting to make me feel good because that was one heavy bar stool you pushed over. There was no earthquake, no wind and no one near the stool and it fell over and hit the ground. Again, I said that was my daughter. I believe it was you, Kels. It was a good night at work. I had a good workout at the gym, too. I spent a lot of time talking to Tawnia. Things are going well with Hawaii. Don't you love what he wrote to you on Myspace? We are getting along so well, honey. Do you like him? Do you think he's good to me? I see me spending my life with him. I only wish you and Digger and I and he could have been a family. He says you're a blessing. I love you.

She Is Here

A shot glass flies off the bar, a bar stool is knocked over and no one is near it and it's obvious it was you.

July 2, 2007, Monday • Scale: 2

Dear Kelsea Lyn, so today Lonnie was at the gym and he said to me, "Next month will be a year." My brain has not wrapped itself around this whole thing yet. Then, I had to drive by the old house and through your old stomping ground and it triggered a tidal wave. I will always remember how mad you got when I cried and I know it was only because you loved me so much. I experienced crying, the lump in my throat, chest pains, and my finger writing OCD is back.

You're supposed to be here to tell me to stop writing. Digger and I are fighting a lot right now. I just wish he would reach out for some help in his grieving process, you know? Honestly, I can't even think about the waves that are going to roll in over the next 2 months. I think I will go see the doctor and see about getting some medication to get me through the 22nd of August. I know how to reach out and you know I'm not too proud. I love you.

She Is Missed

A drive past the house, a tidal wave hits. . . .

July 3, 2007, Tuesday • Scale: 3

Dear Kels, well, the physical signs of grief have been here for 2 days in a row now. My stomach has been sick and food flies through me. Today has been okay. I've been questioning a lot of things today. I haven't spoken to your brother now in over 24 hours. Do you realize I have never gone that long without talking to him? Can you please watch over him extra close for me? I feel like I'm losing him and I can't do that because I would die for sure then. If I lost the both of you, there would be no purpose in life. I know God has made me strong but I just couldn't do it. I'm going out with Colleen tonight. I know you'll be with us. Do you like the letters so far? Do they make you smile even when they are sad? It's just me spending the last few minutes of each day with you before I go to sleep. I've been told journaling is a good tool in grieving. I don't know, though, because I've always written to you and I couldn't imagine not spending this time with you every night. I love you. Kisses.

She Is Missed

Anxiety . . . lingering all day making me physically sick.

July 4, 2007, Wednesday • Scale: 3

Dear Kelsea, so is it true? Do you have like the best seat for all the fireworks? Personally, I chose to work tonight. This holiday didn't really mean too much anyways. I heard all the fire works going off but I didn't even step outside. I try to explain and tell people that there is so much in life I just don't care about anymore. I'm still struggling to be responsible. I still have such a hard time paying bills, making phone calls, appointments, just day-to-day living responsibilities. Remember how much I loved babies? I struggle now. I see babies and I just don't have the love or desire I had before. Why would God want to take that away from someone? It's like my love of life and the things in it are so jaded. Everything is mundane and gray. I don't really see much color in life anymore. I look at my eyes in the mirror and they just look empty. I'm sorry, Kelsea. I love you.

She Is Missed

Another holiday spent without you.

July 5, 2007, Thursday • Scale: 3

Hi Honey, I know I skipped group tonight but it was that double-edged sword. I was working, you know, all day with Hawaii, and then we went to the beach. It was a nice break yet part of me felt guilty for not going to group. Maybe I just didn't want to deal with all the sadness and pain because I know what's going to creep up on me over the next 6 weeks . . .

a road to hell. Kelsea, I can't stand this. I can't stand you not being here. It's like this grief thing just intensifies trivial shit in my life. The smallest thing can send me into a spiral downward fall.

People don't understand that even though I look "okay" on the outside, inside I am torn apart. My heart is empty. The tears and crying are never ending inside my body. I hate all this. I want you. I want you. I want you here. How or why has this happened to me? Why me, Kelsea? Why my life? Why my beautiful daughter? I can't do it. I love you and this hurts so bad.

She Is Missed

My mind was on a vacation today from you because sometimes the pain is so deep.

July 6, 2007, Friday • Scale: 3

Dear Kelsea Lyn, did you see how crazy work was tonight? It was steady and busy and I liked that. Maybe because I didn't have a lot of opportunity to talk about you. I did tell some guys, though, when they called me afraid that I fear nothing. Seriously, what do I have to fear? Because the truth is if I was to die I would be with you. I don't want to die right this minute but there are still times I want to die. It's funny how the loss of a child brings that out in a parent. Yet, every parent I have met who has lost a child says the same things about death. I had a nice day with Hawaii though. It's so relaxing sometimes just to hang out.

Since the other night and my fight with Hawaii, it's as if it brought us closer together. But it should I think. I'm going to go see you tomorrow. I always come away from visiting you wiser! I think because I hear what you say to me. Thank you for your help and guidance and watching over me and Digger. I love you.

She Is Honored

Your picture displayed so proudly at the bar for everyone to see.

July 7, 2007, Saturday • *Scale: 3*

Hi Honey, I hope you loved the colored roses I brought you. I see someone else came to see you, too. You are so missed by all. Did you see how well my spit cleaned up your stone? Do you know I was told you are the only one in that town there with that type of stone? You're so spoiled but you deserve it. All you ever had to do was flash me those blue eyes and I melted. It was pretty hot out there today. I can't believe it's the middle of summer already. It's almost like time is faster now. Almost a year and it's like, how? It feels like yesterday. Is it because I visit you every week and write to you every night? Can it be that my love for you continues to grow every day? Do you hear me when I call for you? Did you hear me yell out your name at your pad? Did you see the hard tears I cried? Do you see my OCD is back? You're supposed to be here telling me to stop writing . . . come to me in a dream, please . . . I need it.

She Is Honored and Here

A trip to your pad as I talk to you . . . sounds of cats meowing so loudly in the distance.

July 8, 2007, Sunday • *Scale: 4*

Hello Kelsea Lyn . . . well, today I met a woman who I believe is part of our purpose in this journey. She has endured trials the same as me and has learned to be a positive drive in her life and the life for her daughter. She hasn't lost a child, but she's been a victim, too. I think it's that blessing of hope I have been praying for. Today had been one of my better days in awhile and I think it's because I spent the day with Hawaii. I really need that one-on-one time with him. Digger's gone to church with me 3 weeks in a row and I think he is hearing things being said. You know, just like I have never given up on you, I will never give up on him. Today is the first day I haven't had anxiety in awhile and it felt good. I can't even imagine, honey, how hard life was for you with your mania. Everyone always thought you were just happy, but I know it was your illness and I'm sorry for that. I don't understand why God inflicts that on someone. I love you. Kisses.

She Will Be Honored

I received an introduction to a woman who understands, a woman to help me, so you will be honored.

July 9, 2007, Monday • Scale: 4

Hi Baby girl. . . . I don't know what it was today but for a few minutes I couldn't shut up talking about you and I was smiling with the stories, your stitches, your hairy legs, your tumors and hematoma! They all made me smile. I spent the day again with Hawaii. We are spending a lot of time together and getting closer. He is so understanding to my grief and I don't think there are too many men who would accept a grieving mother. I am a broken woman at times and most people have no idea what to say or do. Maybe part of my or OUR purpose in all this, honey, is to educate people on the loss of a child. There is no greater loss and sometimes I wish I wasn't so strong. I question and wonder if I wasn't strong, would you still be here? But I simply don't have a choice, do I? So many choices we can make through life, yet this one we can't and it's so unfair. Will I ever understand? I know I will NEVER accept this, ever! I love you.

She Is Honored

So many stories shared with Hawaii about you. I found myself smiling and laughing as I talked about you.

July 10, 2007, Tuesday • Scale: 4

Dear Kelsea, did you realize every day I start my day with you, in prayer, and every night I write you a letter, and all the hours in between you are with me, too. But, all that aside, it does not change the aching pain of not being able to physically see you in front of me, touch you, smell you or even yell at you. Do you realize how much stress was removed from my life? But I swear to you I would change and give it all back to have you in my life with all the arguments, laughs, wondering, doctor appointments, and 3 am phone calls. All in a heartbeat, I would take every fiber of stress back. At work tonight, Daisy said her husband's little brother would have been so good for you.

There are so many boys' hearts broken that they couldn't be good to you. Whose wedding am I going to plan? Whose dress am I going to help pick out? It's not fair. I love and miss you.

She Is Missed

I just miss you so very much, Kelsea Lyn.

July 11, 2007, Wednesday • Scale: 4

Hi Baby, so it's Hawaii's birthday today. Good news . . . his daughter and I talked today and things are better. I shared with him how important it was to me to be accepted by his children. I'm sorry you didn't accept my last relationship. You never shared with me your true feelings. I had to hear it from Tawnia but its okay. I still always stood my ground when it came to you guys. I'm going to get your yearbook and diploma this week. One of your friends from school came up to me at Walmart today. She finally graduated and is going to take a career assessment test. Remember yours? You little fashion designer. . . . I found out the grand opening for my support group is on August 22nd. I don't know what I'm going to do yet that day. Hopefully, wake up and be able to function. I love you, Kelsea Lyn Phelps. Watch over Digger and bless Hawaii somehow tonight for his birthday. Kisses from Mama.

She Is Here

As I blow dry my hair, a noise from the shower. Something knocked off the bathroom shelf inside the shower but there's no wind and no earthquake. . . .

July 12, 2007, Thursday • Scale: 4

Dear Kelsea Lyn, well, did you see how good Hawaii's birthday party went? I'm so thankful God answered my prayer for guidance in what to do, you know?

They all loved my poem that I wrote to Hawaii. You were blessed, too, you know, with the ability to write. I will have all your journaling and poems published in our bipolar book. I hope that we will be able to help others, somehow. But you were supposed to be with me through this education. We would have made such a great team to talk to people. Both of us as strong and outspoken as we are . . . I guess I taught you that. You had such a big, loving, caring heart and everyone knew it. Why did she have to give you those pills? How can someone do that to a child? You trusted her, Kels. Why couldn't I have known and stopped this from happening? How can God have needed you more than me? I love you.

She Is Honored

Constant prayer for justice. . . .

July 13, 2007, Friday • Scale: 4

Dear Tat, I'm sorry our visit was interrupted. At first I thought, that poor grounds keeper just needed to vent to someone. But, after talking for over a solid hour, I got frustrated. I just didn't get my quiet time with you but I didn't want to be rude to him either. At least I got a few minutes with you. My workouts have been lagging a little lately. At least I feel like that. I see moms with their daughters at the gym and I have to look away. I don't want to be jealous or envious, but how can I not? They have their daughter and I don't and I still don't understand, why me? Why a mother who dedicated her life to her children? Why any mother or father? I know we all have to die one day but not at 17 years old, not as a baby or child. Not here one day and literally gone the next. No warning, no preparing, just gone. I don't understand. I love you. Help me . . .

She Is Loved

Reading *The Department* reminded me of how much I fought for you because I love you.

July 14, 2007, Saturday • Scale: 1.5

Hi Honey, another day I'm reminded of how raw I am, so sensitive, so fragile. How long am I going to be this fragile, Kels? I hate it. I miss you so much and I KNOW people just don't understand. But I don't want them to understand because they would have to lose a child and I don't wish that on anyone in this world. I can't breathe. It hurts. It's Over the Line this weekend and you were there last year. I wish you could be there this year. I wish I could take you for Carne Asada Fries. I wish my kitchen was full of your dirty dishes. I wish I could tickle you and dye your hair black again. I wish we still shared a room together. I wish Tawnia could have given you her truck on your 18th birthday and you were driving and working. I wish I didn't have to cry every day. I wish I was with you.

I love you.

She Is Missed

Constant tears, a lump in the throat and horrific pain today.

July 15, 2007, Sunday • Scale: 3

Hi Baby, did you see 4 weeks in a row Digger was in church with us. Do you think he's heading toward the good path? Please don't give up on him and help me guide him. Today has been a pretty calm day. It's hard to look at your Myspace sometimes but I have to write you there, too. I go see Dr. Johnson this week. I am going to have to get something for anxiety the next couple months.

I've been so raw lately and Hawaii is getting the butt end of some of my anger and it's not fair to him. As much as I thought he understood, though, last night I realized he doesn't. He kind of attacked my behavior but doesn't understand the way I am processing your loss. No one can understand how a parent feels losing a child, not an uncle, aunt, mother or friend but a child. People need to be educated, patient, compassionate and not afraid. I love you more than the law allows. Kisses.

She Is Loved

A television commercial: Abe Lincoln, a weasel and an "under the sea" space man. I remember you looked at me and said, "What the hell?" We laughed. It was just on and it made me smile.

July 16, 2007, Monday • Scale: 2.7

Hi Sweetheart, I enjoyed our visit but I have to tell you, the Big N' Tastee from McDonalds wasn't that good. I got one to eat at your pad with you because it was your favorite. Did you like that? Tawnia shared with me her Carne Asada Fries anxiety and Reba McEntire's "Fancy" song story. Dang, you were definitely with her all day last Saturday. She wants to know if you enjoyed the Over the Line Tournament. She said you're lucky she doesn't drink Bacardi since they pulled their tent from the tournament. Your brother seems to be doing better. Do you think my persistent prayers are being answered? He's been working out again. I hope you hold his hands and lead him to the good path. Do you see, though, how raw my emotions and thoughts are? It's like my head keeps playing bad games on me. I keep crashing and my mind is going 100 miles and hour with Hawaii. I know it's all my anxiety. I need help honey. I don't want to jeopardize my love for him. You know? I love you, tons.

She Is Honored

My first Big N' Tastee from McDonalds shared with you at your pad.

July 17, 2007, Tuesday • Scale: 3

Dear Kelsea, how is my baby girl? How wonderful and beautiful is heaven? I wish you could tell me so I could have some peace in my heart and soul. I talked to a guy at the gym today and I have decided that life is becoming "softer." But, I've learned that my trust level is gone. I think I'm struggling with trust because I trusted you would be here with me and you're not. It's like before when I would talk to everyone; now I really avoid people because I don't want to talk to them. I had to go to Sonrise today and pray. I dropped to my knees and cried out for help. I really am struggling right now and I'm trying not to. I'm trying to stay strong but the anxiety attacks are getting more frequent and I hate them. I hate not trusting. I have constant chest pains. I was told I need to get angry because I haven't yet. I think because I just don't believe it yet. I miss you and love you.

She Is Missed and Loved

A prayer at Sonrise . . . just me, you and God.

July 18, 2007, Wednesday • Scale: 3

Dear Kels, I did it today. I got some medication for my anxiety. My blood pressure today was 140/82, way too high for me. I took one today to see how I felt and it was a little better. I'm going to have to be careful, though, with them. I didn't do too much today; it was a lazy day. I didn't work out but I met with Susan. I think I will be with her on the 22nd. I had to drive through the old neighborhood today and I just got sick. I can't do that. I went to your high school, too, for your yearbook and no one was there. So, do you think you would have been working at Hooters yet? You're so funny. You would have been such a flirt but you already know that, hah? It's hard to believe just a year ago you were so happy and doing so well at ECAL. You would have made it, no doubt. How about getting some LMM (Love My Mom) dust for Hawaii? I can use all the help I can get. I wish you were here with me. I miss you so much I am sick. I love you, kisses.

She Is Missed

A doctor visit for help—so much anxiety. . . .

July 19, 2007, Thursday • Scale: 2.5

Hi Honey, I made it to group tonight. It's really hard though because I just cry almost the whole time. I talked about your one year coming up and it also being the foundation's Grand Opening. How ironic and God's will is that? I mean I didn't even want to wake up that day and now Ken wants to do something special, too, for you. Now I have a purpose for that day. I've been struggling but to be honest, I feel better right now about it coming up. I feel stronger for some reason. Your brother has been working out a lot and not gambling. Thank God! I thought about what I have endured the last 11 months of my life: your death, a divorce, cancer, the loss of 2 jobs and now I'm being sued. And I'm still able to stand up and walk. Are you giving me the strength to survive? I can't lie down and die; I need to know my purpose to fulfill it. Help me see it, Kelsea, please? I love you more than a lot of laws . . . kisses.

She Is Honored

Group, rough but a necessity.

July 20, 2007, Friday • Scale: 3

Dear Tat, so I've realized now how important group is on Thursday nights. I felt a little better today because to be honest, honey, this has been a really hard week. This whole year thing is killing me and messing with my head. I went to the court house to file papers on being sued and I got over whelmed and a headache and I had to leave. I still don't have a lot of energy to do things. I had to go into work early tonight though. I worked 10 hours and it wasn't bad. How many jobs do you know that allow you to drink while you work? I actually drank a lot tonight because my week really sucked. It's funny, though, because I drink a lot of "blasters" with Rockstar so I don't really ever feel the alcohol. I wish I could have taken you drinking when you turned 21. We would have had fun. I'll have to do it anyways, hah? I love you more than the law allows and think of you constantly. Kisses.

She Is Honored

A moment of silence at the Sports Bar . . . six of us in total silence.

July 21, 2007, Saturday • Scale: 3

Hi Sweetheart, long night at work last night and I was tired all day long. So, you had to have loved the moment of silence dedicated to you last night at work. It warmed my heart for that guy to do that for you and he didn't even know you. I have to say that the people who come into the bar are very nice and compassionate. It is the perfect job for me right now. It's too much for me to think about, what I'll be doing a year from now. I think about tomorrow being 11 months and I don't know where the days, weeks and months have gone. All I know is I pray every day for the strength to walk, talk, function, focus and breathe and God keeps giving it to me. I have to work again tonight and I need you there with me, keeping me safe. I haven't been on the computer lately, it's too hard right now. I hope you are happy now. I love and miss you.

She Is Honored

A skull and crossbones ring, worn proudly on my wedding band finger, simply for you.

July 22, 2007, Sunday • Scale: 2

Dear Kelsea Lyn, how can it be 11 months ago? Just writing that simple sentence turns my stomach. Today, I have had fleeting thoughts of you in my brain and I have to push them away right away. I almost had to take some medication today but I didn't. I tried keeping myself busy with Hawaii today.

Church was okay. I was really tired from working so late all weekend. I didn't have much focus in church to hear a lot. We did sing 2 of your favorite songs though, "Evermore." I don't know, Kels; I really don't think my brain has absorbed all this. I know I'm not still numb but sometimes I think I am. I just hope people don't start throwing the whole, "Well, it's been a year now," thing at me. A year is NOTHING. A year is *yesterday*. My insides are still so very raw that just seeing a bus today was a trigger. The bus you and Digger rode to church when you were little. I still hate all this. I love you.

She Is Missed

Thoughts of you all day making my stomach ill . . .

MONTHLY JOURNAL: NO ANNIVERSARIES

It was at the beginning of this month that a long time friend of mine, who knew Kelsea very well and loved her, said to me, "Next month will be a year." It was that simple comment, that innocent comment that sent me spiraling. You see, I hadn't even thought about that until he said something. How could I? I hadn't even made it to the 11th-month mark yet, let alone a year.

Over the next couple weeks, my days got very dark. In my head I couldn't comprehend that it was going to be a year soon. My brain still cannot wrap itself around that concept. I don't know if it is denial? Is it still sheer disbelief? I just don't know yet.

I found myself struggling with this "year" concept. People would ask me what I am going to do on August 22nd and all I could think about was just being able to get out of bed. I know people mark the "year" date as an anniversary. I have such a hard time with that, though, because in my mind an anniversary is a joyous occasion.

You have wedding anniversaries, birthdays celebrated, anniversaries of divorces (which some people celebrate, if you asked, I would imagine) but the death of a child to me is not an anniversary. In fact, it is more of a day I don't ever want to acknowledge. If I could go to sleep the day before and wake up the day after I would be perfectly satisfied. Unfortunately, I cannot do that so I have been faced with what to do.

I missed my support group 2 weeks in a row also due to work one night and a family event. I thought at first, no big deal I don't need it. I was so wrong. It was the two weeks after the one year comment was made that I missed.

You see, group, as I have said before, is such a double-edged sword. I found myself struggling to go because of how sad and painful it was, yet I knew I needed it. So, when I missed the 2 weeks in a row, I thought no big deal. Then, I went the third week and realized how incredibly important it was to me. I left there feeling "softer."

Softer has become a good word to me. When people ask, "Are things getting better," it is an innocent question. No. In my mind, things will never be "better" because Kelsea will never physically be here with me again. I heard someone in group one night say things seem "softer" and that made sense to me. Even the word "easier" is hard to use because it's not easier; we are just learning to deal with this new life handed to us. So, I use "softer" a lot and explain to people and they understand and appreciate it.

I have found that most people honestly do not know how to deal with, talk to or comfort a person who is grieving. When you throw in the fact that it is a child, the simple truth is it makes it even harder. I know that it can be hard for someone who has lost a mother, father, cousin or best friend because they hurt, too. I understand that. But, the truth is no one ever has a child and expects or thinks or even imagines having to bury them. It's not the normal way a life is supposed to go. You're not supposed to out live your own child.

I can honestly say, I NEVER in my life ever thought one of my children would pass away. NEVER. I have actually never lost anyone close to me in my life and then the first loss I encounter is my beautiful 17-year-old daughter. I am still trying to get the answer of why?

In my prayer every single day, I ask God to open my heart up to understand. I tell Him I love Him, trust Him, believe in Him, have faith in Him, and I want Him to bless me with the simple answer of why, so I can understand. I believe one day I will understand, but for now it is so very difficult.

I know I have a new purpose in life and I just want to know what it is so I can accomplish it. I have not gotten mad at God yet and I have been told I need to get mad at Him and that it is okay to get mad at God. I know that and maybe one day I will but for now I am not mad; I just want understanding.

I don't think people understand how raw I still am. I know it's because they see me on a day-to-day basis living, working, walking, breathing and occasionally smiling. It makes it very easy to forget that my daughter passed away just months ago but the fact still remains . . . when even something so trivial takes place it has the ability to scratch the wounds I still carry with me and send me spiraling into my deepest grief still.

Philippians 4:6
Don't worry about anything; instead pray about everything.
Tell God what you need and thank Him for all he has done.

✒

CHAPTER TWELVE

July 23, 2007, Monday • Scale: 3

Dear Kels, Hawaii's daughter finished my book today and she liked it. If people only knew the struggles we endured . . . sometimes I wonder how difficult life would have been for you. I see other bipolar people or parents of bipolar children and so many of them took their own lives. Bipolar is an illness and I wanted you and I to educate society on this illness. I know your bipolar was not the reason that THIS happened. I know that, through your trial coming up, they are going to try to make you look like a bad, out of control girl. Sure, you had some struggles but you were a good girl. I promise you, I will make sure the whole world knows the truth about you. I will clear your name and honor you to the very best of my ability. We have a rough road ahead of us but I know you will give me the strength and your Father will guide me and justice will prevail. I love you, Tat. Kisses.

She Is Honored

Mystical Perfume, always wearing it, knowing it's what you loved.

July 24, 2007, Tuesday • Scale: 3

Dear Tat, I have to say that these days, these last few days, I've been trying to push down all the thoughts. It's like I think about what's happened, my eyes squint and my brain just does not comprehend it. Then, my stomach gets sick so I just don't want to think. A guy at work tonight, once he found out about what happened, said I am the strongest woman he's ever met. He has 3 girls. I always thought Cara was the strongest woman alive and now I realize there are so many of us out there; it is so sad. It's not supposed to be like this. I can't even count how much I have been saying,

"I can do all things through Christ who strengthens me." That is my refuge. I can't even fathom, still, the rest of my life. How do we parents do it, Kels? Why do we have to journey this path when we didn't ask for it? I love you.

She Is Honored

A jalapeño and cream cheese taquito from 7-11; my first one since you went Home.

July 25, 2007, Wednesday • Scale: 3

Hi Honey, did you see me in the ocean today? It still scares me but Hawaii held my hand and made it better. I've really been avoiding thinking. I know you know what I mean. I haven't cried in a couple days but only because I am on another "mind vacation" now. I think because subconsciously I know what I'm getting ready to face over the next few months. As I sat down tonight and my brain had a chance to think, I thought of how I could have had so much fun today. How could I have gone for a couple hours today without feeling grief? Because as soon as I realized I had gone a couple hours without the pain, my brain goes back to disbelief. I swear I still feel like you're just somewhere else right now and you will be back again one day. I can't imagine when reality truly sets in because it's still all not real. I need you in my dreams, please. I love you, kisses.

She Is Missed

I still live with disbelief and am unable to let thoughts into my head.

July 26, 2007, Thursday • Scale: 3

Dear Kelsea, I love you with all my heart but I'm sure you know that. I enjoyed our visit and I hope you love the pinwheel, pretty cute. Don't you think? Did you see how much I spoke at group tonight? I think I spoke more than I ever have and I barely cried. We talked about tomorrow. I'm not sure what to expect. I just pray for strength. Ken talked a lot about me being "coached" for when the trial starts. He talked about keeping my composure and I just don't know. I know I won't have a choice though.

I'm not afraid for tomorrow or what's coming up. I just don't want them to make you look bad. You're the victim, Kels. I promise to clear your name. I promise to fight till the end and further if I have to. Susan will be with me too. I see someone came and left you a pink bear and a cigarette . . . that so makes me smile to see a cigarette left for you. I miss you, Kelsea so damn much. Kisses.

She Is Honored

Flowers at your pad, group and so many words spoken . . .

July 27, 2007, Friday • Scale: 3

My Dearest Kelsea, I miss you so very much. It was a short court date but I was there. It's going to be another 2 months now till pretrial but I am confident in justice and God's will. I know it will be a brutal fight but I will be ready. Did you see how beautiful it was out at the beach today? I did pretty dang good for awhile. I'm not sure what the trigger was for the wave but it came. I think just the reality of seeing all the families and remembering how much I loved taking you and Digger to that very beach. I just sat in the sand and cried and prayed and tried to understand and I just don't. I'm so thankful for Hawaii and his family and being able to share their closeness. I just wish I could have given all that to you and Digger. I tried to have us be a family. I'm sorry I didn't do a better job. Please forgive me and show me you are with me still. I love you more than the law allows. Kisses and hugs.

She Is Honored and Missed

A court appearance, a sunset at the beach with many tears . . .

July 28, 2007, Saturday • Scale: 4

Dear Kelsea, what a lazy day. I didn't even leave the house today. I laid down in the afternoon and even took a nap. Hawaii pointed out to me how relaxed I am today to have been able to sleep without taking a pill. We watched 2 movies today and I watched another alone. I made myself laugh tonight because Hawaii said something and I repeated it back to him and

I swear it was you. I sounded just like you when you would do that to me. Sometimes, I can tell a story about you and it makes me laugh. Those are the good memories, I know that.

Sometimes I still feel like you're just at a friend's house and that's' why I haven't seen you. Sometimes I can't look at your picture because I get so sad. I'm not looking forward to next month. I just don't want people to think because it's been a year, I'm okay . . . that will make me mad. I love you, miss you, want you and need you. Hugs.

She Is Missed

I look at your picture and an overwhelming sadness surrounds me.

July 29, 2007, Sunday • Scale: 4

Hi baby girl, did you see Digger at church with me *again*? Pretty cool, hah? It's crazy to think one of my spiritual gifts is faith. Is that why God took you so young? I wish I knew right now my purpose. I'm going to start on another book. It's going to be all about your trial. I want to journal about every single step I take, breath I take, inch of pain I feel so I can help someone else. I want to be able to publicly talk about giving someone else's child medication. I want to save a child and his or her parent from this hell I was thrown into. I feel like I have to let the world know all about you, who you were, your life, your struggles, my struggles, simply our story because we have one to tell and I need your help when I sit down and write. Speak through me, honey. Give me your talent, your thoughts, your life. Sometimes I still catch my breath so shallow, so slow and I have to remember to breathe. I love you, Kelsea. Be with me always. Big kiss.

She Is Missed

Tears as I drive my car and remember . . .

July 30, 2007, Monday • Scale: 3

Dear Kelsea Lyn, I read the interview and confession today. How can she have told so many lies? I find myself sitting alone, crying and broken. I think how humbled I am to be so broken and yet so strong. I mean, I have to be strong, right? I mean, to even be able to breathe. I've had chest pains today.

Sometimes I look at certain pictures of you and I just break down. You were so beautiful and full of so much life for someone to take that away from you. I just can't understand. I've been alone a lot today and it's not been good. You never know, though, when all this pain is going to hit. It's not a physical pain but it's pain. I have such a headache right now from crying. I'm sorry, honey, I know you hate me crying but I just can't stop. Maybe if you came into a dream and I could see you I might be okay for a day. Please? I need you really bad. I love you. Kisses.

She Is Honored

Coloring your little red box, going over every line you drew . . . keeping it alive.

July 31, 2007, Tuesday • Scale: 3

Dear Kels, 11 months ago today I stood in the church as we all honored you, cried for you, spoke about you and remembered our love for you. Thank your Father for the blessing today. I had to file bankruptcy today and the attorney is doing it all for free—yet another testimony of a blessing. I realized today I have not been listening to any music in my car while driving. I call it silent pain.

Tomorrow we move into August. It's your dad's birthday. Can you believe he is 50? I hope you're with him tomorrow. I took Digger dinner tonight at work and he showed me around and what he does. He gets his wisdom tooth pulled on August 22nd. I think it's going to help us through that day. He planned on taking it off work anyways and I am, too. I'm coming to see you tomorrow. I think your new address is there. I have to polish and seal it. Have I told you today how much I love you? I pray you're happy in heaven. . . . Kisses.

She Is Missed

I found myself driving around all day with no music; I call it silent pain.

August 1, 2007, Wednesday • Scale: 4

Hi Honey, did you wish your dad a happy birthday? It's August now. So much happens in this month. I have to bring the civil attorney your investigation tomorrow. I put a lot of your pictures in the binder because I want your face vivid in his mind to give him more passion. I still haven't been able to turn my radio on. It's strange, Kels; the last few days it's like I haven't allowed myself to think about you *at all*. I guess it protects me from the pain. I've been told it's our bodies own natural way of protecting ourselves from the grief. I'm going camping this weekend with Hawaii and his family. We've never camped, hah? Well, I guess you did at the desert. I hope I'll be okay, no big waves. I think Digger's going a couple days, too. Will you be there with us? Please? I really need to feel your presence. I need to see it somehow. I just need it, Kels. I love you tons.

She Is Honored

Pictures for your case binder, a face to a crime, more passion . . .

August 2, 2007, Thursday • Scale: 1

Dear Kelsea, can you believe the trials being thrown at me? How many times, Kels, am I supposed to turn my cheek with Hawaii? It's like I had so much anger toward him today I didn't have time to think about you. I'm sorry, although I've never screamed as loud as I did in the car today. It was anger at him and the loss of you. I couldn't eat all day and at group I found myself not feeling an ounce of compassion for any other parent even when they cried. I got annoyed even at one parent crying. My head hurt and I barely heard what was being said. I knew I could turn to you and vent. You would be so pissed at Hawaii right now. Still, no music playing in the car and it's getting close. Clint from the 105.3 Rock is going to do something on the air on the 22nd for you. I still can't fathom a year already. I still hate this all. I love you forever, hugs.

She Is Honored

A rock radio station is going to dedicate the 22nd to you.

August 3, 2007, Friday • Scale: 2

Dear Kels, how is my baby girl doing? Do you miss me as much as I miss you? Do you even remember what this world is like? What's it like not to have violence, drugs, hate, thieves, pain, sadness, hunger, addiction and sickness? Is it all as wonderful as we are taught here on earth, this place called heaven? You know I am not afraid to die, right? I know your brother needs me, though, and I need him, too. I need to figure out what I'm supposed to do with all this stuff. I'm camping now and the beach is always beautiful. You could go into the water no matter how cold it was. I wish you were here with me. I'm sorry I couldn't afford to take you and Digger on any vacations. I'm sorry for so many things. I'm struggling, you know, with Hawaii and I wish I had you here because you would hug me and tell me its going to be okay no matter what happens. I love you, Kelsea Lyn, with all my heart.

She Is Missed

A family camping trip with Hawaii's family . . . all sitting around the fire talking; my testimony of faith in your Father, knowing I will see you again.

August 4, 2007, Saturday • Scale: 2

Hi Honey, so here I am camping still at the beach. It's okay and I'm sure if you were here, and Dig, too, it would be fine. I'm not really sure who knows about my loss in this family and who doesn't. I guess it doesn't really make a difference. They may understand a little better, though, why I isolate myself. It's so sad to think that the Tracy that lived 346 days ago is gone. I could try my hardest to get her back but it's simply not possible. A part of me died the very second you did. I have to question, why? Why does this happen to parents who love and live for their child? Yet, there are parents who don't even care about their kids, why me?

Why take a child away from a mother who gave every second of every minute to her child? I just don't get it, Kels. I just don't know about life as it is right now. I don't know what I'm supposed to be doing right now. I know I'm camping with a huge, close, loving family and I wish I could have given it all to you. I ache, Kelsea. Help me breathe and go on . . . I love you.

She Is Honored

A piña colada for you.

August 5, 2007, Sunday • Scale: 2

Dear Kels, still at the beach . . . today I actually got on a soft board and paddled about a $^1/_4$ mile out into the deep ocean. I had to concentrate on not thinking about what was below me in the water, but I did it. I've got more color right now than I have had in 8 years and I know you would be so mad at me. I haven't really had the opportunity to talk about you here. Maybe it is because I don't want to make anyone sad or uncomfortable. This whole grief thing is so hard to comprehend for the person who hasn't lost a child. No one understands and they say that they couldn't even imagine, and they can't. I NEVER for a second thought this would happen to me. I will say I am going to try my hardest to make the one year mark a good day for you. I haven't had to take the medication I got from the doctor yet for the anxiety. My finger is still writing but I don't care about that right now. My concern is being able to get up every day and simply walk, talk, function, focus and breathe. I miss you, Kelsea Lyn, with all my heart, soul and being. I love you, kisses.

She Is Missed and Loved

Thoughts of you in my mind, all day, everyday . . .

August 6, 2007, Monday • Scale: 2

Hi Honey, it's nice to be back home. Did you see how hard I did cardio today? It felt good to get back into the gym. I know, I only missed it 3 days and I'm a freak. Do you see the turmoil in my life right now? I mean, its not like I don't already have enough B. S. in my life and I have Hawaii drama, too. I hate drama, Kels. I talked to the owner of Lakes Market and he said we can put another flyer up for your "1st Year Marker" night in his store. Your day is going to be special, I promise. My emotions are a wreck. This grief thing just intensifies any other bullshit thrown your way. You cry and it's about mixed things. You get angry and I wanted to hit myself today. Remember the day you frustrated me so bad I sat in the kitchen and cut my wrists? I'm sorry for that. I just snapped. I love you, Kelsea, and want you here on earth to experience love, marriage and a baby. Kisses.

She Is Honored

A coffee at Starbucks and when they ask me my name, I say Kelsea.

August 7, 2007, Tuesday • Scale: 3

Hi Honey, so did you see me with Peyton at the beach? It reminded me of when I would take you and Digger all the time. So, I thought about who I used to be . . . outgoing, friendly, a love for children, a smile for everyone, loving life and saying hello to everyone . . . and who I am now: quiet, not wanting to talk to people, avoiding them on purpose, not interested in children and someone on Myspace referred to me as a "broken woman." She's right but she doesn't have to tell everyone, you know? I saw a girl in the gym today for the first time in a couple months and I just did not want to talk to her. Do you think I will ever have a true love for life again? I have to work tonight and I am glad. I need a distraction to my life in whole right now. Not only have I lost trust in innocence but in someone I truly trusted and I just don't know how or if he can get it back from me. Talk to your Father to help us, please, honey? I love you tons and tons.

She Is Honored

Constant journaling to you here and to your Myspace.

August 8, 2007, Wednesday • Scale: 1

Dear Kelsea, I can't tell you how painful today has been . . . more episodes of the surface of my skin being scratched, opening up the deep, raw wounds that lie deep in my soul. I looked in the mirror today and I saw the emptiness in my eyes that I had in the beginning. It's as if my eyes are empty and the pain is so visible in them, so deep. You know none of us is perfect, including Hawaii. But, I believe the lessons I am learning right now are in forgiveness. I felt so much better after he and I talked. I know I am far from perfect, too, and have made some poor choices. That's why

I am not going to be so judgmental. These are lessons I wish I could be teaching you as I live them. But, I know you see everything going on right now. I just hope I am putting a smile on your face with my actions. I just want to be the best person I can be and I know your Father will continue to bless me even amidst all the trials He has put before me this last 12 months. I love you, Angel.

She Is Missed

So many tears today . . . so very much pain.

JAMES 5:11
As you know, we consider blessed those who have persevered.
Amen.

August 9, 2007, Thursday • Scale: 2.5

Dear Kelsea Lyn, happy birthday to Digger. Were you with him today? It's crazy how quick a wave comes over you. In the store I heard a man in the next line talking about how he just had another grandchild born. That lead to thoughts of you, thoughts of you not getting married, not having a baby and I began to cry. I got to my car and balled and I miss you so much. I had chest pains today, the lump in my throat, all of it while sitting in my car. I have to tell myself to breathe.

I wipe the tears off my eyes and face and I walk into the next store as if life is okay. But no one knows what I just went through. I want to tell someone so they can acknowledge my pain but there is no one. I had a good talk with Susan though. Did you see how spoiled Digger was for his birthday? Did you see my resting heart rate at Walmart . . . 56! I laughed because I would have kicked your butt! I love you, Kels. I need you. I want you back but I can't and I hate that.

She Is Honored

A coffee at Starbucks, using your name and I heard it called out 3 times . . .

August 10-11-12, 2007, Fri/Sat/Sun • Scale: 3

Hi Honey, do you realize this is the first time I have gone 3 days without writing to you every night? As much as I hate to admit it, I think it is a sign of healing. I've somewhat made amends with Hawaii and he truly does make life a little easier for me. Your brother has his own life now and I have accepted that. So, it's like all I have really is myself because I really don't have any responsibilities anymore with you and your brother. I struggle being responsible and disciplined at times. So, I guess when I am with Hawaii, like the last 3 days, he helps me live again.

But, it's so crazy, though, how one minute I am living and the next minute I want and feel dead. On Saturday I was in Walmart and I heard a mom and daughter talking and shopping together or I see them driving together and my heart aches. I see teenage boys driving their big trucks with a girlfriend and I flash on how that should be you. At church on Sunday, it was horribly difficult. Another bereaved mother sat with me. I cried so hard. It's like if my arm was cut off, people would know I was hurt and ask if I'm okay, but when the injury is deep in your heart and soul . . . no one knows. Sometimes I want to tell everyone about my loss and pain and other times I don't want to tell, let alone talk to, anyone. It's almost been a year and I still get chest pains and a lump in my throat. I don't really know why but I haven't turned my radio on in my car in a couple weeks now. Did you see how good I did at work last night? I am thankful for that job and know your laughing at my good wits. Your new address stone is perfect. I'm thankful it is in now. I promise to polish it every week so you have the cleanest pad in your neighborhood. I love you, Kelsea . . . kisses.

She Is Missed

Still, no music played in my car . . .

August 13, 2007, Monday • Scale: 2

Dear Kelsea, did you see me hard at work last night? I contacted all 5 news stations about your ceremony on the 22nd. I also contacted the newspaper. I want you honored in the *biggest* way. I will do all I can to make it all happen. With days like I had today, Kels, I wish I was with you. Do you really have no sorrow or tears anymore? Because I had both today with Hawaii and I just wish sometimes all I knew was joy, love and happiness with no more trials. Your brother has a girlfriend and I need to be here for him. Sometimes, I wonder if my behavior toward Hawaii is one of grief and pain and mistrust in life in general. I just know when he's not with me and we fight, the grief is so much harder and the pain so much deeper. I know you would have loved him. I miss you so much and I'm crying a lot again but no medication yet. I guess I'm trying to do it on my own. Give me your strength. I love you so much. Kisses and hugs.

She Is Honored

Contacts to all the news stations in San Diego for your 1-year marker.

August 14, 2007, Tuesday • Scale: 3

Dear Kelsea Lyn, it's still hard to believe that a year ago you were here, hanging out with Josue, checking in with me and so excited to start East County Academy of Learning (ECAL). I'm scared for next week. I'm more scared for the day before because I know that was my last day with you. Can you see Tawnia's struggles right now? Please help her because if anyone is close to feeling my pain it is her. Also, when I think about your friends thinking about you, I feel their pain, too. I feel everyone's pain. I've been catching myself a lot lately making smartass comments like you, same tone of voice, same comments. I tell Hawaii that was all Kelsea. Do you think that shows I am "healing?" And what exactly, Kels, does it mean to "heal?" You never heal from the loss of a child, though, because the simple truth is you are not coming back here to me. Do you know how hard that is to write? I hate reality. I still hate this new and different life I have been given. I want you back. How long do I have to wait? I love you, kisses.

She Is Loved and Honored

Each day more and more, I say things with your attitude, tone and wits.

August 15, 2007, Wednesday • Scale: 3

Dear Kels, I've been communicating a lot with Bill Menish. Remember the reporter who interviewed me when I was boxing? I hope they will do something in a week for you. I think I've been so busy with Hawaii and our issues I haven't been able to think about what's coming up. I have a lot to do still between now and next week. Give me your strength, okay? I really hate when I have time on my hands because that's when the grief creeps into your soul. So slowly, yet all of a sudden you're down and the waves over your head and you're gasping for a breath of air, to breathe . . . it sucks, Kels. Sometimes it's really hard to write to you every night but it's our time together. I guess there are parents who go days or longer without talking to their child and I talk to you every night. I know it helps keep my relationship with you fresh. I miss the hell out of you, Kelsea Lyn. Is heaven really that great? Will I ever have an answer as to why us? I love you, kisses.

She Is Honored

Bill Menish, news in San Diego wanting to cover our story with an interview . . .

August 16, 2007, Thursday • Scale: 3

Dear Kelsea Lyn, did you see all the flyers I put up around town for your memorial? Can you believe the news will be here in the morning? I hope you're looking down on me and smiling at everything I am trying to get done for next week. I have things I want to do and Susan gave me some good suggestions. I saw Jeanie's mom today and she started crying, still. I didn't go to group today or meet with Susan. A part of me felt guilty but a part of me sees it as healing and doing "better" for lack of a better word. I don't know where I am getting the strength to put together your ceremony. I just know what I want for you and I will make it happen and then I can stumble and fall. But for now, you will be honored. I'm nervous about being interviewed. I just want everyone to know your story and what a good girl you really were. I love you with all my heart, hugs.

She Is Honored

Flyers put up all over town.

August 17, 2007, Friday • Scale: 3

Hi Honey, well I got more done today. Do you like the pink balloons I got for your ceremony? I've had a hard time finding the candles but I'll get them, I promise.

Do you think the interview with Bill went well? He remembered you when you were only 10 years old during the interview he did with me when I coached football. A couple times in the interview, I thought he was going to cry with me. It's surreal to think this is really our story being told. Bill said he wants it to be a story about life and as the criminal side comes up he will continue to follow it. It was pretty overwhelming and, after the fact, I thought of more stuff to say.

Susan was with me of course. Do you like all the attention you are getting? I know you're smiling in heaven. I just wish I could see it. Was I slammed at work tonight or what?! There are so many customers from the bar going on Wednesday to support me, even though they didn't know you. How cool is that? I tell everyone you were the spitting image of me and they smile. I love you so much, Kels. Kiss.

She Is Honored

Balloons bought, string, a tank and candles found . . . all in preparation.

August 18, 2007, Saturday • Scale: 3

Dear Tat, can you believe your dad and I would have been married 23 years today? I hope he is doing okay. Do you spend a lot of time with him at all? How do you do it? Can you like just fly from one place to another in a second? Can you be with more than one person at a time? Is your hair long or short? How old are you and do you stay that age or can you be whatever age you want? Do you hear everyone when they talk to you? Can you read our thoughts or do we have to talk out loud? Was it you that protected your brother from hitting that wall?

Can you pop another balloon for us at your ceremony? Do you get to eat in heaven? Is there incredible food? Are the streets made of gold? Are there mansions? Do people wear crowns of jewels? Have you met the crocodile guy? Are there animals in heaven? Have you seen our little Poohdunk? I'm taking good care of Sassy Girl for you. See how skinny she is now? I love you and can't wait for all the answers to my questions . . . hugs.

She Is Honored

Your flyer up at work outside, people signing it and writing to you, perfect strangers . . .

August 19, 2007, Sunday • Scale: 2

Hi Honey, I prayed so much today in church for understanding and comfort. I cried a lot and could not concentrate on the message. Do you see me hold your picture high in the air when I'm singing in church? I miss you. They baptized a little girl around 10 years old and I'm sorry I didn't baptize you. Can you forgive me? I had another good night at work again. I really like my job and I hope I make you proud. This purple pen reminds me so much of you. I had a pretty calm day just chillin' at Hawaii's. We talked about marriage . . . what do you think? Should I marry him if he asks? He's inviting his children to your ceremony. I hope it turns out well. I'm going to try my hardest, okay? I've got so much to do the next 3 days; give me strength and guidance. I can do all things through Christ who strengthens me. I say it every day as soon as I think you are gone. I still don't believe it, as crazy as that sounds. I need you in a dream, please? I love you forever, kisses and hugs.

She Is Missed

Constant prayer and tears in church today.

August 20, 2007, Monday • Scale: 3

Dear Kelsea Lyn, I'm almost done getting everything for your ceremony. I picked up the candles today. Someone told me one day that lighting a candle is like music to the angels in heaven. Well, in a couple days I will have an orchestra for you. I had a guy in the bar tonight who, when he saw your flyer, began to cry.

Tears rolled down his cheeks and he couldn't speak. Do you see how unfair this all is, Kels? Do you see how even people who didn't know you are touched? I'm sorry for being so selfish, honey, but I would rather have you here now with me than to touch all these people. I want you back. At lunch today I started crying and told Hawaii, I wish he could have known the woman I was before this happened because I'm just a broken woman now. I know people don't agree, but it's because they don't understand who I was then and who I am now. This wasn't my choice and I hate that. I love you, kisses.

She Is Honored

A trip downtown to get all the candles for your ceremony . . .

August 21, 2007, Tuesday • Scale: 2

Dear Kels, I decided to take the day off of work tonight. I stopped by the Santee substation and spoke to Richard. He was so rude to me, honey, it sent me into a spiral down and I realized how emotional today was going to be. I did some finishing touches for tomorrow. I'm thinking it's going to be very nice for you. I know it is going to be bitter sweet. Bitter because you are not here, but sweet because of all the love you will be shown. As I sat watching TV at night with Hawaii, I glanced at the time. It was 8:13 pm and I realized it was one year ago in 17 minutes that I spoke to you, alive. I crumbled. I spent the next 45 minutes crying and so emotionally wiped out and drained. I just went home and wanted to take my good sleeping pills. I've been taking them a lot more than before.

Just the Trazodone, lately. I told Hawaii I was afraid to go to sleep and I was. . . . I don't want to wake up tomorrow, knowing a year ago a part of me died forever.

Help me, Kels. I love you.

She Is Honored and Missed

Still more preparation for tomorrow . . . tears all day.

August 22, 2007, Wednesday • Scale: 2

My Dearest Little Girl, how is it that I have been without you now for a year when the longest I ever went without my girl was maybe 10 days? How is it my brain does not allow me to grasp this concept? How is it that most of the time I just don't think about all this pain because, when I allow myself to, it's unbearable?

How have I been able to wake up each day for the last 365 days and function? It's absolutely beautiful out here at your pad today. There's a nice breeze and it's sunny. Did you see the argument I had with that rude woman? That woman who had no compassion and a dark heart? I wanted to pull her through her car window, Kels! You know my mind is whacked today. I probably shouldn't be driving. I tried explaining to her I just lost you a year ago and when she didn't care my anger raged! I hope she is at home and watches the story about us and feels like *shit*. I really do. Lord, help her.

So Kels, did you see the turnout at your ceremony? There were even old neighbors from our apartments. I'll bet there were easily 100 people and it's a year later. Did you like what I wrote and read? I held it together pretty well I think. It's amazing to see everyone, even the people who didn't know you, write a message to you. Everyone was amazed at how all the balloons stayed together, too, as they floated up to you . . . I should have gotten 2 boxes of candles. I'm glad channel 9 news came and covered it. It wasn't too long of a story but it was still recognition and honoring to you. It warmed my heart, too. All the people from my work showed up, too. It was amazing because they all only met me 4 months ago, yet they totally supported me tonight. I hope you were proud of what I put together for you. There isn't an hour that goes by that you are not missed, loved, longed for . . . they even acknowledged it on 105.3 Rock Station. So, now that it's over, I'm going to sleep and just be thankful for the success of your 1-year marker ceremony. I love you more than life itself and I meant it when I said I would have given my life for you that day. Kisses and Hugs.

She Is Honored, Missed and Loved

Visits to your pad from your friends leaving flowers . . . Tawnia and all the kids sharing a Starbucks at your pad . . . giving a cheeseburger and some money to a homeless woman at Walmart in your honor . . . a dozen roses, bouquet and balloons at your pad from me . . . so many tears at your pad along with anger . . .

Your ceremony: balloons with messages, candles lit, a moment of silence, the news covering your ceremony, 100+ people all at the park for you, tears from people who didn't' even know you . . .

All Year Long . . . you are loved, you are missed and you are ALWAYS honored.

JOURNAL: ONE YEAR OF SURVIVAL

Here it is . . . one year later and I'm still here. As I approached the 1-year marker I had no plans for this day. Hawaii's oldest daughter asked me about 2 weeks before this day what I was going to do. I told her I just want to be able to get up out of bed and be productive and be there for my son. I'm not sure why but it was after that conversation that I suddenly got strength to honor Kelsea.

I began researching where to get candles for a candle light ceremony. I made flyers up and put them all over East County. I contacted the TV news stations and radio stations about this ceremony I was going to have at the park for Kelsea. I bought balloons so everyone could write Kelsea a message and we could all release them together. I had no idea what kind of turn out I would have. I bought 100 candles for everyone, thinking that would be enough. I wrote what I wanted to say on a piece of paper so I would not forget.

I have to say, I struggle sometimes with the lack of compassion from people. I think I got angrier today than I ever have. As I was driving around today trying to get everything set for tonight, I turned in front of a woman coming out of the parking lot at Walmart. My mind was spinning and I didn't see her.

She stopped her car and began shaking her fist at me and yelling. I put my car in park, got out of the car and walked over to her window to apologize and let her know what this day was. She didn't care. She had no compassion that I just lost my daughter one year ago. Cars were now backing up. As one car drove by, he yelled, "I just called the cops!"

I looked over at him as he drove by and yelled, "I am a f-ing cop" and then I turned to the woman in the car and did not have the kindest words for her and it took everything in me to not pull her through her car window. As I got back into my car, I was shaking. My anger was through-the-roof and I probably had no right driving around with my mind on another planet, but I had no choice. I did not plan that 1 year ago today my daughter would have passed away at the hands of another mother, but I will say it felt *good* to yell at her.

The night came and I ran out of candles. One local news station was there to film the ceremony. One local rock radio station broadcasted the ceremony, time and place during the day for me. People told me they heard about Kelsea's memorial on the radio and came. There were more people than I ever expected.

As everyone showed up, they took a helium filled balloon and wrote Kelsea a message. Everyone mingled around sharing Sharpie pens as they wrote their messages. When everyone was done writing, we all gathered in the park and held our balloons up high. I said a few words and at the same time, we all released the balloons. We watched in amazement as 100 balloons floated so effortlessly into the sky, together as if maybe Kelsea had her arms reached out to catch them all.

After the release, we lit our candles and I spoke to everyone. It warmed my heart to see the love and support a year later. I cried. Everyone cried. I was thankful for the strength Hawaii's daughter gave me in that simple question about what I was going to do that day. At the end, a local news station interviewed a couple people and me. I had to be careful what I said and was thankful they honored Kelsea with us.

As I sit here now, knowing the first year is over, all I can think about is now I get to enter year 2 of hell. Now I get to go through another year without Kelsea. Now what do I do? I'm angry. I want her back and I'm still waiting for her to walk in the front door and come home to me. I don't know if those thoughts will ever leave or if I will eventually accept that she is not going to walk in my door again. I don't think I will ever be able to accept this because that makes it real . . . and I'm not ready for reality yet.

I know over the next several months I will have to be strong. I will have to be patient. I will have to trust in the justice system and Kelsea's attorney. I will have to continue breathing and living until that sun that keeps coming up every day just decides to stay down. Then, I will see Kelsea's smile, hear her laugh, see her beautiful blue eyes and feel her arms wrapped tightly around me as she once again professes her love to me.

MATTHEW 11:28-30
*Then Jesus said, "Come to me, all of you who are weary
and carry heavy burdens, and I will give you rest."*

CHAPTER THIRTEEN

ANOTHER 9 DAYS OF HELL

August 23, 2007, Thursday • Scale: 1

Dear Kelsea, okay, so now that it's been 1 year I want to know when you are coming back? I woke up today and thought to myself, *Now what?* Now I enter into the second year? No. I want you. You're supposed to come home now. It's like, okay it's been a year . . . come home. Yet, I realize you can't. I slept all day and stayed on the couch. I had no energy, no motivation; I had nothing after last night. It was such an emotional let down day. I hate it. I made myself get up and go to group though. I told everyone how good yesterday went. They all want to go to court with me when it starts. I just don't get what I'm supposed to do now? Enter into another year? Then another and forever? It still feels like yesterday, yet like forever too. You were so loved, Kels. You still are; my love for you still grows every day. I miss you . . . hugs.

August 24, 2007, Friday • Scale: 2

Hi Honey, my life is a mess right now with Hawaii. I really need you to talk to your Father about what Hawaii and I are supposed to be doing. How many times, honey, am I supposed to forgive? I know, every single time, hah? I hate to say this but I have been so stressed about Hawaii that I haven't had time to think about my pain with you. Is that part of your Father's plan, to give me a break from the pain, sadness and hurt by occupying my thoughts somewhere else? I've been praying so much lately. I mean, for the first time in my life I drove straight to the liquor store for alcohol to get drunk and I GOT drunk but at least I was at home, right? So help me, honey. Work your magic. Give me some KCD right now because I'm pretty mad. I wonder what you would tell me to do right now? Help me because I love you . . .

August 25, 2007, Saturday • Scale: 2

Hi Honey, at least I was a little productive today. I wrote and delivered thank-you cards to all the businesses that helped me. It felt good. I also went out to a Charger bar, Georges, by myself. I knew I would know someone in there and I did. I was hoping to see Hawaii there but he didn't show. Tawnia drove me and picked me up. I am so blessed to have her in our lives. She has been a Saint to me so many times and you were her daughter, too. I'm trying to talk Adam and her into having another baby, a little girl. I think that's probably the only girl I would ever be able to bond with and love. I just feel nothing, Kels, for other kids now. Will I ever get that back? Maybe when Digger has kids. I'm, still fighting with Hawaii. I'm angry and I need your Father to help take that anger away so I can love him again. I love you.

August 26, 2007, Sunday • Scale: 2

Dear Kelsea Lyn, I've found myself under so much Hawaii Stress I can't grieve. I have to wonder if it's supposed to be like this. I mean, I hate to admit this to you and I hope you forgive me but I haven't thought about you today or the last few days and I haven't cried either. Work was rough too . . . till Hawaii came in for 5 minutes. Thanks for talking to your Father for me. I talked to a few of the guys at work about the trial and they are pissed at how Laura Wion could give you *any* medication. I can't see a jury not feeling the same way. Did you hear Hawaii's Myspace song? Do you like Fergie? I never heard her before but it's a great song. So now that I've entered the second year of hell, is this a year that I just completely don't allow myself to think about you? I'm struggling and I hate my life right now but I love you.

August 27, 2007, Monday • Scale: 2

Hi Honey, so I'm getting my hair done tomorrow and my nails the next day. I don't' know if I have the money, but right now, I don't care. Bill Menish said your story will be aired tomorrow night. I can't wait. I know he did a great job for you. I feel really guilty, Kels, because I feel like I've been so pre-occupied with B. S. stuff I haven't been grieving. I feel like once your ceremony was over, I just shut the switch off and I haven't cried or anything. I'm scared for the next wave. My weight is still down but I want to drop 3 more pounds. I know it's all vanity pounds but I don't care. I've been home all day doing basically nothing. I hate not seeing Hawaii because we spent so much time together that now I get bored when I'm not with him. I need to start on our bipolar book. It's just hard to sit down and start it. I miss you, I love you and I want you back, kiss.

August 28, 2007, Tuesday • Scale: 3

Dear Kels, do you love my hair? It's so dark underneath, just like you liked it. I feel myself getting a little stronger every day with Hawaii and making better choices. We have our date in a couple days but I'm a little scared because I don't want to fight with him. All I can do is pray, right? I watched your story on the 6 pm news and, honey, it was perfect. Bill did such a wonderful job letting people know you were loved. I was home alone and had to watch it alone. I cried the whole time, then I had to pull it together and go into work and it was rough. I have so much support there, though, and I'm so thankful work was okay and not too busy. I hate that you and I will never be able to sit and drink a beer together. I don't even want to start on all the things I hate and that you are not going to experience now. My brain is still protecting me right now, but you know I still love you forever.

August 29, 2007, Wednesday • Scale: 3

Hi Tat . . . I've been spoiling myself the last couple days, hah? I don't know why but I've got my hair, nails and eyebrows all done. I probably can't afford it but I'm in an "I-don't-care" mode. I was driving this morning and realized how much I have pushed you out of my mind since the 22nd. I felt like I didn't even have a daughter, let alone one who passed away. It's just my brain's way of protecting me but I feel guilty. I haven't really cried in a week or so. I feel tiny waves and I'm finding myself getting mad at other parents with their kids. I have to tell myself to stop. I still avoid so many people in the gym because I just don't want to talk to them. Susan wants me to work on building relationships with other women. I just can't see it. I can't even bond with Cheyenne. I've lost the only girl in my life I truly loved and cared for. Why would God do that to me? Can you answer me? I love you.

August 30, 2007, Thursday • Scale: 3

Hi Honey, so what did you think of the Charger game? It was okay, hah? It was nice being with Hawaii for the day. He always tries to tell me and get me to see your passing away as a blessing. He talks about how many people you have helped and lives you have touched and continue to touch. It's like my head hears what he is saying but the selfishness in me would rather you be here and not have helped who you have. My heart is still ripped out and I just don't see it as a blessing. I feel like I'm afraid to "accept" this because I'd feel guilty. I feel like then it would be okay and it will never be okay. That Laura Wion killed you because that's what she did. So . . . 56,000 people at the Charger game and the cops have to give your brother a "Minor in Possession" ticket for carrying a beer. What is God's plan for Digger? Watch over him, Kels, he's got a lot of anger deep down. I love you so very much.

August 31, 2007, Friday • Scale: 1

Dear Kelsea Lyn, today has been rough. I've had the lump in the throat, chest pains and anxiety. Your funeral was a year ago today. It was hot at your pad today but I had to spend the day with you there. There was another funeral today; well I'm sure you've met Darlene by now, your newest neighbor. It was actually nice to have had that funeral there because it was like a memorial for you a year ago. But I feel more lost now, Kels, than before. I hate that a year is over because I keep asking myself, now what? What am I supposed to be doing now? I guess all I can do is take 1 day at a time and sometimes, like today, 1 hour at a time. I have to work tonight; can you please be with me and give me some KCD? I know I've been crying all day and you hate it, but I just miss you so damn much . . . I hate it . . . come into my dreams. I love you.

CHAPTER FOURTEEN

IT'S NOW BEEN 2 YEARS

August 22, 2008, Friday • Scale: 7

Dear Kelsea Lyn, how is heaven treating you? I'll bet it's crazy having no "time" in heaven like we still have here. I'd have to say that when you lose someone, time is one of your greatest enemies here. It's been exactly 2 years today since your funeral and my brain just cannot wrap itself around that concept. I've had chest pains today. Actually, I've had them for the last week and a half but I'm sure that's just because I knew I was coming up on the 2-year marker and all. I hadn't had the lump in my throat, chest pains, headaches or any of the physical signs of grief for quite awhile. I keep telling Hawaii about the pains but he is right, just because I don't feel stressed doesn't mean I'm not. I guess I'm just going to have to get used to this every year. Do you think as time goes on that they will subside? I remember after the first year ended and I began the second year, I was pissed. I thought, okay so I made it through this year. Now what?

Now I have another year to go through this hell I'm in?

That's exactly, Kels, what happened. I went through this last year, the second year, in a different kind of hell though. You know, the first year was the year of survival. The second year was the year of the fight. Now, I believe this third year will be the year of honoring you. What do you think? Would that make you proud and happy? You have to admit, all the attention you thought you weren't getting here on earth, you're definitely getting it now. I guess I still don't understand why you didn't think you got any attention . . . you were the queen of attention, honey.

Why, Kels, did God have to take you? I still don't understand. I guess that's a question I will have to wait for the answer, until I see you and your heavenly Father. I just wish I knew how long I had to wait.

It was nice visiting your pad today. I hope you love the pink and white roses. I really had to groom your pad though; it was getting out of control! It just warms my heart to see your friends leaving you things when they visit. Can you believe there were 4 cigarettes left for you? I know some people may look down on that and the fact you smoked, but you know I loved you no matter what, right? I can't imagine not visiting you every single week. I promised you the best looking pad in the neighborhood and that's what you will continue to have because you deserve it and deserve to be spoiled.

Did you see me crying in church last night? I haven't cried that hard in a very long time and it felt good. I actually go for long periods at a time now, Kels, without crying. You're not mad at that, are you? I mean, in the beginning I thought it was disrespectful toward you if I didn't cry every single day. . . . even though I knew how much you hated me crying.

It doesn't mean I don't still love you or miss you or still need you here with me. I guess it's just part of this whole grief process thing I'm going through.

Well sweetheart, I have a big day tomorrow. Fox News Channel 5 is coming to talk to me about my book to you, *Letters to Kelsea.* I hope you are living that everlasting life that is full of joy and happiness. I can't wait to hold you again, touch your face, look at those piercing blue eyes, smell your scent, hear your laugh, see your smile and tell you how very much I love you.

JOURNAL: JUSTICE FOR KELSEA, SURVIVING THE FIGHT • AUGUST 22, 2008

So, here I am exactly 2 years later, 2 years of living without my daughter, 2 years of struggling to breathe, 2 years of fighting to survive, but I made it. I just spent the last year fighting for what was right, fighting for justice.

As the year began and court dates were set I had no idea how grueling the next year would be. I learned very well the process of the justice system. I found it frustrating at times but knew I had to be patient for justice to truly prevail. Over a period of approximately 18 months, I never once missed a court date. I told Kelsea's attorney I would be there even if it took 30 seconds. Many times there were "continuances" in which everything I had prepared myself for was thrown out the window only to put me through several more weeks of hell in this fight.

In the end, though, on July 25, 2008 Laura Wion was sentenced to 6 years in the California state prison system. I had written the judge prior to her sentencing and told him what would bring me some peace. Hearing the judge sentence her to the full 6 years and hearing him say, "Remand into custody" and seeing the bailiffs take her immediately was justice. That is exactly what the judge did and it was that night that I was able to take my first full breath.

I stopped going to my group during the second year shortly after the first year ended. In the beginning I found solace in the group. I found that after that first year passed group was getting harder and harder to attend. As I was trying to live my life, be productive, learn my new purpose, I found group so draining. It was so unbelievably sad and painful I just couldn't bring myself to go. I stayed away for 8 months when I decided to return as the trial was approaching. I knew I would need the support from the only people who knew how I felt.

I've now been back to group for almost 4 months and I have found that now, instead of being the newest member to this choice less group, I was not and the pain that I felt in the beginning belonged to someone else now. When I hear their stories and see their pain, it brings mine right back to the surface again but in a different way. Now the pain I feel is *their* pain. I know that's a hard concept to understand but I honestly feel their pain with them.

The things I do talk about now in group are things I want to say to help the newer parents. They are things to bring them hope, which is something I had nothing of the first and second year of this new life. I know I keep saying "new life" but that is really what it is. Before, I was a mother of 2 children, now I have 1.

Before, I had a daughter to go shopping with, eat out with, share secrets with, go to the gym with, watch TV with. Now I don't. Before, I dreamed of my daughter's prom, graduation, college, wedding and grandchildren. Now those dreams are gone, forever. No holiday will ever be the same, no birthday, no days will be the same.

It hasn't been until the last month that I feel as if I am finding some meaning now in this life. I have to believe that God has a plan for me now. As time goes on I believe I see that plan unfolding before me. I have had people all over the world who have become familiar with this court case and who have contacted me with their support. I have had young adults contact me and tell me that Kelsea has changed their lives. I have had people contact me to tell me how strong I am.

That I still struggle with at times because I revert back to the same thought I had the first year: *Maybe if I wasn't this strong, I would still have my little girl.*

I still question God as to why I couldn't have helped all the people and Kelsea couldn't have touched so many lives without losing her. Why we couldn't have worked together like we had planned and traveled with our book about Kelsea's bipolar illness. We had aspirations of writing this book together to educate people about mental illness and to tour the world doing this.

Instead, I find myself dedicated to doing this alone. Although Kelsea is in heaven now, I have continued my relationship with her. I still visit her pad every week. I still talk to her every day. I still carry her picture with me wherever I go. I still tell her I love her every single day. Sometimes I think I may even be closer to her now because there is not an hour that goes by that she is not on my mind. She is not physically here with me anymore, but she is always in my thoughts and obviously, heart.

I used to and still do have a little bit of a hard time with that saying, "she's always in your heart." Yes, she is but at times the physical craving of wanting to hold my daughter or talk to her or laugh with her overtakes me. The pain that is a few layers under my skin comes ripping through and I'm right back to that first day.

The difference now is before the pain would last for days. However, that pain now comes but it dissipates much quicker than in the beginning. Thank you, God.

Then of course, there is the saying, "Time heals all wounds." I have learned over 2 years that time does not "heal." A grieving parent is never healed because our child never comes back to us. My life has gotten "softer." My life has become more manageable. I haven't had anyone say to me lately that saying about time, but when they do I have learned to politely explain to them that some wounds will never heal.

I have experienced the people over the last year that absolutely have no idea what to say to me still, so they just walk past me and look the other way and that's okay. There have been times also, though, that I have looked the other way, even with my own friends because I was in that dark place that hour and wanted nothing to do with anyone. Those days still happen, just not as frequently.

I can say that within the last week I have felt a peace about me that I have not felt since I lost Kelsea Lyn. It's brought me hope. I know that I am not in the clear by any means. I know that still beneath my skin is a real rawness. I think this hope is emerging because I see myself helping others through these writings. I have just had a tribute to Kelsea written in the *San Diego Union Tribune* focusing on this book, *Letters.*

I had an interview today with a television news reporter who read the newspaper article and wanted to do a human interest story again about this book, *Letters.* This woman was compassionate and I could see the passion she has for her job. At one point in the interview as I was speaking and crying, her eyes filled with tears and she felt my pain. That's what I mean when it's right there.

I still get angry when I think about not having Kelsea here and having a 5-year marker, or 10-year or even 20-year marker. I refuse to call them anniversaries because anniversaries are something to celebrate. August 22, 2006, will never be a day to celebrate. It is simply another mark on a calendar as another year passes. To put things into perspective there are parents still attending my support group 3, 5, 6, 9 and even 12 years later.

You see, it never goes away but I can say that 2 years later, I can breathe a little better. 2 years later, I am able to work again, granted not full time but still work. 2 years later, I have found a man to accept this broken woman. A man who loves his children and appreciates them more than ever because of my loss and my grief. 2 years later, I am able to occasionally remember the good times I had with Kelsea without the pain drowning the memory out. 2 years later, I can laugh without feeling guilty. 2 years later, I have hope in my life now and a desire to help others.

Am I cured? Has my life "moved on?" Is everything "better" now? No. I will never be cured. Life doesn't move on. It gets softer and it will never be better because Kelsea will never be with me here on earth again. I do know, though, that I am finding a passion in this new life. It is a passion to help others. I hope that when this book is read, people will be able to identify with the same thoughts, feelings, darkness, guilt, hope and happiness that I have experienced at different levels, at different times and on no set schedule. Grief has a life of its own. I was told in the very beginning, one day the love will outweigh the pain and that is when you will begin to live again.

Some days I feel life now. Some days I feel happy. Some days I feel the love for Kelsea. I know that the life ahead of me will still be a roller coaster. I know my tears are not gone, just hiding. I know that my life has forever changed but I also know that one day, by the grace of God, I will be holding my daughter in my arms again and that is what keeps me alive today. I am trying to be the best person I can and I owe that all to Kelsea Lyn.

CHAPTER FIFTEEN

JOURNAL: A BUMP IN THE ROAD

March 14, 2011

I've gone back. Once again, I have found myself in therapy and attending my support group. It started when I was watching TV with my roommate. She was talking about something on TV and it started irritating me. Her actions and words were simple but my inner being raged. I snapped and in a moment I was spewing harsh words at her that she did not deserve. I didn't apologize though. I got up, said good-night and went to my room. The next morning I knew I needed help again.

I made an appointment with a therapist and spent an hour with him explaining what had happened with my roommate, what was going on in my life with my boyfriend and what happened with Kelsea Lyn. My emotions ranged from talking to crying to anger back to crying. The roller coaster I had stepped on was exhausting me. But I finished the hour learning 1 thing. I absolutely needed to be there.

I went back the following week and it was the third week in therapy when it all started becoming clear. My anger wasn't about my relationship with my boyfriend, like I thought. It was about the fact that I am approaching the 5-year marker and I don't know where 5 years have gone. It is about the fact that Laura Wion gets out of prison in $11^1/_2$ weeks and gets to go home to her family, yet Kelsea is still gone. It's about me facing my grief again when I have been able to manage it for so long now. I was told it was time for me to revisit my support group as well.

April 7, 2011

The day was here for me to go back to group. I did not want to go but knew I absolutely needed to go. All day I was thinking about what I wanted to say. I thought about how long it had been since I was there. I thought about all the new parents who would be there with fresh losses.

As I drove there I began having chest pains. They were all too familiar and I knew it was simply the stress of me driving to group and having to walk in again. I parked my jeep and walked into the building. I took a deep breath as I slowly walked up the stairs to the second floor. I contemplated going to the bathroom first but knew I really didn't have to go. I was just stalling.

As I opened the doors the room was full of all new faces. It was the next generation of parents now living a choice less life. Ken smiled at me, welcomed me and explained to everyone how nice it was to have someone walk back through the doors that he hadn't seen in a couple years. Wow, had it really been that long? Of course I knew it had but for him to recognize it was amazing. He simply said, "My prayer is that you are not here because of more tragedy" and I told him, no. I sat down and again I could not breathe. I closed my eyes and the tears swelled in my eyes as they began to roll down my cheeks. I had my head down so no one could see and so I did not have to look at the pain on these new parents' faces.

I sat and listened to Ken's calm, soft voice as he prepared us all for the next couple hours. He softly brought us all into the same place, a place of refuge. With my head down, I listened to his words and he was able to help me slow everything down. Eventually, I was able to stop the tears from taking over my cheeks and look up into the room.

I listened to parents talk about what they were feeling. Nothing that was said was new to me. All the feelings being felt by everyone in the room were real, fresh, raw and very, very familiar. I had seniority in the room. I had the most "time" under my belt. Everyone's losses were under a year and I remembered that dark place. I sat and listened. I thought to myself, I can't talk because I felt if I did I would give these parents a sense of absolutely no hope. I thought they would look at me coming up on five years and think to themselves, "I'm screwed, she's at five years and is still that much of a wreck?"

Then, there came a moment when I decided to talk. I looked at Ken and I explained to him how angry I was. My fists were clenched, my leg was bouncing and I felt like I wanted to scream because I couldn't put into words how mad I was. I told him I don't know where 5 years have gone or what I've done. I told him I was pissed that Laura Wion was getting out of prison in 11 weeks. The tears were rolling down my face and our eyes were locked. All of a sudden it was just Ken and I in the room. I lost all awareness of the other parents.

After I spoke, Ken looked at me and said, "How dare you be angry because the woman that killed your daughter is getting out of prison in 11 weeks." He said it over and over again as I cried harder and harder. He told me to look around the room. He said, "Do you see any other parents in here experiencing having to deal with the woman that took their daughter's life getting out of prison in 11 weeks?" As I looked around the room at these other parents, my tears slowed and I realized what he was saying. I had every right to be angry at Laura Wion getting out of prison in 11 weeks. It was absolutely okay for me to be feeling what I was and it was completely normal and understandable to everyone in the room.

Over the next half hour, the whole group began to strategize to help me through this. Here is what we all came up with:

1. Come to support group.

2. Manage "triggers" throughout the day.

3. Change route to avoid encounters (with Wion once she is out of prison).

4. Remove concept of time.

5. Forgive myself.

6. Use my talents to honor Kelsea; give back my experience.

7. Remember I am human and take care of myself.

It was amazing to hear these parents, who were in darkness, forget about their pain for a few minutes to help someone they just met with their pain. I think by far the most important thing I learned from group tonight was this statement: time is a 4-letter word to a grieving parent.

See, as I explained to my new therapist about the loss of a child, he didn't quite seem to get the concept of how unique our loss is to any other loss. He said to me that everyone who loses a loved one experiences "loss." He said that even in my support group all the children die in different ways, so why is it so different than losing someone else? I said because the 1 common thread that we all have is it's our CHILD and there is no greater loss, ever.

I realize this may sound selfish or cold to someone who has suffered a loved one's loss other than a child. I can only speak from my experience. My dad passed away 10 months ago now. I loved my dad dearly and had a close relationship with him but the loss was so very different and I can honestly say losing my dad didn't compare to losing Kelsea.

So for now, I will return back to group next week. I will make a concentrated effort to make it there no matter how I am feeling. Ken also reminded me of my ability to write. He said this is the time for me to write again so I can help others.

So I can hopefully bring peace to others who might be facing the same thing I am, someone finishing their prison sentence and getting out of prison when our child still cannot walk in the front door of our homes EVER again.

I will embrace my anger and allow myself to feel it and work through it and understand it. I will continue therapy and group to help me through the next four months of this roller coaster I have stepped back onto. I will continue journaling in hopes of passing on bits of hope, peace and wisdom to anyone willing to dive into this world we as grieving parents now live. Till next week . . .

April 14, 2011

I checked out today. I went to work in the morning and put my 4 hours in then I attempted to work out and cut it short. I went home and just checked out. I climbed into bed, pulled the covers up over my head and went to sleep. I slept the afternoon away until I had to get up and get ready to go to group.

The drive this week wasn't as anxiety ridden as the week before. I didn't have any chest pains and didn't cry on the way. Instead, today I prayed the whole way. I prayed for a blanket of peace and comfort for every parent attending group that tonight. I prayed for the wisdom and words to use when and if I spoke. I pulled up and the parking was horrible and I found myself getting angry.

As I walked up to the building, I heard the loudness of all the people enjoying themselves at the restaurant that sits directly below the office for our group. It's an Italian restaurant with seating outside and ambiance radiating everywhere. I looked at the people laughing, drinking, eating and again I got angry. I was jealous. I thought how unfair it was that I was walking into a support group for parents who have lost a child and they all got to sit there enjoying themselves. Then, I realized how unfair those thoughts were. After all, it wasn't their fault they had not suffered the tragedy I experienced.

As I walked up the stairs to group I realized I was still breathing and I wasn't already crying. I walked into the room to find 2 parents from my generation there and they immediately both embraced me. I looked around the room and here again was sitting the new generation of parents. I was glad they had all made it back another week. They are learning what I learned 4 years ago. The best way to honor our children is to first take care of ourselves in the midst of darkness and hopelessness by mustering up the strength to come to group every week. Then we were choosing to live.

I found myself tonight in a much better place than I was last week. I didn't cry as much and I was able to keep my head up the whole time. I always found myself burying my head, with my eyes closed and tears rolling down my cheeks, unable to look at anyone during group. But, tonight I actually felt like I helped. I felt like I was able to give some words of encouragement.

We touched on the subject of "anniversaries." I reiterated to this new generation that I refuse to call certain dates that word. I just told them each year is another year without my Kelsea Lyn and another mark on a calendar. So I call them "Markers." We touched on things getting "better." I reiterated that to me, it never gets "better" but it has gotten "softer." When I used that word it was as if a light in many of the parents' heads lit up. I could see in their faces that they understood what I had just said and that brought me joy to know I just made a connection only we could truly understand.

Yes, tonight was very different for me at group. I'm so glad I made the decision to return back to group last week. I am glad I was able to spew my feelings and emotions without being judged. I was able to cry and not care but feel the compassion from 13 other parents whom I had just met. I was able to cleanse myself last week of all the built-up, pushed deep inside me emotions. But tonight was extremely cathartic.

Tonight, I felt like I helped. I felt like the bits and pieces of my grief that I shared hit home and shed some light into this new life and journey for this new generation. I was honest tonight in what I have experienced throughout almost 5 years of grief. Would I call the place I live now still "hell?" No and that is going to be the hope I feel I can bring into group.

So, I will make it through yet another week of grief searching for words and ways to be able to help this new generation survive each passing hour, knowing that their choice to live is honoring their child to the fullest.

Over the last $2^{1}/_{2}$ years, I have lived somewhat life again. When I reflect back it does not mean I have not grieved, but that the pain has gone from debilitating to manageable. I never thought I would be saying something like that and a bit of guilt does go along with that statement. But I have gotten to a place where I am able to work and financially support myself.

CHAPTER SIXTEEN

THE 7-YEAR MARKER

August 22, 2013, Scale: 8

My Dearest Kelsea Lyn, What can I say other than I love you and that will never change. I wasn't sure how today was going to go but I enjoyed my time with you. Even though 7 years ago today was the darkest day in my life. Now, when I wake up in the morning on this day, I know what I am going to do and I just do it.

Did you like the flowers and balloon? I know butterflies haven't ever really meant anything special to us but it was huge and I thought a nice touch to your pad. It was pretty hot out there and I got a bit sun burned but it was worth it. Of course, it didn't go un noticed by your brother and he was a bit upset with me because of the Melanoma I've had in the past. I never realized until later in life the affect it had on you when I got the cancer the first time. I'm sorry that was so hard on you.

Can you believe I'm married now? Do you like our house? I know it was a long time coming but I think you would love Hawaii as much as I do. I know you would have made him laugh ALL the time! I always laughed no matter how mad you made me when you crinkled your nose! You had that look on your face and would shrug your shoulders a little bit at the same time and that was all it took to put me in the palm of your hand.

It was nice going to dinner with Digger tonight, too, even if he was drunk. I have to admit, though, it really didn't bother me. I mean hell, Kels, we lost you on this day and that will never change. At least he called me to pick him up, right? We had a good conversation, too, actually. Did you hear him when he said "Can you believe it's been 7 years, Mom?" He has never said that before. I think going out for dinner somewhere is something we will start doing each year for you.

My life, Kelsea Lyn, is very blessed now. I honestly couldn't have imagined making it 7 years without you and yet here I am. I wish you were here, though, to help me with my business. I could just imagine you and I showing up at a home to deliver a Margarita machine and talking to the customer way too long! We would have had them laughing and not wanting us to go or inviting us back to their party!

I hope that you are proud of who I have become, Kels. I hope that you look down at me and the things I do and it makes you smile. I have to wonder what you would be doing right now. Where you would be working? Where you would be living? Would you be married or have a baby yet? You were a young girl when you went to heaven and now you would be a young lady, a woman. How has it been 7 years, Kels? How?

I have to admit, Kels, that today was a peaceful day even with the sadness it brings. I am glad the day is over though. Once again, I will go to sleep and wake up tomorrow morning to begin another day, another month, another year without you. But, there is peace in knowing that with each year that passes I am that much closer to being with you again. The beauty of it all, Kelsea Lyn, is that when I see you again, it will be an Everlasting Life with love, joy, peace, no tears, no pain and for eternity.

I love you more than the law allows. . . . Kisses from Mama.

THE FINAL JOURNAL ENTRY: LIFE

It amazes me to think that I am still here walking, talking, functioning, focusing and breathing . . . 7 years later. It amazes me to know the utter darkness and death I experienced when Kelsea passed away. I died with her that day. It amazes me that, once again, I have a life.

In the beginning, it was hard to think past each day, let alone a week, month or God forbid a year. Yet, each year, August 22nd still came around. Although my life seemed to have stopped, the people around me who never experienced such a loss kept moving forward with each day. At times it made me so angry, but now I am living a "normal" life.

I now have a business that will honor and have Kelsea's name on it forever: A Kelsea Lyn Phelps Company: EZ Pour Drinks. I never realized the opportunity I would have to share my story with customers. It's not something I begin talking about everytime I pull up to a home. But if a customer asks who Kelsea is I am able to share my daughter's story. Many times they have a child who can read what happened to Kelsea. I look at it as simply educating others and their children so no one has to experience the journey I began. A journey that was out of my control.

On July 21, 2013, I got married to Hawaii. He came into my life just 4 months into the darkness and carried me for so very long. No one knows the journey and darkness, emotional roller coaster, anger or the moments of laughter, hope and now life again than Hawaii. He stuck through every second of grief with me, supported me and loves me wholeheartedly. For 7 years, I lived from house to house, renting rooms from friends. I felt like a wanderer but now I live in a home with my husband. Words cannot express the peace I feel having a home again.

I have continued to attend my church every Sunday with my husband. The support and prayer I received there is a large part of my place in life today. I know that many, many times it is hard to believe in God when you lose a child or anyone for that matter. You want to ask God, why? You get angry with Him and many times simply lose all faith. I am thankful to say, though, that I did not ever turn my back on God. When I was in the darkness I cried out to Him. In the first year I practically chanted "I can do all things though Christ who strengthens me" (Philippians 4:13) on a daily basis. Today, I find refuge not only in that verse, but also knowing that it is not something I have to say every day now.

Yes, my faith has carried me over the last 7 years. I honestly do not think I could have navigated my way through the last 7 years on my own. I praise God and thank God every morning for the blessed life I now have.

Did I ever think I would call my life blessed with the loss of my daughter? No. But my heart has began healing. There are certain things and sayings that in the beginning I hated to hear. The most important one I believe was the saying, "Time heals all wounds." Although sometimes it still comes with guilt, I can honestly say that time HAS begun to heal my heart. I don't believe it will ever be whole again because Kelsea held a large part of my heart in her hands. I do believe though that after 7 years I am alive again.

I'm not sure if "healed" is a good word or if I still think "softer" is more appropriate, but I know that I am in a much better place today than I have been in seven years.

I'm not going to say that my life is perfect or that I am in the same place as I was before all this happened. I still have waves that come in, but they are more like small swells of water that hit my legs and buckle my legs. At times, it is difficult to see a mom and daughter together, but instead of great anger I feel sadness. If you actually take a moment to think about that statement, you understand anger is deep grief and sadness is the beginning of healing.

My goal in writing my thoughts, feelings, day-to-day moments, grief and journey is to hopefully bring some peace to anyone in the grief of losing a child. I have said this before, there is no greater loss in life than the loss of one's child. I stand by that.

But, I am here to tell you that one day you will be able to smile and even laugh out loud. You will be able to breathe and think clearly. You will be able to work again and have a social life that includes friends and family. You will be able to go to the gym again, grocery shop and even go to the mall. You will meet new people brought into your life solely through your loss who will become a confidant. Then one day, you in turn will be that person for someone else. You will be able to stop taking the medication to help you get through the pain because the pain will subside one day. It may not be today or tomorrow or in the first year or 5 but it will come.

I believe I can honestly say that you are going to be okay again, one day. I never believed I would be at the place I am in life today. It took me 7 years but I have come a long, long way in this journey. I would like to say I can promise you that with supportive people, a good support group, many tears, a good therapist, medication at times, self-compassion and, most important, God in your life, the journey may be long but you will survive. You will love again, laugh again, feel joy and with each passing hour, day, week and year have hope grow within your soul.

Please, accept my condolences in your loss and know that my prayer is that God continues to give us an abundance of hope in our lives as we heal and live to honor our children, Amen!

PHILIPPIANS 4:12–13

I know how to live on almost nothing or with everything.
I have learned the secret of living in every situation,
whether it is with a full stomach or empty, with plenty or little.
For I can do everything with the help of Christ
who gives me the strength I need.

BEFORE, DURING AND AFTER

Kelsea's junior year was complete and for the first time, she was going to attend summer school. She was going to be spending her senior year at a charter school named East County Academy of Learning or ECAL. This school was for students who were struggling for a variety of reasons in a traditional school. It offered more supervision and one on one teaching in each classroom. Kelsea had been diagnosed bipolar at the age of 12 and struggled in school at times.

We pulled up to ECAL one sunny June afternoon to tour the school, meet the teachers and simply make a decision if this would be good for Kelsea. The teachers were amazing and hit it off with Kels immediately. We walked around the school grounds and it was quiet with tree's everywhere. The principal came to us and invited us to his office. We sat there and he made Kelsea feel unbelievably comfortable as well as myself. I thing Kelsea and I both felt peace.

When we were done we walked together to the car in silence. I was thinking, *This school is perfect.* We got into the car and Kelsea looked at me with a glimmer in her eyes. Her first words to me were, "Wow Mom, this school is a blessing," and I said, "Yes, it is."

Over the next several weeks, our routine consisted of getting up early enough to be able to stop at the local 7-11 by ECAL so Kelsea could get coffee to go with her cream and sugar! I would make my coffee in less than a minute, then I would watch Kelsea make a concoction of different flavored creams, sugar and add a splash of coffee to it all! We would laugh every day we walked out with the coffee and I always said, "Why don't you have some coffee with your cream?!"

Kelsea brought home schoolwork every day and diligently sat down to finish it for the next day. I do not ever remember her being so disciplined in her school career as she was in ECAL. Her confidence grew daily and she was very happy in this new school and was looking forward to her senior year at ECAL and for the first time she was getting good grades on the work she was doing.

Kelsea was in therapy at this time because of her bipolar disorder. So once a week after I picked her up after school we would go see Chris. He had been Kelsea's therapist for over a year and she loved him! He was fairly young, handsome and made us both very comfortable.

Kelsea was nearing the end of summer school and, one day with Chris, I mentioned to him that I made a deal with my children that if either one of them got straight A's on a report card I would pay them $500.00! We laughed about it because I had a feeling Kelsea could very easily pull it off with the 3 summer school classes she took. He looked at Kelsea at that moment and said, "You know what, Kels? I will add another $100.00 to that if you get straight As!" There is no word to describe the look on Kelsea's face other than love. She looked at Chris with a smile beaming and said thank you.

We ended the session talking about Kelsea finishing the summer school session and we established a plan for her over the 10 days between summer school ending and her senior year beginning. With this in place we said good bye to Chris and he said, "See you in a couple weeks!" He was going on vacation for a couple weeks and we were to see him after Kelsea started her senior year.

On the last day of summer session, we were handed Kelsea's grades and I came the closest I EVER did to owing her $500.00! She received 2 A's and one solid B for her efforts. I could not have been prouder because for the first time in 17 years my daughter was excited about going to school and it showed in her effort and grades.

Over the next week Kelsea enjoyed her break and looked forward to a new beginning in this new school. She knew she would be meeting new friends, teachers and her outlook on life was incredible!

You see, because of Kelsea's bipolar disorder she truly did struggle in school. She was also diagnosed with attention deficit disorder (ADD) which made it difficult for her to concentrate in school. Throughout school she was monitored and placed on an I.E.P., which is an Individual Education Program.

Kelsea was placed in special classes in school yet she still struggled. That is why, as we walked to our car that first day, Kelsea commented on what a blessing ECAL was going to be for her.

On August 22, 2006, Kelsea was to have her first day of her senior year at ECAL. Instead, I walked into her room and my life was FOREVER changed. My life at that moment ended and I began a life that I never asked for, imagined or would wish on my worst enemy in life. . . .

I sit here today, though, in a place I never imagined I would be after that horrid day.

Today I am married again. Today I own a small business that is named after Kelsea. Today I am able to smile and laugh again without guilt. Today I can go places without triggers taking me down to my knees. Today I can look at pictures of Kelsea without tears of pain. Today I do not consciously step into a torture chamber and allow myself to stay there. Today I can talk about Kelsea and remember how beautiful her heart was. Today I go longer than 1 hour without thinking about Kelsea because it does not consume me. Today I have realized that the pain that I felt and carried with me for years has now transitioned into sadness.

I miss Kelsea every second of every minute of every day; that has not changed. However, I can honestly say with all my heart that I have hope in my life now.

Hope for continued healing and a future. Hope that in this travesty of life that others will be handed in the loss of their child, by my words, they will find hope, too.

When someone today asks me, how are you? I look them in the eyes and say, "Never in my life would I have ever thought that I could be as blessed as I am today."

REFERENCES

The Book: A special edition of The New Living Translation.

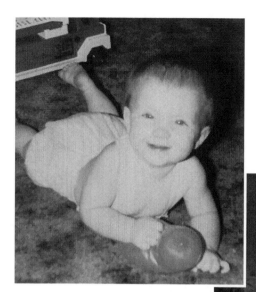

My 8-month-old
sky-blue-eyed girl.

One year old and blowing
kisses already.

I love you more, Mama.

Already inseparable . . .

My two angels . . . cheese!

Flower girl and ring bearer at
their Godmother's wedding (1999).

Yes Mom, it's your underwear
on our heads!

Mission Beach,
San Diego, a
roller-coaster and
snow-cone. Kelsea's
favorite things!

At the beach again showing off
her muscles "like you Mama!"

Halloween pumpkin carving
(1999).

Pop Warner El Cajon Braves
thirsty cheerleader.

Picture-perfect
cheerleader.

What, Mom?
I'm trying to
work out . . .

Out to eat for Digger's
15th birthday, Kansas City.

Vacationing in Spokane,
Washington—devious smile!

Thanksgiving 2003—
so much love for
each other.

We loved taking pictures together for no reason (2004).

Old-fashioned picture day bonding (2005).

Digger and me out for
Christmas dinner (2016).

Celebrating Digger's 29th
birthday; always missing Kelsea.

Kelsea's "Pad"

IN EVERLASTING LIFE

TRACY LYN PHELPS   KELSEA LYN PHELPS

MARCH 27, 1963   JANUARY 3, 1989

   AUGUST 22, 2006

   "JESUS FREAK"   "TAT"

"I LOVE YOU MORE THAN THE LAW ALLOWS"

Rest in Peace,
Kelsea Lyn Phelps

45989431R00176

Made in the USA
San Bernardino, CA
22 February 2017